D0849752

NEW YORK

State and City

Also by David Maldwyn Ellis:

Landlords and Farmers in the Mohawk-Hudson Region, 1790–1850
The Saratoga Campaign

Co-author:

A Short History of New York State
A History of New York State
New York: The Empire State

Editor:

The Developing Frontier: Essays in Honor of Paul Wallace Gates

NEW YORK

State and City

David Maldwyn Ellis

Cornell University Press

Ithaca and London

First published 1979 by Cornell University Press.
Published in the United Kingdom by Cornell University Press Ltd.,
2–4 Brook Street, London W1Y 1AA.

International Standard Book Number 0-8014-1180-7
Library of Congress Catalog Card Number 78-15759
Printed in the United States of America
Librarians: Library of Congress cataloging information appears on the last page of the book.

For my students at
Hamilton College

Contents

Maps

Illustrations

Preface

If New York's population, finance, trade, manufacturing, transportation, politics, and the arts command national attention, it is because the Empire State has usually led in these areas during much of the nation's history. Its failures have also been conspicuous, whether one looks at housing for immigrants, safety in the streets, efficiency in government administration, or equality of opportunity. New York's shortcomings, like its achievements, have been gargantuan.

I have tried to indicate the highlights of New York State history and to explore its major themes, including wherever possible references to local events and important personalities. Since Michael Kammen and others have recently presented us with careful reexaminations of colonial New York, I have chosen to give greater emphasis to the period since the Revolution.

I was born, reared, and educated in central New York, and I have taught history for over three decades at Hamilton College, several of whose graduates, notably Carl Carmer, Samuel Hopkins Adams, and Harold Thompson, have written outstanding books dealing with New York history, folklore, and literature. Perhaps the landscape and local lore have had a subliminal effect upon Hamilton students and other central New Yorkers, such as James Fenimore Cooper, Walter Edmonds, and Edmund Wilson. At any rate, I confess a deep affection for New York's lovely countryside, its colorful history, and its inhabitants, including its rogues and its fools.

The York State character has intrigued me for years. We New Yorkers pride ourselves on our hardheadedness and our practical outlook. Intangibles have also played their part in creating the New York character, as Washington Irving so ably demonstrated.

I have tried to uncover the characteristics that have differentiated New Yorkers from other Americans and the features they have shared with them.

The old complaint that New York's history has been neglected became progressively less valid during the 1970s, when the bicentennial spurred many historians to collect data and compile the histories of their communities. Their research has been valuable to me. But to encompass the basic features of Empire State history in one modest-sized volume, I have been forced to compress many developments and to omit significant and fascinating material. No doubt specialists and local enthusiasts will feel that I have scanted some important events, ignored their communities, and slighted scores of personalities. They are correct. For example, I have mentioned fewer than a third of our governors and commented on fewer than a tenth of them. Whether or not I have made the best selections to illustrate historical trends and to reflect New York's special characteristics is something each reader must decide.

Two other problems have complicated my task: the role of New York City, and the state's relationships with both the nation and the world. New York City's population of roughly eight million exceeds that of forty-three states. If I have not given the city equal time with upstate, I have nonetheless attempted to weave its story into that of the state and also of the nation. Chapter 8 deals with the intermittent feuding between upstate and downstate, while the chapters on population, culture, economics, and politics pay considerable attention to metropolitan developments.

I have examined reciprocal relationships between New York State and national as well as international politics. Happenings in Ireland, Israel, and Germany have had great impact on the affairs of metropolis and state. Conversely, the statements of New York officials and their actions toward foreign leaders, whether the Prince of Wales, King Faisal, or Adolf Hitler, have complicated American foreign relations and sometimes jolted the State Department. The state has always served as a bridgehead for foreign goods and ideas, and at the same time it has provided the major gateway to and from the great interior of this country.

Historians will recognize my indebtedness to fellow workers in the vineyard. I wish to thank Michael Kammen of Cornell University for reading my chapter on provincial New York and making valuable suggestions. Thomas F. O'Donnell of the State University of New York College at Brockport has corrected and improved my material on New York literature. I am grateful to my sisters, Sarah Ellis Ward and Margaret Ellis Blabey, for assistance and suggestions.

I wish to thank Prentice-Hall, Inc., for permission to reprint five maps from *New York: The Empire State,* of which I am co-author.

DAVID MALDWYN ELLIS

Clinton, New York

NEW YORK

State and City

1

The New York Character

Scores of historians, hundreds of foreign observers, and millions of ordinary visitors have tried to make generalizations about the traits of New Yorkers and their institutions. Because diversity has been the outstanding feature, they have failed to capture New York's essence, too changeable to pin down, too elusive to grasp. How does one encapsulate in one history both upstate and metropolitan New York? Like a massive geological fault, the rivalry between these two sections has ruptured state unity for centuries.

The term "New Yorker" evokes certain images that filmmakers, television producers, novelists, and even politicians have made familiar: the cab driver with his trenchant commentary on current personalities, the addlepated or clever secretary with an accent allegedly common in Brooklyn, the Madison Avenue hustler, the Greenwich Village dropout, and the business tycoon. Father Knickerbocker and the Tammany tiger, the creations of Thomas Nast's fertile brain and skillful pen, have become stock figures in American iconography. Upstaters, however, cannot boast of readily recognizable images or characters. Perhaps the only exception is David Harum, the shrewd banker in Edward Westcott's novel, but Homer's horse trader could pass for a small-town businessman almost anywhere in New England.

Geography has shaped New York's development to an unusual extent by making it one of the world's great thoroughfares. Mountains, rivers, and lakes have separated New York from Canada and neighboring states, especially in the period before automobile and air travel. To the north, hostile forces—French, British, and Indian—crouched behind Lakes Ontario and Erie.

1

Although the international border became one of the most peaceful in the world, it did mark off from New York such distinct societies as French Quebec and English-speaking Ontario. For decades most New Yorkers had little contact with Pennsylvania, although pioneers did float logs and farm products down the Delaware, Susquehanna, and Allegheny rivers. The main lines of trade and travel in both New York and Pennsylvania ran east–west; the Allegheny Plateau, a rugged terrain with a scattered population, raised an effective barrier between the major cities of Pennsylvania and the urban corridor stretching from Albany to Buffalo. Similarly, rough country in northern New Jersey and in southeastern New York limited contact between these two regions except along the Hudson and Delaware valleys.

To the east, mountain ranges separated colonial New York from New England. Although Lake Champlain was more of a unifying factor than a barrier for the sparse population on its shores, the Adirondacks formed a wall between northern New England and the more fertile parts of central and western New York. In addition the Berkshires in western Massachusetts and the Taconics, a range running down the border between New York and Connecticut, obstructed westering Yankees until after the Revolution.

New York became the major gateway to the North American continent and also a thoroughfare to the interior. Early settlements fringed the Hudson River, which is tidal as far as Albany. The Erie Canal magnified the value of the Hudson-Mohawk gateway by extending it westward to Rochester and Buffalo. The canal, reinforced by railroads, sparked urban growth along this route. By 1900 more than four out of five New Yorkers lived in a twenty-mile-wide corridor running from New York City northward to Albany, then west to Buffalo.

Although diversity and change have marked the way of life of New Yorkers, several other features have emerged in almost every generation. What New York is today, it always was: commercial almost to the point of crassness, cosmopolitan and basically tolerant despite recurrent outbreaks of tribalism, urban-centered and open to intellectual and cultural currents flowing in from Europe and the American hinterland. Although talented newcomers in every generation have broken into the highest echelons of politics and business, a powerful elite has usually set the tone in social and cultural affairs. The landed grandees of colonial New York gradually yielded their leadership role to commercial titans such as A. T. Stewart and John Jacob Astor, who in turn were succeeded by the Rockefellers, Morgans, and Harrimans.

New York Means Business. So runs the slogan of the New York State Department of Commerce, which has recently had to underscore this point to business firms contemplating moves to other states. From the outset residents have applied themselves to trade and allied pursuits—in fact, almost any activity that promised gain. As early as 1794 Talleyrand stated that New York was the best place in the world to make money fast. Visitors by the hundreds have repeated his observation.

The Dutch West India Company, chartered in 1621, founded the colony as trading posts on Manhattan and near the present site of Albany. A nation of shopkeepers, the English captured New Netherland largely because Dutch traders undermined the navigation acts that protected British trade with the colonies. The provincial seal soon displayed the figure of a beaver and a mill, representing growing exports of furs and flour. After the Revolution hundreds of thousands of New Englanders reinvigorated the commercial spirit and soon dominated the business life of both New York City and its upstate satellites. As we shall see, Manhattan's merchants grasped control of the transatlantic, coastal, and interior trade routes and transformed their city into the supreme mart of the Western Hemisphere. By 1820 New Yorkers had even surpassed Philadelphia bankers in finance. Wall Street came to symbolize the money capital of the country, if not the world, after World War II. When businessmen began to form giant corporations around the turn of this century, they relied on J. P. Morgan and other Wall Street bankers for assistance. Roughly one-third of the five hundred largest corporations established their headquarters in metropolitan New York. Upstate, too, had its large firms: Eastman Kodak, International Business Machines, Bausch and Lomb, General Electric. Upstate produced an unusual number of business leaders, including the first billionaire, John D. Rockefeller.

A random sampling will illustrate the significant role of New

York's citizens in various business fields. Cornelius Vanderbilt, a native of Staten Island, took over the New York Central after making a fortune in shipping. All of the Big Four who built the Central Pacific in California—Collis P. Huntington, Leland Stanford, Mark Hopkins, and Charles Crocker—hailed from the Empire State. By 1910 a Long Islander, Edward Harriman, had assembled the largest railroad empire in the United States and had plans for a railroad in China. Jay Gould, from Delaware County, and Daniel Drew, a Putnam County drover, became infamous as Wall Street plungers who proved as talented in watering stock as in manipulating politicians.

Clearly something in the New York environment brought out commercial talent and the inventive abilities of its citizens. George Eastman of Waterville developed the dry plate for photography and George Westinghouse of Schoharie County built up a massive corporation around his invention of air brakes. Thomas B. Watson created the fabulous IBM (International Business Machines) company, which has revolutionized business practices throughout the world with its computers and other office equipment.

New York has also attracted from other states and countries outstanding businessmen: steel barons (Andrew Carnegie, Charles Schwab), copper kings (the Guggenheims), newspaper publishers (Adolph Ochs from Chattanooga, Joseph Pulitzer from St. Louis, William Randolph Hearst from San Francisco). Able young people from all over the country moved to New York hoping to strike it rich. Of course, most enjoyed only modest success, but a few climbed to the top of the slippery pole.

Commerce ordinarily takes place in urban centers, and ever since the Dutch established two trading posts on the Hudson, a substantial proportion of New Yorkers have lived in cities. Colonial New York surpassed Massachusetts and rivaled Pennsylvania in the proportion of its citizens who were city dwellers. Large landholders maintained homes and businesses in New York City and Albany, where their children intermarried with the merchant aristocracy. New York City grew sharply after 1754 and especially after the Revolution, gaining national leadership by 1820. No less spectacular was the growth of scores of upstate centers, and several along the Erie Canal became major cities. When the guns roared at Fort Sumter in 1861, about half of New Yorkers were living in cities. When the twentieth century opened, a majority of upstaters were urban. Since World War II well over four-fifths of the population have lived in six clusters along the "urban streak" running from Buffalo to Albany, down to New York City, then east into Nassau County.

More striking even than its commercial and urban character has been the heterogeneous population of New York. Wave after wave of immigrants have swept into the state from every continent and nation. Before 1950 the foreign-born and their children constituted a majority of city dwellers upstate. Certain cities still show the imprint of particular groups, among the most conspicuous being the Swedes of Jamestown, the Poles of Buffalo, the Italians of Utica and Rochester, the Irish of Albany, and the Czechs of Binghamton.

But the countryside has also attracted a wide variety of nationalities. One can find German Mennonites on the farms of the Black River valley, Italian truck farmers around Rome and Canastota, French-Canadians in the north country, Welsh farmers in central New York. Black migrants by the tens of thousands made their way into the state after 1940, when World War II created a labor shortage. Gradually they drifted from the fields of the South to New York's cities, where they populated large neighborhoods.

Two elements in New York's population deserve special attention. First, approximately three million or one-half of American Jews live within the state's borders, with the greatest concentration in the metropolis. Their contributions to the arts, science, professions, education, theater, and business need no elaboration. Second, three out of four mainland Puerto Ricans have made their homes in New York. Together with the hundreds of thousands of other Latin Americans in New York City, they have established a strong enclave of Spanish-American culture.

Citizens of New York have generally shown a spirit of tolerance even though they have not necessarily loved each other. Each new wave of newcomers has faced a certain amount of social harassment before they have been "accepted." Unlike the people of most seventeenth-century societies, Dutch citizens placed profits ahead of conformity. When Governor Peter Stuyvesant began to persecute Jews, his superiors restrained his hand. British officials were more interested in getting land patents, fighting the French, placating the Iroquois, and increasing the provincial revenues than in policing nonconformists.

The leadership of New York in high culture is largely a by-product of the rise of New York City to commercial and financial supremacy. Throughout history some members of wealthy families have become patrons of the arts, partly out of vanity and self-indulgence and partly because of a genuine interest. Obviously the average citizen of the Empire State, like his counterparts in the South and West, did not understand or appreciate the masterpieces collected by a handful of aristocrats, but thousands of musicians, artists, and writers from Europe and the hinterland found their greatest opportunities in the metropolis. Actors and actresses of the London stage made Broadway their first stop on American tours. P. T. Barnum in the middle years of the nineteenth century brought more popular entertainment to the masses, but he occasionally added a fillip of "culture," as when he presented Jenny Lind, the Swedish nightingale, to captivated audiences in 1850.

Manhattan became the capital of the creative arts with music at the Metropolitan Opera, ballet at Lincoln Center, and paintings at scores of galleries and museums. After the Civil War, most of the nation's books and magazines were published in New York. Interestingly enough, most of the major publishers grew up in communities far from the metropolis. New York City attracted the talent of the nation and the world, and gave it the opportunity to develop.

Upstate has also participated in the culture boom that most parts of the country have experienced since World War II. In scores of communities, devotees of the arts have enlisted patrons and sponsored symphonies, theater groups, and art museums. The numbers attending art fairs vie with audiences attracted to the more traditional county fairs with horse races, exhibits, and sideshows. New York was the first state to set up a Council on the Arts to support musical, dramatic, and ballet groups. The Performing Arts Center at Saratoga and the Lewiston Art Park near Buffalo have received much encouragement and state support.

One can add compassion to the list of New York's characteristics. Allan Nevins found humanitarian reform and concern for the ill, underprivileged, and downtrodden the "golden thread" in New York City's history. More recently another urban historian, Bayrd Still, has noted that New York City has provided many more urban services than other major American cities.[1] In addition to the usual municipal services such as police and fire protection, they include a wide range of educational, cultural, recreational, and medical amenities. One can trace this liberality to generations of altruistic reformers, the strong evangelical impulse of the nineteenth century reinforced by the liberal inclinations of the sizable Jewish community, the need to provide for indigent newcomers, the power of pressure groups, and the rush to seize matching grants from both state and federal governments.

New York City is the headquarters for hundreds of humanitarian organizations, from the American Bible Society to the Urban League. The United Nations, the National Council of Churches, and the large foundations employ thousands of persons who aid millions throughout the nation and the world. Only Boston has as many humanitarian associations in proportion to its population.

Upstate spawned a large number of reform movements in the three decades before the Civil War. In 1825 Charles Finney began his famous revivals and urged converts not only to seek salvation but to regenerate society. Harkening to this message, citizens in central New York embarked on a host of reforms. They organized Sunday schools and handed out thousands of tracts. Demon rum, which held thousands in its grip, became their favorite target. They supported academies where young people could help pay for their education by working in the fields. Eventually they made the destruction of slavery their main goal, and whenever they could they rescued runaway slaves from slave-catching marshals. At Seneca Falls in 1848, women drew up the Declaration of Sentiments and Resolutions of the First Woman's Rights Convention to proclaim their rights as human beings and as citizens.

The reformers ran into resistance offered by saloonkeepers, politicians in league with southerners, and conservatives who objected to any change. But reform sent down deep roots. How else can one explain the remarkable hamlet of South Butler in Wayne County, which in the 1850s hired a woman preacher (Antoinette Brown Blackwell), a black preacher, and later a woman doctor?

The fires of reform were banked after the Civil War, when energetic and motivated individuals tended to seek fulfillment in making money and creating large business enterprises. Still, upstaters continued to produce an occasional champion of the underdog. Margaret Sanger, who grew up in Corning, challenged church authorities and public opinion by advocating birth control. Elbert Hubbard of East Aurora preached a revival of crafts, which several other individuals were urging in Woodstock. Walter Rauschenbusch of Rochester, later of New York City, demanded that Christian principles be applied to social and business life. Thousands of unknown reformers worked in various localities to bring about better schools, clinics, sanitation, and civil service.

The fact that New York had the largest bloc of electoral votes for 150 years before the 1970s gave its governors a head start in the presidential sweepstakes. New York has also had its share—perhaps more—of scoundrels and rascals. Aaron Burr and William Tweed head a long list of crooks, charlatans, and demagogues, most of whom have retreated to history's shadowy corridors. What can one say to excuse the political and administrative bumbling that paralyzed New York City in 1975?

Of course, New York did nurture an occasional giant of statecraft: Alexander Hamilton, who wrote about fifty of the eighty-five *Federalist Papers*; John Jay, who framed the first state constitution; De Witt Clinton, the testy governor whose Erie Canal was the greatest single achievement on the state level in the nineteenth century. In addition, Samuel Tilden, Grover Cleveland, Horatio Seymour, and Theodore Roosevelt raised the level of public service and brought about important reforms.

In the twentieth century New York State's governors look rather impressive when compared with those of other states.

A women's rights convention. *Harper's Weekly*, June 11, 1859.

Among them have been Charles Evans Hughes, Alfred E. Smith, Franklin D. Roosevelt, Herbert H. Lehman, Thomas E. Dewey, and Nelson Rockefeller, all men of national stature. Each of these men has his critics, but one must recognize their overall ability, integrity, and devotion to the public welfare. Sometimes they cajoled, sometimes they coerced the legislators to adopt social legislation. Perhaps the cost was too high: the highest per capita tax load of any state.

New Yorkers surpass most Americans in interest in foreign affairs, a quality regarded as vaguely un-American in some parts of the country. Obviously the foreign-born and their children, who have formed such a high percentage of the citizens of the Empire State, account for much of this interest. Jews have agonized over Hitler's holocaust, the threat to Israel's security, and anti-Semitism in the Soviet Union. Blacks, searching for their roots, have watched with growing pride the emergence of African nations. Puerto Ricans and other Spanish-speaking inhabitants have close ties with the entire Hispanic world, and newcomers continually strengthen those ties. American Irish have taken up the cause of an independent Ireland.

New York's leading role in foreign trade and travel has also made its citizens and especially its businessmen interested in events overseas. Its great newspapers and magazines have emphasized foreign news, while the major banks and multinational corporations have investments and customers on every continent. The presence of the United Nations has stimulated concern over threats to peace and human rights throughout the world.

In one sense, New York has served as a bridge between this nation and the rest of the world. In 1892 a French economist wrote that New York could best be understood as the connecting link between two very different worlds: "For Europeans New York is America but for Americans it is the beginning of Europe."[2] In its own way upstate joined the metropolis in performing this function. François Chateaubriand and J. Hector St. John de Crèvecoeur found on the upstate frontier Rousseau's "noble savage." New York State provided the basic landscape and cityscape that entered the consciousness of foreigners. As Howard Mumford Jones has noted, James Fenimore Cooper's novels "fixed the image of America for thousands of Europeans." Travelers—and they wrote hundreds of accounts of their journeys—gave the most generous attention to Niagara Falls, the lordly Hudson, and especially Manhattan's skyline, symbol of modern technocracy.

New York, although recently challenged by California, has set the pace in most aspects of economic, cultural, and social life. But New York, especially the metropolis, has seldom won any popularity prizes, as was clearly shown when it sought federal aid during the crisis of 1975. As Kenneth Jackson has observed, "most Americans," including many upstaters, have and will continue to regard New York City "as a mismanaged ant heap, unfit for human habitation."[3] In the 1890s William Jennings Bryan thundered against the "gold bugs" of Wall Street. In the 1920s citizens in the Bible Belt regarded Gotham as Sodom and Gomorrah incarnate. More recently Governor George Wallace of Alabama inveighed against the "pointy-headed liberals" of New York, while Barry Goldwater and Richard Nixon denounced the news media centered there.

No doubt the overweening pretensions of New Yorkers in the worlds of business, entertainment, and journalism have caused much of the resentment west of the Hudson. Part of this hatred stems from fear that other communities will follow New Yorkers into such strange and loathsome activities as the drug culture, pornography, and organized crime. Still, New York City has a compelling fascination even for those most offended by its intensity, extremes, and threats. Where else have there been so many opportunities, so many choices, so much vitality in a climate of tolerance? Thomas Wolfe, who came from North Carolina to write in New York, declared that the city "lays hand upon a man's bowels; he grows drunk with ecstasy; he grows young and full of glory; he feels that he can never die."[4]

Natives of New England and their children formed well over half of the population of New York State in the formative decades when upstate took form and its institutions became rooted. A Georgia-born merchant, Gazaway Bugg Lamar, complained in March 1861 that "New England education, New England doctrines, New England men control that great state and suck its life blood out of it. . . ."[5] Even if one discounts his words as exaggerated by the imminence of civil war, one cannot deny that the Yankee imprint lay heavily upon all sections of New York State, including the metropolis. New Englanders held dominant positions in business, manufacturing, professions, journalism, and politics.

Obviously we must examine more closely the hallmarks of New England civilization, an inquiry that thousands of authors have attempted without complete success. On the popular level we all share images of laconic Vermonters, flinty lobstermen, and earnest Boston reformers. Upon closer examination the Yankee character displays a variety of contrasting attitudes: idealistic and materialistic, puritanical and hedonistic, rational and emotional, aristocratic and democratic, individualistic and community-minded. A people of paradox, New Englanders developed king-sized consciences and a spiritual pride that outsiders called arrogant and hypocritical.

Behind the puritan ethos was a grim acceptance of life as a time of testing imposed by a Calvinist God upon his people, with whom he had made a covenant. To demonstrate that they were among the elect chosen for salvation by this transcendent God, men had to submit to discipline, in effect to become moral athletes.

To survive the harsh winters and to extract a modest living from the grudging soil, New Englanders had to work hard, husband every resource, and plan carefully. If a French farmer's wealth was judged by the size of his manure pile, the New Englander's foresight was measured by the size of his woodpile.

But New England traits and institutions have kept evolving over the centuries. Traders who haggled with English, French, and Spanish merchants observed and copied other life-styles, and some acquired wealth, Satan's most beguiling temptress. The ideas of Enlightenment—liberty, equality, progress, toleration—filtered into New England, where democratic procedures had already been established in congregational and town meetings.

The Puritans' emphasis on literacy and their reliance on rationalism opened their minds to new currents of thought. By the end of the eighteenth century many merchants, lawyers, and even divines in the Boston area had repudiated the tenets of Calvin. Meanwhile the Great Awakening had stirred the dry bones of the churches, and this outpouring of the spirit split congregations into Old Lights and New Lights. New Light congregations asserted their independence, while Baptists and Methodists, the latter stressing free will and plenteous grace for all repentant sinners, won many converts. Thousands of farmers migrated to the frontiers to escape the watchful eyes of the orthodox and the censorious comment of their neighbors in the compact communities of eastern and southern New England.

A striking example of the transplanting of New England values to New York may be seen in John Brown, a merchant of Providence, Rhode Island, who in 1799 divided his tract in northern Herkimer County into eight townships and named them Industry, Enterprise, Perseverance, Unanimity, Frugality, Sobriety, Economy, and Regularity. Despite this systematic testimonial to the Protestant ethic, the Brown land attracted few pioneers and yielded no income to the Brown family.

The upstate character was thus a variant of the Yankee character, but few communities in New York were able to reproduce the formal and informal restrictions that remained so powerful in the New England countryside. Upstaters sloughed off some of the narrowness and miserliness of their forebears if only because the Empire State had a more fluid society and offered more opportunities.

In the nineteenth century the two regions kept diverging for a variety of reasons. Whereas textile manufacturing became the dominant industry in New England, milling, meat-packing, and other food-processing activities became more important in New York, whose manufacturers engaged in a much broader range of activity.

The specter of deserted fields and vacant farmsteads stalked New England before rural decline became a major concern in New York. When Yankees saw their children and more vigorous neighbors depart for western farms, factory jobs, or lives before the mast, their businessmen became more cautious and the old spirit of "can do" evaporated. By contrast, New Yorkers, their numbers growing by leaps and bounds, filled communities with their optimism and confidence. Next year, they exulted, they would break new records—more sales, more profits, more jobs. While Connecticut leaders took pride in describing their state as "the land of steady habits," New York's decision makers hailed change itself as a positive good.

New England's leaders, old families, and institutions harked back to the heroic days of the Pilgrim and Puritan founders and to the glorious events of the Revolution. Writing about the past became a major occupation of New Englanders. Most upstaters, however, had little sense of identity with or affection for New York's Dutch founders; Washington Irving was not the only one to ridicule them and their traditions. Whereas New Yorkers gloried in their cosmopolitan communities, New Englanders had difficulty in absorbing Irish immigrants into their society, which remained remarkably homogeneous for over two centuries.

New Yorkers found the future more exciting than the past that an increasing number of Yankees considered themselves duty-bound to preserve and celebrate. Post-Revolutionary New York constituted a brand-new country, the Empire State. Its citizens greeted Fulton's new steamboat with bonfires; they shot off skyrockets when De Witt Clinton's barge passed; they hailed the first railroad that puffed its way from Albany to Schenectady.

New Yorkers worshiped progress as a new deity that required its adherents to keep improving institutions and expanding the economy. When Sam Patch, a native of Pawtucket, came to New York, he attracted huge crowds by leaping into such rivers as the Niagara. In 1827 he jumped into the Genesee River below the falls at Rochester, and his failure to surface brought into question his slogan, "Some things can be done as well as others." Yet his words bespoke the true Yankee-Yorker spirit: self-confident, risk-taking, enterprising.

As immigrants poured into the state, the Yankee-Yorker stock became a small minority in the major cities, although its members remained dominant in small towns and the countryside. Interestingly enough, most newcomers adopted the value system of the native stock, their rate of acceptance or adaptation varying with their educational level and skills, and with the amount of opposition they encountered. Who, for example, would deny the trading skills of such immigrants as Italians, Jews, Lebanese, Chinese, Greeks? Even illiterate peasants from hierarchical societies found it possible to get ahead with a speed that astonished their families in the Old World. They and their children soon saw the advantage of learning the three R's in public schools and evening classes. Today many of the most zealous examplars of the so-called puritan ethic are persons of Jewish and Roman Catholic background.

While De Witt Clinton was writing his famous call for the Erie Canal in 1816, he was also, as president of the American Academy of Fine Arts, urging its members to observe the countryside.

Can there be any country in the world better calculated than ours to exercise and to exalt the imagination—to call into activity the creative power of the mind, and to afford just views of the beautiful, the wonderful, and the sublime? Here nature has conducted her operations on a magnificent scale; extensive and elevated mountains, lakes of oceanic size, rivers of prodigious magnitude, cataracts unequalled for volume of water, and boundless forests filled with wild beasts and savage men and covered with the tall oak and the aspiring pine. . . .[6]

Soon a series of aquatints of mountains and streams appeared in *Picturesque Views of American Scenery*. Thomas Doughty, who colored the plates, embarked upon a career as landscape painter. His views of the Hudson Valley intrigued and fascinated Thomas Cole, another English immigrant, who moved to Catskill and set up his studio there.

After the Civil War the literary history of the state bifurcates because the writers in and about New York City had little in common with those dealing with upstate. Furthermore, as the upstate cities grew and kept absorbing larger numbers of immigrants from Europe, they projected a blurred image that writers found difficult to describe. Authors tended to retreat to the countryside in search of local color and tradition.

New York's landscape has matched its population in diversity and variety. The Empire State is composed of many subregions—indeed, of thousands of distinctive localities and neighborhoods—which travelers, geologists, geographers, de-

mographers, political scientists, historians, and students of literature have recognized. No one should miss E. B. White's delight-
ful essay on New York City, in which he points out: "The city is
literally a composite of tens of thousands of tiny neighborhood
units. . . . Each neighborhood is virtually self-sufficient. Usually
it is no more than two or three blocks long and a couple of blocks
wide. Each area is a city within a city within a city."[7] In 1976
approximately 10,000 block associations had emerged, with
building captains, beautification boards, and security patrols.
Citizens distrusted City Hall and big government, which had
failed to meet their needs in education, housing, police protection, and trash collection.

Geologists and geographers have divided the state sometimes
into drainage basins, sometimes according to elevation and phys-
ical features—mountains, plateaus, lowlands. These units have
exerted a powerful influence on the location of population, on
economic activities, on transportation routes, and even on the
cultural milieu. John H. Thompson has made the most careful
analysis of regionalism within the state, but his criteria largely
ignore the dimensions of folklore and history except as they are
influenced by economic developments. He outlines eight "composite regions," that is, areas that "exhibit similarities in resource
base, history of use, current characteristics and problems, and
developmental potential."[8] Before presenting his list of "optimum
administrative districts," he discusses eight composite regions
that have uniform characteristics: the Adirondack Wilderness,
the Appalachian Country (an enlarged Southern Tier), the Upstate Heartland (roughly the Lake Ontario plain and the Finger
Lakes), the Middle Mohawk, the Hudson Valley, the North
Country (St. Lawrence Valley and Lake Champlain country),
Tug Hill Wilderness (an upland area west of the Black River),
and Metropolitan New York (the lower Hudson, New York City,
and Long Island).

Demographers have tended to define the state in terms of
population clusters: Greater Buffalo, the Capital District, Greater
New York, and so on. Political scientists have subdivided the
state according to functions: counties, park districts, even income tax groupings.

Few persons have spent so much time and thought on the New York spirit as Carl Carmer, who had a keen awareness of place as well as a command of the literary associations. He collected selections from a hundred authors for his volume *The Tavern Lamps Are Burning: Literary Journeys through Six Regions and Four Centuries of New York State*. Dismissing Long Island and New York City as outside his scope (a significant decision in itself), Carmer settled on six regions: the Hudson Valley, including the Catskills; the Adirondacks, including the St. Lawrence Valley and Lake Champlain; the Mohawk Valley and the Erie Canal; the Finger Lakes; Western New York; and the Southern Tier.

Let me try my hand at naming regions that have a quality of their own, blending geography, economic development, history, folklore, and literature. "Old" New York—that is, the area partially laid out in tracts and lightly settled before the Revolution—breaks into easily identifiable units: Long Island, New York City, the Hudson Valley, the Catskills, and the Adirondack area, including the St. Lawrence Valley and Lake Champlain. "New" New York, that part of the state settled after the Revolution, has less sharply defined regions. Who can really draw a line between the Finger Lakes and the Southern Tier? And where does Western New York begin? At Lake Seneca? At the Genesee River?

The urban corridor stretching from Albany through the Mohawk Valley to Rochester may be regarded as a separate region. These cities absorbed large numbers of immigrants and have been linked together by the Erie Canal, the New York Central Railroad, and the Thruway. Buffalo has been excluded because this city with its environs is large and distinctive enough to stand by itself. The remaining territory has been arbitrarily divided into two regions: the Finger Lakes, including the upper Genesee Valley, and the Southwest Gateway. A brief description of these regions provides a sense of the remarkable diversity of the Empire State. It may even uncover clues as to what makes New Yorkers tick.

Long Island. Before the Civil War the basic population of the island east of Brooklyn was almost exclusively New England by derivation. The sea shaped the contours of Long Island and

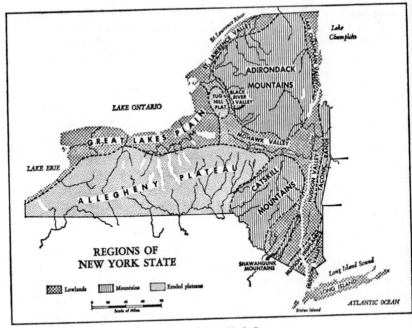

Regions of New York State

greatly influenced the livelihood of its people for over two centuries. The local poet Walt Whitman captured a feeling for his
native Long Island's dependence upon the ocean.

Sea-beauty! stretch'd and basking!
One side thy inland ocean laving, broad, with copious commerce, steam-
ers, sails,
And one the Atlantic's wind caressing, fierce or gentle-mighty hulls
dark-gliding in the distance.
Isle of sweet brooks of drinking water-healthy air and soil!
Isle of the salty shore and breeze and brine![9]

The iron horse helped break down isolation in the 1840s and
stimulated Long Islanders to produce foodstuffs for the city market. After the Civil War many rich New Yorkers acquired large
estates where they could hunt, play, and entertain. In this century Robert Moses revolutionized Long Island with his parks and
highways. Developers have gobbled up thousands of farms, laid

out streets, and erected houses by the thousands. The process of suburbanization has spilled well beyond Nassau County into Suffolk, whose citizens, especially those in the still rural easternmost section, fear the encroachment of developers and suburban problems.

New York City. The metropolis, an empire in itself, has presented to visitors and to insiders a multifaceted personality. A magical place, it has been the center of commerce, culture, and conviviality. The city is composed of hundreds of neighborhoods. Chinatown, Harlem, Brooklyn Heights, Wall Street, Greenwich Village are only a few of the most widely known.

One will search long and hard for "York Statism" in the metropolis, where change has remained the most persistent characteristic. As John Jay Chapman wrote about the city, "The present in New York is so powerful that the past is lost."[10] Since 1850 New York City has belonged more to the nation and the world than to the rest of the state; yet the residents of the Big Apple have discovered, sometimes with a rude shock, that Albany, no less than Washington, has crucial authority over their destiny. The events of the 1970s shook the confidence of the citizens of Baghdad-on-the-Hudson. Nevertheless, Gotham and its inhabitants—chastened, leaner, less exuberant—will survive.

The Hudson Valley. Early European travelers often compared the Hudson River with the Rhine because of its grand views, historic landmarks, and storied associations. Actually an arm of the sea, the Hudson became an important artery of trade and travel, a vital link in the route to the interior. Sloops continued to tack up and down the Hudson even after 1807, when the *Clermont* belched heavy smoke on its first voyage. Steamboats carried more than a million passengers in 1851, the first year a train chugged from Manhattan to Greenbush, opposite Albany.

Most colonial New Yorkers lived within a few miles of the Hudson. The British sought control of the river and its frowning fortress at West Point during the Revolution, but the patriots at Saratoga, on the upper Hudson, frustrated their efforts. Washington Irving and the painters of the Hudson River School enveloped the landscape in a soft romantic haze. Wealthy families built fine mansions along the eastern banks, their ranks continually enlarged by those newly enriched in trade, manufacturing, and finance. By the mid–twentieth century, many of these estates had slipped back to public or semipublic agencies: state parks and national monuments, hospitals, colleges, convents, and retreats.

The Adirondacks. The landscape in the northeastern part of New York, in Edmund Wilson's phrase, "overwhelms the people," a fact that city dwellers in the whole Northeast increasingly appreciate. Only a few people have chosen to live in the rugged Adirondacks, whose stony slopes and short growing season have discouraged farming. To be sure, the magnificent stands of timber have supported several thousand loggers and lumbermen, especially in the nineteenth century. Residents among these lonely mountains and hills have developed an independent spirit bordering on eccentricity. Visitors have told tall stories about the peculiarities as well as the skill of their guides and handymen.

Lake Champlain and its approaches provided the backdrop for dozens of raiding parties and military expeditions from 1609, when Samuel Champlain shot three Mohawk chiefs, to 1814, when Thomas MacDonough won the Battle of Plattsburg. The narrow band of fertile land bordering the south shore of the St. Lawrence River never attracted many people, even after the construction of the Seaway. Hunters, hikers, and vacationers discovered the beauties of the North Country and the Adirondacks, and millions of visitors have patronized such resorts as the Thousand Islands, Ausable Chasm, Lake Placid, and Lake George. Writers have woven many stories about the military struggles, the natural wonders of the north woods, and the idiosyncrasies of hosts, guides, and guests in resort communities.

The Catskills. Overlooking the Hudson Valley are the Catskills, a mountainous region that gradually merges into the Allegheny Plateau. The spirit of Rip van Winkle hovers over these mountains, made familiar to Americans in the paintings of Thomas Cole and his successors. Later John Burroughs not only recorded the flora and fauna of the region but also conveyed his feeling for the Catskill terrain.

The stone houses at New Paltz, Kingston, and Hurley enable

us to reconstruct genteel life of the seventeenth century. Most Catskill farms and villages, however, reflect the domestic arrangements of settlers who arrived after 1800. Because of its proximity to New York City and its growing middle class, the Catskills became a playground for tens of thousands. Resorts sprang up to cater to peoples of almost every background: Jewish, Irish, Russian, Negro, German, Polish. In Sullivan County, Jewish businessmen constructed famous hotels whose amenities and entertainment have attracted many non-Jews as well.

The Erie Canal and Urban Corridor. Transportation is the key element in the corridor of cities and towns running from Albany through the Mohawk Valley to Utica and Rome, then westward along the Lake Ontario plain to Rochester and Buffalo. Governor De Witt Clinton and others dreamed of building a waterway through this water-level route to the interior. Not only did their dreams come true beyond their wildest expectations, but the people who constructed and operated the canal became a great source of folklore—in fact, the mother lode for authors who have written about the Empire State in this century. Walter Edmonds, Samuel Hopkins Adams, Carl Carmer, and others have concocted tales of pathos, courage, and comedy around Clinton's Big Ditch, the Horse Ocean, the Big Giddap. Each upstate center projects a distinct personality, which its citizens recognize and alternately cherish and bemoan. For some—Little Falls, for example—location has proved decisive; for others, particular industries have stamped their imprint. Governmental policy has obviously shaped the destiny of such cities as Albany and Lockport. Each city in the state has a somewhat different ethnic mix and each has had its strong personalities.

Albany lived off the commerce of the Hudson River and the Erie Canal until well into the nineteenth century. Although it became the state capital in 1797, it did not become a fief of the state government until the days of Governor Alfred E. Smith. In the 1960s Nelson A. Rockefeller greatly expanded the services and inflated the costs of state government. In 1959 a Dutch princess arrived to celebrate the 350th anniversary of Henry Hudson's voyage. Embarrassed by the seedy look of the area south of the state capitol, Governor Rockefeller decided to create the "most spectacularly beautiful seat of government in the world." Soon the bulldozers knocked down ninety-nine acres of buildings and contractors slowly constructed the South Mall. The Mall proved a most impressive aggregation of structures, but it still could not house all of the vast state bureaucracy, and many taxpayers have questioned the wisdom or necessity of spending over $1 billion for this project. Locally, Albany's O'Connell machine provides the most durable example of the old politics: favoritism and niggardly public services made palatable by low taxes.

Before World War I the Mohawk Valley included many cities devoted to textiles and knit goods. Changing styles, inefficient old buildings, rising labor and energy costs, and competition from new mills in the South undermined these old industries, and they withered and died. New enterprises only partially filled the weatherbeaten old factories and replaced the jobs that had vanished. Manufacturers of electronic devices and business machines settled in the valley and became the largest employers in Utica and Herkimer as well as in Schenectady, the home of General Electric. Rome, the Copper City, made a strong bid to become a tourist mecca with the reconstruction of Fort Stanwix and the establishment of a canal village.

Syracuse, a crossway of canals, railroads, and now highways, distributes goods over a wide area. Its five hundred or so manufacturing plants produce a wide range of products—drugs, automobile parts, china, air conditioners. Its newspapers and political leaders have preached a vigorous brand of old-fashioned conservatism, which, however, has not drowned out voices of protest in the Syracuse University and black communities.

Rochester, which began as a flour-milling center, became a boom town with the coming of the Erie Canal. The arrival of George Eastman, who made epochal discoveries in photography, revolutionized its industrial development. Eastman Kodak, one of the fifty largest corporations in the United States, employs more than 100,000 people. Another miracle company is Xerox, the manufacturer of the copier whose name has become a verb in offices around the world.

Enjoying one of the highest per capita incomes of all the state's urban centers and the lowest unemployment rate, Rochester has projected an image of prosperity. Its business leaders, noted for their booster spirit, have gone further in rebuilding their city's downtown area than businessmen in most other cities in the state or the country. Because local families founded and kept most of the control of most of the industries, they have had the means to support such institutions as the University of Rochester, local hospitals, and museums.

The Finger Lakes. The state's Lake Country, like that of old England, has attracted the attention of the scribbling fraternity. Its landscape is one of surpassing loveliness—deep blue lakes, rolling hills, prosperous farms, and spectacular gorges. As a vacationland it offers superb boating, swimming, sailing, hiking, and riding.

The area has a certain finished look because many villages and towns reached their peak before the Civil War. One can observe on the main streets of Geneva, Canandaigua, Bath, and other towns fine examples of nineteenth-century architecture, including magnificent Greek Revival homes. The main flow of trade and travel passed north of the region, along the route of the Erie Canal and the New York Central. The Erie Railroad did provide an alternate route to the west through the southern tier of counties, and in recent years Route 17 has attracted a growing volume of cars and trucks.

The Niagara Frontier. French explorers were the first Europeans to note the strategic importance of the Niagara region. Fort Niagara, the outlet of the famous Niagara River, allowed French officials to intimidate the Senecas and claim control over trade coming down the lakes. Both American and British armies fought many battles in this area during the Revolution and the War of 1812.

The Erie Canal, railroads, and lake transport combined to make Buffalo a major center to which heavy industry gravitated. Its flour mills grind more flour than those of any other city in the world; the steel mills in Lackawanna sprang up where Pennsylvania coal met the iron ore moving down from the Mesabi Range of Minnesota. For many decades Buffalo appeared to itself and to outsiders as a rough, tough town, full of smoky factories, immigrants (especially Poles), wildly enthusiastic sports fans, and Democratic politics. As in most cities, its downtown area has become run-down with the exodus of many middle-class citizens and businesses; even the University of Buffalo has moved to the suburbs. The Niagara Frontier has several educational institutions, an exceptional museum in the Albright-Knox, and musical groups of distinction. In the last generation, culture has filtered down to a large number of citizens. In the nineteenth century, Niagara Falls became synonymous with honeymoons. Tourists still flock to the falls, and heavy industry has sought the hydroelectric energy generated nearby.

The Southwest Gateway. This sparsely populated area includes three counties: Chautauqua, Cattaraugus, and Allegheny. Among their outstanding features are the Chautauqua Institute, the 65,000-acre Allegheny State Park, Seneca Indian reservations, and a few oil wells.

Carl Carmer captured the flavor of the New York countryside in his tales of residents and studies of various localities. Boldly he asserted: "York State is a country." Seldom did he analyze in precise terms what constitutes this embryonic nation. In *Dark Trees to the Wind* he lowered his guard a bit: "People are both a region and a way of life. Landscape becomes a part of them and they become a part of each other. Generations and institutions enter into this developing pattern but the pattern, present or past, is always people."[11]

Wherever we look, we encounter Carmer's people, who have formed a society of infinite variety, complexity, and change. As America's society grows increasingly pluralistic, it may be able to forecast its future from New York's experiences.

New Yorkers, who have a normal allotment of pride and other frailties, still have never looked upon themselves as a superior race, the elect of God, or the fulfillment of historical processes. Drawing upon the talent of newcomers from every state and nation, they have learned how to balance rival interests, to accommodate change without jettisoning traditional values, to unearth and reward talent, and to take care of those in need. Have New Yorkers created the good society? Probably not. But no one can gainsay the fact that throughout the past two centuries New York has been the place where the action is.

2

The Peoples of New York

The process of Americanizing the immigrant is a phenomenon that continues to intrigue foreign observers and to concern each generation. St. Jean de Crèvecoeur, who lived along the west bank of the lower Hudson just before the Revolution, wrote that the "American" was a "new man" shaped by the free institutions under which he lived. "Here individuals of all nations are melted into a new race of men."[1] In 1908 an English author named Israel Zangwill presented a play called *The Melting Pot,* whose title caught the public fancy. One of his characters declaimed on "how the great Alchemist melts and fuses them [immigrants] with his purging flame! Here shall all unite to build the Republic of Man and the Kingdom of God."[2]

In 1643 William Kieft, the director general of New Netherland, told Father Isaac Jogues that eighteen languages were spoken on Manhattan Island. The seaport had already taken on the cosmopolitan flavor that was to become so prominent in the future. Subsequently millions of people from every continent settled in or passed through New York.

The English annexed approximately 8,000 white subjects in 1664, perhaps two-thirds of them of Dutch background. Population reached 20,000 by the turn of the century and rose to about 73,000 by the middle of the eighteenth century. Thereafter immigration and better times brought about rapid growth to 168,000 in 1771. New York province, however, trailed well behind three of its neighbors, Massachusetts, Connecticut, and Pennsylvania.

Almost all New Yorkers lived within a few miles of the Hudson River, Long Island Sound, and the Atlantic Ocean. A tiny vanguard ventured north of Albany while a few thousand pioneers made clearings in the Schoharie and Mohawk valleys. New York port in 1756 had about 13,000 citizens, far outdistancing Albany, the only other city of any size.

Native Americans, more familiarly known as Indians, probably did not number more than 30,000 in 1609, when Henry Hudson first met them and observed their reaction to alcohol. Firewater (rum or whiskey), disease and epidemics, especially those afflicting children, and warfare sharply reduced their numbers. The Revolution dealt a crushing blow to the Iroquois, most of whom supported the king and had to retreat to Canada after defeat. After 1783 a handful—perhaps some 6,000—caved in when pressed by thousands of land-hungry settlers. Today approximately 9,000 Indians live on the state reservations, but thousands more have drifted to large cities. Hundreds of Indians live in Brooklyn, working on the construction of skyscrapers and bridges.

Africans quickly followed the Dutch- and French-speaking Walloons (Belgians) who settled the first two outposts. The Dutch West India Company found that few Dutch workingmen wished to emigrate to the wilderness at a time when Amsterdam and other Dutch cities were prospering. Therefore they sent eleven male slaves in 1626 to work as servants and craftsmen. Although Dutch masters treated their slaves more mildly then plantation owners in Virginia or the West Indies, officials and owners alike ruthlessly put down any threats to order. In 1712, after some slaves burned down buildings and killed five whites, a special court sentenced eighteen slaves to death.

New York colony had the largest number of slaves north of Maryland. Most blacks, their numbers varying from one-tenth to one-seventh of the population, lived in or close to New York City. Wherever Dutch farmers were numerous, slavery had firm roots.

The arrival of Jews in Manhattan in the 1650s, in the wake of persecution in Brazil and Spain, annoyed Director General Peter Stuyvesant. The directors of the Dutch West India Company, however, were reluctant to irritate Jewish stockholders and vetoed his plan to deport the refugees. The small community grew slowly and before 1700 had established Shearith Israel, the first synagogue.

As early as the 1640s New Englanders sailed across the sound and settled Southampton, East Hampton, and Southold on the eastern end of Long Island and founded villages in Hempstead, Jamaica, and other localities to the west. Once the British flag flew above Manhattan, English officials, soldiers, traders, sailors, and craftsmen migrated directly from the mother country. By 1790 English blood ran in the veins of approximately half of all whites in New York. From the English, New York derived its basic institutions, law, government, language, religion, and culture.

Almost all the Dutch settlers—five to six thousand—chose to stay in New York after the conquest of 1664. The terms of surrender guaranteed them their homes, lands, goods, and inheritances, and in addition they enjoyed freedom of worship. These generous terms, however, did not prevent mutual animosity between Dutch and English, which expressed itself in fistfights, name-calling, and political rivalry.

The Dutch dominated Albany and Schenectady until the Revolution and made settlements around New York bay—Bushwick, Flatbush, Flushing, Brooklyn—as well as in northern New Jersey. They comprised almost half of Manhattan's population as late as 1700 and about one-sixth of New York State's population in 1790.

Dutch customs, names, and sports took firm root and eventually became part of the national heritage. Non-Dutch groups adopted Santa Claus (St. Nicholas was the patron saint of New Amsterdam, the jovial figure who brought presents to children). Names ending in -kill (creek), -bush (woods), -wyck (district), -vleit (stream) still dot the Hudson Valley. *Cookie, stoop*, and *boss* are three Anglicized Dutch terms that still enjoy everyday use. Dutch institutions eroded during the eighteenth century as young people abandoned the language and the Dutch Reformed Church. In 1765 a French visitor observed: "There are still two Churches in which religious worship is performed in [the Dutch] language but the number that talk it Diminishes Daily."[3]

French Protestants took refuge in New York after Louis XIV revoked the Edict of Nantes in 1685. The Huguenots aligned themselves with the English and founded several important families (Jays, De Peysters, De Lanceys). Two small communities, New Paltz and New Rochelle, had a distinct Gallic flavor because French families settled them.

In 1710 ten ships sailed up the Hudson carrying more than 2,500 Palatine Germans, increasing the population of the province by almost 10 percent. When the armies of Louis XIV had driven the Palatines from their homeland, they had fled to London, where their plight embarrassed the government. Needing tar, pitch, and masts for the Royal Navy, officials shipped these refugees to the Hudson Valley, where they could work on forested land made available by an enterprising Scot, Robert Livingston.

The experiment failed. The Germans, disgruntled by poor food, military discipline, hard work, and unfulfilled promises, demanded land. Some became farmers near Rhinebeck, but in 1713 more than one hundred families trudged through deep snow to the Schoharie Valley, a fertile region where they laid out farms and seven villages. Soon Albany speculators, who claimed ownership of this land, threatened to expel them. Angered but resigned, some Palatines signed leases or bought tracts; others fled to Pennsylvania, where William Penn was offering free land to settlers. Still others accepted Governor Robert Hunter's offer of free land in the Mohawk Valley, where the site of their early settlement is known as Palatine Bridge. West of the "little falls," the Mohawk Valley widens into a fertile intervale. Here on German Flats in 1725 other Palatines founded Herkimer, the most westerly settlement in the province of New York.

As one might expect, the Scots often engaged in merchandising though most tilled the soil. Sir William Johnson imported more than a hundred Highlanders to his lands north of the Mohawk River, but they fled to Canada upon the outbreak of the Revolution. The Ulster Irish, noted in both Great Britain and the New World for their aggressive, even ruthless treatment of "natives," founded Cherry Valley. Ulster and Orange counties, along the west bank of the Hudson, bore appropriate names for pioneer families who hailed from northern Ireland.

The forces of acculturation and assimilation first made themselves felt in New York City, although intergroup tensions continued to erupt from time to time. The Germans in the Mohawk Valley, the Dutch communities along the Hudson, and the Yankee towns on Long Island and in Westchester County clung tenaciously to their separate institutions and ways of life. Often separated from other communities by several days' journey, their residents viewed outsiders with suspicion if not hostility.

Peter Kalm, a Swedish botanist who visited Albany in 1749–1750, noted, "The hatred which the English bear against the people of Albany is very great, but that of the Albanians against the English is carried to a ten times higher degree."[4] Nevertheless, Crèvecoeur's comment about a "new race" and other evidence indicate that New Yorkers of varying backgrounds were intermarrying and slowly forming a more homogeneous society. The process took place earliest and proceeded the furthest in New York City, where citizens rubbed shoulders with all kinds of individuals every day.

During the three decades after 1790, New York State's population almost quadrupled, overtaking that of Virginia. In this period New York City, with about one-tenth of the state's population, surpassed Philadelphia.

The percentage of nonwhites declined partly because of a high death rate but primarily because of rapid immigration of whites. By 1820 the proportion of blacks had dropped to less than 3 percent, and the demoralized Indians failed to keep up their numbers.

The influx of New Englanders into New York became a torrent after the Revolution. Although New England had only a million inhabitants in 1790, it was to export about 800,000 persons during the next three decades, most of them to New York. Among the expelling forces were worn-out and stony soils, declining crop yields, large families, and high taxes. The fresh, fertile, and above all cheap lands in New York kept attracting Yankees.

The Yankees reproduced their way of life in New York. In the town of Durham in the Catskills, for example, they built a Presbyterian church, set up stocks, erected a whipping post, and founded a library. In nearby Windham they decreed that "if any person suffer his or her dog to go to meeting he or she shall forfeit the sum of fifty cents for each and every offence."[5] Timothy

Dwight passed through this area and made churlish remarks about older communities with ill-repaired houses, "disagreeable roads," and "clownish" loiterers around the taverns. It warmed his heart to visit Durham, where the land was "thoroughly cleared, well-cultivated, and divided by good enclosures into beautiful farms."[6]

New Englanders almost submerged the older Dutch and German settlements in the Hudson and Mohawk valleys. The Dutch burghers of Albany feared the enterprising zeal of the Yankees who laid out Troy in 1787 and promptly captured much of the trade of the upper Hudson Valley. For decades Troy fought to keep Albany from building a bridge across the Hudson because its merchants wanted to restrict east–west trade to its own bridge.

More shocking still was the intrusion of obstreperous Yankees into Albany itself. Elkanah Watson has left us a graphic description of his encounter of 1789 with Albany's inhabitants: "I settled in Albany, an old traveler, in the midst of the most illiberal portion of the human race—sunk in ignorance—in mud—no lamps— water spouts projecting several feet into the streets—no pavements—no library—nor a public house—or a private boarding house deserving the name. It necessarily followed that no traveller who had the misfortune to reach Albany, remained in the city. . . ."[7]

The newcomers had a tremendous impact upon economic, political, educational, and cultural life. Yankee woodsmen and settlers cleared most of the forests. Yankee clerks kept the ledgers for businessmen who had learned retailing back in Connecticut or Massachusetts. The academies and colleges of New England supplied a high proportion of the men who pounded the pulpit, pleaded before the bar, bled the patient, and applied the birch rod to the unruly student. Milton Hamilton discovered that of 113 printers and editors in New York between 1785 and 1830, 71 hailed from New England. Six of the first seven presidents of Hamilton College had studied at Yale. A majority of the delegates at the constitutional convention of 1821 were natives of Connecticut or the sons of men from the Nutmeg State.

The four decades between 1775 and 1815 saw a blending of the smaller ethnic groups—the Dutch, Germans, Scots, Ulster

Irish, French—into what might be called the old native stock, that is, Protestants of northwestern European origins. Because almost continuous warfare had cut down immigration during that period, these ethnic groups did not receive many reinforcements. New York's population reflected more closely the national composition than it did in earlier days or at any time after the great Irish and German immigration of the 1840s.

The ethnic breakdown for 1820 showed an increase in English representation. The well-informed Timothy Dwight estimated that three-fifths to two-thirds of the state's inhabitants were of Yankee origin. If one adds the British contingent (English, Welsh, Scottish, Ulster Irish), native-stock New Yorkers constituted more than three-fourths of the total.

Population rose sharply from 1,372,812 in 1820 to 3,880,735 in 1860. Approximately half of New Yorkers at the latter date resided in urban centers, with more than one-fourth in New York City and Brooklyn. Mobility reached new peaks. By 1860, 867,032 natives of New York were living outside the state, most of them in Ohio, Michigan, and Wisconsin. Immigration, however, more than offset this loss. In 1855 natives of Europe made up more than one-fourth of the state's population and nearly one-half of the population of the metropolis at the mouth of the Hudson River.

In the nineteenth century New York City became a magnet for European immigrants; during the colonial period most of them would have landed at Philadelphia. The explanation is simple: passenger traffic followed shifting trade routes. Between 1790 and 1815 New York City acquired the major part of the North Atlantic trade, a dominant position in the coastal trade, and after 1825 the best route (the Erie Canal) through the Appalachian barrier. In 1818 the Black Ball Line began packet service on a regular schedule between New York and Liverpool, a convenience welcomed by businessmen and travelers. Meanwhile Philadelphia labored under several disadvantages. Its links to the interior were inferior, and a transatlantic voyage was lengthened by several days when a sailing vessel had to round Cape May and tack up Delaware Bay to the city. Relatively few Europeans settled in southern states, where they faced the competition of slave labor. New England, bulging with surplus young people, had little attraction for immigrants before the 1840s, when Irish and French-Canadians began to find work in textile mills. But in New York the rapid growth of trade, transportation, manufacturing, and finance attracted millions of immigrants.

Most newcomers hailed from Ireland and the German states, but the English, Scots, and Welsh also came in substantial numbers. America had become known as the land of opportunity, where cheap land, good jobs, and religious and political freedom were available to the common man. In Ireland most heads of families were landless peasants who eked out poor livings by working on the great estates. Those fortunate enough to secure a farm had to pay ever increasing rents to the hated English landlords. Suddenly in 1845 the "rot" destroyed the potato crop, the chief source of food. Indeed, the rot was to ruin most of this crop for the next five years. As a result millions fled, many of them settling in New York City and canal towns. Lacking funds, education, and industrial skills, the Irish became menial workers: household servants, laborers, members of construction gangs.

The Germans formed the second largest contingent of foreign-born. Although many found work in the stores, artisan shops, and lofts of Manhattan, a large number also settled in Rochester and Buffalo, where they outnumbered the Irish. Because many Germans had basic education and skills, especially in woodworking, they tended to become craftsmen, tradesmen, and professionals. Coming from many German states, they exhibited a variety of religious and regional traits. Perhaps one-third to one-half belonged to the Roman Catholic church while the other half adhered to several Protestant groups, with Lutherans by far the most numerous. Among the German immigrants were several thousand Jews, most of whom settled in New York City. Although they constituted less than 5 percent of the metropolitan population in 1860, the Jews were already contributing a considerable number of persons to the fields of banking, manufacturing, and education.

Immigrants received at best a lukewarm reception from the old native stock. The influx of Roman Catholics caused smoldering religious resentments to burst into flame. When Bishop John

Hughes demanded public money for parochial schools, Protestants became furious. They could see nothing wrong with public schools whose teachers, textbooks, and readings were more or less anti-Catholic. When the Irish and Germans fought the Sunday closing of saloons and other controls over drinking, evangelical tempers flared. Nativists deplored intemperance, crime, and poverty. Then as now, taxpayers resented relief payments, especially to aliens. The Whigs and Republicans, both of whom flirted with nativists, naturally disliked the Irish and German preference for the Democratic party. Workingmen resented the competition of the foreign-born, who undercut wage levels and sometimes took jobs formerly held by native-born Americans.

Clearly nativist outbursts involved much more than simple religious bigotry, which was of course present on both sides. What was taking place was a confrontation between subcultures, each proud of its traditions and determined to maintain its identity. Members of the old native stock became alarmed because their kind of society was eroding before their eyes. Little Dublins and Kleindeutschlands, each with its own network of churches, schools, newspapers, and clubs, seemed to threaten American nationalism and prevent civic unity.

When investigators asked Americans in the twentieth century to describe Negro characteristics, they often used terms like those used to characterize the Irish Catholics in nineteenth-century New York: primitive morality, laziness, combativeness, religious fanaticism, fondness for gambling and strong drink, tendency toward crimes of violence, ignorance, lack of responsibility, emotional instability.

Hardened by English persecution, disciplined by their devoted priests, convinced of eventual victory either on this earth or in the hereafter, the Irish called for the reconversion of America to the True Faith. To the nativists Bishop John Hughes issued a stern warning: if a single Catholic church were burned in New York, the city would become "a second Moscow."[8] No nativist dared test his resolution.

Meanwhile assimilation of the foreign-born proceeded slowly and unevenly. The old tensions such as the English–Dutch feud faded away in the face of the more pressing immigrant threat. In general the children of the foreign-born adopted American ways more rapidly than their parents. They learned English in school, in the streets, and on the job. Newcomers were instructed in the complexities of ward politics by Democratic politicians, who also exposed them to the high-flown rhetoric of the Fourth of July. Meanwhile, immigrants were shaping American society in countless ways from diet to music. To cite but one example, the arrival of the Irish and immigrants from the Continent brought about the end of the Puritan Sabbath in upstate cities.

The period 1860 to 1914 saw a very large increase in population, most of it concentrated in urban centers. The approximately 3.9 million persons of the 1860s grew to about 6 million in 1890 and 9.1 million twenty years later. Similarly New York City's population rose dramatically, especially after 1898, when it acquired Brooklyn, Staten Island, the Bronx, and Queens County. In 1910 the metropolis had 4.8 million people, over half of the state total. Meanwhile, rural population, which reached its peak in 1880, started to decline, and during the 1880s nearly every rural town lost people, a trend also evident in New England.

The Irish and Germans each accounted for approximately a third of the immigrants between 1860 and 1890, with the British trailing well behind. The census of 1890 listed about 100,000 Slavs and 64,000 Italians, harbingers of the massive influx of these groups during the next two and a half decades.

Before 1882 almost nine out of ten immigrants came from northwestern Europe. Sometimes called the "old" immigration, this group slowly lost its overwhelming share, until by 1896 the "new" immigration from southern and eastern Europe took the lead. Contemporaries exaggerated the differences between the educational level, skills, and sex imbalance of the two waves. Actually the expelling forces—a worsening agriculture, industrialization, the spread of railroads and steamship lines—remained very much the same after 1882 as they had been before. Once again the pulling forces proved too alluring to resist: cheap land, cheap transportation, and jobs in American industry, which surpassed those of all other nations after 1890. The familial and kinship system continued to play an important role. Of the 12,000 Italians in Buffalo in 1905, for example, about 10,000 had come from two south Italian villages.

The rise of Pan-Slavism spelled persecution for minorities living in the western provinces of Russia, whose officials harassed Jews, Finns, Poles, Lithuanians, Latvians, and Estonians. Anti-Jewish riots and laws stimulated a massive exodus, and New York became the promised city. Meanwhile in Italy millions of villagers and landless peasants south of Naples and in Sicily came to America and found work as unskilled laborers, shopkeepers, and construction workers.

Although the bulk of foreigners settled in New York City, tens of thousands made their homes in upstate cities. Italians became the largest immigrant group in Utica and Rochester, while Poles became the dominant element in Buffalo.

Black population grew slowly; indeed, its position relative to the total population declined because the influx of Europeans was so great. Nevertheless, Negro population more than doubled between 1900 and 1920. In 1920 the black total of about 200,000 was less than 2 percent of total population. Three out of four blacks lived in New York City, and Harlem was becoming known as the cultural and entertainment capital of black America.

The influx of foreigners rekindled old nativist misgivings and fears. Old charges were dusted off: high crime rates, heavy relief costs, threats to the living standards of American labor, illiteracy, boss manipulation of voters. Muckrakers, social workers, and progressives became increasingly concerned about urban problems, which the inrush of immigrants certainly complicated. In place of the religious argument, nativists trotted out the dogma of Nordic supremacy: peoples from northwest Europe, they claimed, had more ability and more emotional stability than persons from southern and eastern Europe. Both in the countryside and among the urban middle class, nativists complained about and criticized the alien and unruly population of New York City and other centers. The cry arose for "100 percent Americanism." Educators sought to turn children into pliant "Americans." The commissioner of common schools in New York City declared in 1896, "I consider it the paramount duty of our public schools, apart from the educational knowledge to be instilled in our pupils, to form American citizens of them, to take up and gather together all the heterogeneous elements of this cosmopolitan population. . . ."[9]

Immigrants climbing the iron stairs to the reception hall at Ellis Island in 1905. Photo by Lewis Hine. George Eastman House Collection.

Nativists called for a literacy test for immigrants, a somewhat devious tactic since such a test would penalize immigrants from southern and eastern Europe. Congress debated and passed this measure in 1896–1897 but failed to override the veto of President Cleveland.

Some patricians of the old stock swung to the side of immigration restriction, although others wanted to keep unchecked the flow of the cheap factory labor. Madison Grant, an upper-class clubman who posed as an amateur scientist, complained in 1916 of "a large and increasing number of the weak, the broken, and the mentally crippled of all races drawn from the lowest stratum of the Mediterranean basin and the Balkans, together with hordes of the wretched, submerged populations of the Polish Ghettos. . . . Our jails, insane asylums and almshouses were filled with this human flotsam.[10]

Assimilation took place at varying speeds, depending upon a large number of factors: educational and economic level, the size and location of the immigrant community, religion, nationality. Each individual in varying degree was exposed to many factors. Should children obey their parents? Or should they strike out on their own, move out of the old neighborhood, marry whom they liked, change their name or religion? Such questions tortured immigrants and especially their children. Jews developed Yiddish terms to designate various types: *deitschuks* were the assimilated (German) Jews: *alrightniks* were climbers on the make; *lodgniks* were joiners; and *radikalke* were emancipated women.

The rate of exogamy—that is, marriage outside the core group—is a significant although not a perfect index of assimilation. Julius Drachsler studied 100,000 marriage licenses in New York City in 1910 and discovered that second-generation men and women married outside their group two or three times as often as those of the first generation. The rate of exogamy differed from group to group, depending on its size, date of arrival, and religion. Very few eastern European Jews married outside the group, at least before 1914. By contrast, in the 1970s, rabbis were deploring the trend of college-educated Jews to marry Gentiles. Although less than 4 percent of southern Italians married outside the group, Drachsler found that 30 to 50 percent of northern Italians, Irish, Czechs, and Poles did so. Scandinavians, Hungarians, British, and Canadians of the second generation paid little attention to nationality lines. Religion, however, restricted many persons from straying even if they jumped ethnic lines. Thus Polish men would marry Irish Catholic women more readily than Swedish Lutherans. Still, most members of ethnic groups married within the group.

The number of state residents has continued to grow since 1914 but at a declining rate. World War I damned the flood of immigrants, some of whom actually sailed home to fight for king and country. The draft and war boom created a labor shortage that caused many people to move from farms and small towns to the cities. The hostilities over, Europeans once again booked passage to America, prosperous and relatively untouched by the ravages of war. Nativists and labor leaders became alarmed at the influx, and welcomed new allies among businessmen who worried about the presence of anarchists and Communists among the newcomers.

Congress, pressed by these groups and disturbed by the depression of 1921, decided to cut annual immigration to 357,000. Three years later it limited immigration from any European country to 2 percent of the population of that nationality registered in the census of 1890. Even more important, an "apportionment" based upon the "national origins" of American residents in 1920 was to become the basis for a maximum quota of 150,000 persons a year. Obviously this national-origins provision would strike a body blow against Italians, Poles, Jews, and other recent immigrants. Interestingly enough, the Empire State attracted an increasing share of the immigration that continued.

State population (10.4 million in 1920) increased more than 2 million in the prosperous twenties, but grew by less than 1 million during the depression decade. Most cities showed no gains, but New York City continued to grow by attracting half of the increase.

The return of prosperity after 1940 led to more rapid population growth. War workers used their savings and veterans married, bought houses under the GI Bill of Rights, and fathered many children. New York along with the rest of the United States experienced a baby boom that strained housing, educational, and medical resources. During the 1950s New York State added almost 2 million people, almost all of them in suburbs. The birth rate started to decline after 1966 and population growth slowed. In 1976, estimates of population ran fractionally lower than the census total of 1970.

Five metropolitan areas—Buffalo, Elmira, Binghamton, Utica–Rome, and New York City—lost population in the 1970s. The sharp drop in manufacturing employment caused large numbers of young workers and blacks to move to other states, and thousands of senior citizens moved to Florida and other Sunbelt states in search of warmth and lower taxes. After the paralyzing winter of 1976–1977, many Buffalo residents declared their intention of heading southward.

New Yorkers have had some difficulty adjusting to life in a "steady state" with zero population growth. Businessmen, labor leaders, and politicians blame one another for the end of New York's three and a half centuries of growth. Gone is some of the exuberance and boosterism that New Yorkers have exhibited throughout their history.

The composition of the state's population has undergone significant changes since 1914. The nonwhite element has risen from less than 2 percent in 1920 to 13.2 percent in 1970, when its total exceeded 2.4 million. Four out of five nonwhites lived in metropolitan New York, where they formed almost one-fourth of the total population.

Blacks, of course, constituted the overwhelming majority of nonwhites. In 1970 they numbered 1.6 million, enough to cause an English observer in 1973 to state that New York is "turning black."[11] The rising percentage is as much an index of white flight (over a million in the 1960s) as an indication of the influx of blacks from the South. Incidentally, roughly one-tenth of black New Yorkers have migrated from a foreign country, the great majority from the West Indies, especially Jamaica, Barbados, and Haiti.

Harlem has enjoyed the distinction of serving as capital of black America since World War I, though the black communities in the Bedford-Stuyvesant, Brownsville, and Crown Heights sections of Brooklyn contain a much larger concentration of people. Residential patterns indicate an increasing ghettoization within New York City.

Blacks in New York City have attracted the attention of sociologists, historians, journalists, and educationists. Their conclusions support almost any position one chooses to take. If one wishes to stress shocking conditions and the "tangle of pathologies," to quote Kenneth Clark, he can find ample support. If one wishes to cite examples of dramatic gains, he can footnote his conclusions copiously.

Although blacks clearly improved their lot during the 1960s and 1970s, the rate of improvement slowed after 1969. Rising educational levels and civil rights legislation have enabled thousands to secure employment in banks, stores, offices, and the civil services. Let us take the transit workers as an example. In 1934 the Irish, led by Mike Quill, held almost two-thirds of the transit jobs; four decades later blacks held almost half of the positions. While a substantial minority (about one-third) remain locked in poverty, a majority have made their way into the middle class. The percentage of black college graduates has doubled in the past decade, and young black families have closed the income gap.

During the 1960s militants staged protests against conditions in schools, housing, and employment. They preached separatism, with emphasis on "African" hairstyle, dress, and diet. More recently leaders have urged black students to penetrate the economic world. Sound as this advice has been, it has done little to aid the large underclass of poverty-stricken families. Male unemployment, generally double that of whites, has been a major cause of family instability, and as a result about half of all black children grow up in female-headed households.

The immigration act of 1965 has had a substantial impact on the number of immigrants, especially on nonwhite immigrants. Most striking of all has been the influx of Asians. By 1970 the Chinese population of New York City had climbed to 69,324, making its Chinatown larger than that of San Francisco. Indians, Koreans, and Filipinos have sharply increased in numbers in New York State. More than 40,000 Japanese live in Greater New York, most of them representing business firms.

More than 2 million people claimed Latin American origin in 1970. Most had come from Puerto Rico, Cuba, and the Dominican Republic; substantial numbers had also come from Colombia, Chile, and other South American countries. The influx of these newcomers has "Latinized" large sections of New York City and dramatically influenced its diet, speech patterns, and fashions. Hispanics form approximately half of the adherents of the Roman Catholic church, which has seen many communicants of Irish, German, and Slavic descent migrate to the suburbs.

Puerto Ricans, those born on the island and their children, totaled over 800,000 in 1970. If one were to include members of the third generation, one could count close to 1.3 million persons of Puerto Rican origin in the Greater New York area, which includes northern New Jersey. Upstate, colonies of Puerto Ricans have settled in the larger cities.

Why did these American citizens leave their beautiful island? Basically, for jobs. In this semitropical paradise unemployment has usually exceeded 10 percent, a figure that understates the number of jobless and ignores the great amount of underemployment. When the people in the slums of San Juan and on the small farms heard about jobs in the hotels, restaurants, garment factories, and hospitals of New York City, they flocked northward. During World War II airlines began to provide direct and relatively cheap flights to New York City; soon planes were leaving almost hourly from San Juan. During most of the 1950s more than two thousand islanders arrived in New York each week. Meanwhile Puerto Rico itself was experiencing an economic "miracle" based upon the tourist trade and the expansion of light manufacturing. Although it became a pocket of prosperity among the Caribbean islands, Puerto Rico with its rapidly growing population was unable to employ all of its increasingly numerous job seekers. The more education and skills the islanders acquired, the more eager they became to fly north, where greater opportunities beckoned.

These newcomers, accustomed to another climate, language, and culture, have found the process of assimilation rather painful. Although citizens of the United States, they have often felt like foreigners and sometimes have been treated as such. In the more racially conscious society on the mainland, they have found themselves to be considered not quite white, although they themselves do not consider themselves black, whatever their actual color. Because of their poverty (some 40 percent of welfare payments in New York City in the early 1970s went to Puerto Ricans), they have felt left out of American abundance. Cherishing their Hispanic heritage, reinforced by a network of restaurants, clubs, motion picture houses, radio stations, and frequent visits back home, they find their children experiencing language problems in school and exposed to temptations on the streets.

Fidel Castro's revolution, like so many revolutions before, uprooted hundreds of thousands of Cubans, who fled to Miami and other centers; by 1970, 63,000 had settled in New York. Well educated and often skilled in business and professions, Cubans have established newspapers, stores, and businesses, and have become leaders among the Spanish-speaking population. Their prominence has not always been appreciated by less successful Latin Americans.

The population of the Dominican Republic has lived for centuries in desperate poverty and usually under despotic rule. Thousands have fled to the United States, with perhaps 150,000 to 200,000 settling in New York City. Many have entered this country illegally, a fact that makes their status even more precarious. Fear of expulsion has made it difficult for them to fight the discrimination they often meet. Lacking education and modern skills, most Dominicans have had to take menial and disagreeable jobs.

Colombians have also left poverty and political turmoil in their homeland to seek jobs in New York City. Estimates of their number range from 50,000 to 150,000. Several thousand persons from almost all of the Latin American countries have made their homes in New York. Each has left its imprint upon the food, music, fashions, indeed the basic life-style of the metropolis.

Meanwhile the percentage of foreign-born, especially those of European origin, has kept falling as death has claimed members of the great wave of immigrants arriving before 1914. One can derive from the 1950 census a fairly accurate picture of persons born abroad or who were children of a foreign-born parent. Some 4.3 million persons fitted that category. Of that group, approximately 1.5 million came from Italy, 800,000 from Russia, 700,000 from Germany, 650,000 from both Ireland and Poland, and 400,000 from Great Britain. Almost one-fourth of all foreign-born in the United States in 1950 resided within New York State.

Another way of looking at foreign stock is to consider the mother tongues of foreign-born and native-born persons. This method is more useful in indicating the size of the Jewish immigration than a listing of the mere numbers of immigrants from the Soviet Union. On the other hand, the Irish contingent becomes swallowed up in the English category, a development not calculated to please either group. In 1970 roughly one-third of all New Yorkers had a mother tongue other than English, an astonishing fact. Of course, the high Spanish total reflects the large migration of citizens from Puerto Rico to the mainland.

For decades after the Civil War, the rural areas north and south of the urban corridor underwent a considerable decline in population. Twenty counties showed losses between 1910 and 1940, but thereafter most registered small to moderate increases. Three counties bordering the Adirondacks, however,—Essex, Franklin, Montgomery—continued to decline during the 1960s. While the state's farm population has continued its century-long decline to about 2 percent of the total, rural nonfarm population has increased. About six of every seven families living in the open countryside and small villages do not derive their chief income from raising crops or animals. Some serve commercial farmers

Foreign-born and native-born population of New York State, by mother tongue, 1970

Mother tongue	Foreign-born	Native-born
Italian	356,595	920,777
English	377,824	11,508,409
German	252,248	357,629
Yiddish	213,669	484,049
Polish	90,532	300,174
Spanish	250,529	1,016,126
Russian	41,749	34,469
French	125,649	83,152

as truck drivers, specialists, and distributors; others drive long distances to urban jobs. The greatest increases in nonfarm rural population between 1940 and 1970 occurred in those counties that lie closest to large cities.

Suburbanization, a process that we can trace far back into the nineteenth century in New York, accelerated after middle- and working-class people could afford to own automobiles. As early as 1820 Hezekiah B. Pierrepont was touting Brooklyn Heights as a nightly haven for Manhattan merchants. His selling points,— "health and comfort" of families, a "select neighborhood and circle of society"—anticipated those put forward by developers in recent times. Railways—horse, steam, and elevated—carried commuters up Manhattan Island and into the Bronx. Similar changes were taking place around Buffalo, Rochester, Syracuse, and Albany.

When middle-class families purchased automobiles, they soon looked for a green spot in the country. Westchester County, an area of hills and lakes north of the Bronx, tripled its population between 1900 and 1930. Here commuters lived in affluent communities such as Scarsdale, Larchmont, and Chappaqua. Soon Robert Moses began his mighty works: tunnels, bridges, expressways, parkways, parks. He outflanked the landed barons on Long Island and thrust a series of parkways through their estates. Once the roads were built, developers such as William Levitt bought up potato farms and cut them into lots. Levitt alone brought some 80,000 persons into his developments. Since 1940 Nassau and Suffolk counties have added 1.6 million residents.

The federal government has stimulated suburban development in a number of ways. It has lent money at low interest rates to communities that wish to put in sewers, water facilities, and roads. It has encouraged homeownership by guaranteeing Federal Housing Authority mortgages and making real estate taxes and interest payments on mortgages deductible from income taxes. Congress helped to build arterials and expressways, thus permitting many commuters to reach their offices or factories in less than half an hour. Meanwhile banks, following FHA standards, refused to make loans in inner-city areas, where the poor congregated in old structures.

The urban crisis, marked by crime, congestion, pollution, the deterioration of schools, and the influx of minorities, propelled hundreds of thousands of white families to the safety and quiet of the suburbs. Like most visions, reality failed to live up to expectations because the same problems reappeared.

Soon stores, hotels, and other business firms fled to the outskirts, relocating where they could offer their customers and employees plenty of free parking. Factories also joined the march to take advantage of the opportunity to erect single-level buildings where forklift trucks could be used. Between 1950 and 1975 industrial employees of New York City fell from about 7 percent of the nation's work force to barely 3 percent.

Rochester provides a good illustration of changing population trends among upstate cities. In 1950 its population peaked at 332,488 persons, with another 155,144 residing in the rest of Monroe County. By 1970 the central city had slipped to 293,695, but the rest of the county had acquired another 200,000 residents. Greater Rochester extended its orbit so far as to reverse the decline of population in five rural counties bordering on Monroe. The nonwhite population trebled in the 1950s and doubled again in the next decade. As a result, blacks constituted over 20 percent of Rochester's population, or 52,105, in 1970. They even outnumbered the strong Italian community, which, with its American-born children, still numbered 41,014 in 1960.

After 1960 New York lost more people to than it gained from other states. In 1960 the states containing the largest number of natives of New York were New Jersey (600,000), California (401,000), and Florida (287,000).

The 1960s saw a revival of racial awareness and an upsurge of ethnicity. Infuriated by the slow pace of integration and the persistence of discrimination, many blacks listened to militants who preached separatism and vigorous action. The call for black power shattered the illusion that improving conditions (and American blacks did make striking gains between 1940 and 1970) could quiet "black rage." The more loudly militants denounced their conditions and demanded equal rights, the more alarmed became white citizens, many of whom had worked their way out of poverty only a generation earlier. The ethnics, a new term used to designate Italians, Poles, and other recent immigrants, became uneasy as blacks knocked on the doors of unions and speculators block-busted old neighborhoods. Ethnics felt betrayed when some clergymen seemed more interested in upholding minority rights than in defending parish integrity. Smarting at charges of racial bigotry, ethnics accused upper-class liberals of moving to the suburbs and sending their children to private schools. Open housing and forced busing, they claimed, would ruin their neighborhoods and endanger their children.

Traditionally New York City Jews have provided much of the white support for Negroes in their demands for civil rights and equality. But when blacks demanded community control of schools in 1968, the teachers—many of them Jewish—walked out on strike, temporarily straining Jewish–black relations.

Upstate centers did not escape ethnic and racial tensions. Rochester was rudely shocked in 1964 by an inner-city riot. The precipitating occasion, as in most of the urban riots of the 1960s, was a commonplace incident. The basic causes for unrest were the same found in almost all northern centers: poor housing, discrimination that prevented blacks from moving to better neighborhoods, deteriorating schools, police brutality, high unemployment, especially among teenagers, and discrimination against black jobseekers, many of whom were ill equipped to fill the scientific and technical positions at Eastman Kodak, Xerox, and Bausch & Lomb.

After the fires had died down, many blacks joined FIGHT, an organization dedicated to Freedom, Integration, God, and Honor Today. It called for social justice in the areas of housing, education, employment, poverty, youth, law enforcement, urban renewal, and good government. As a result, many of the companies agreed to recruit and train young blacks.

Because ethnic groups were also interest groups, differences tended to perpetuate themselves. Jews, many of whom had experience as shopkeepers and tailors when they arrived in this country, have continued to excel in retailing and to dominate the garment industry. They have also provided an unusual number of professional people: lawyers, physicians, teachers. The Irish, because of their early interest in Democratic politics, have provided an exceptional number of civil servants, notably policemen.

Italians, many of whom sought out seasonal outdoor work, have become dominant in construction. Blacks and Puerto Ricans, arriving late and bringing few skills and funds, have found it hard to get ahead in a society that insists on the credentials of degrees or training. Nevertheless, blacks have moved more rapidly up the economic ladder in their first generation as New Yorkers than the Irish did in the nineteenth century. Whereas the Irish faced signs in windows saying, "No Irish need apply," the blacks and Puerto Ricans have had the benefit of the Ives-Quinn act of 1945, which places state authority against job discrimination. The federal Civil Rights Act of 1965 also led to various measures against discrimination: quotas for construction jobs, affirmative action for white-collar positions, and the like.

Ethnicity still provides a bastion of support for individuals caught in the anomie of modern life. The tribal instinct is strong and, strangely enough, seems to have had a temporary revival in the turmoil of urban living. In New York, as in other parts of the country, sociologists have found some evidence of the third-generation phenomenon, the nostalgic interest of grandchildren in the lives and world of their grandparents. On the more practical level, the second and third generations have found valuable the hospitals, churches, clubs, and old people's homes that the immigrant generation so painstakingly founded and sacrificially supported.

The long sweep of New York history has witnessed an almost endless parade of ethnic and racial groups passing within and through its borders. Clearly the idea that these groups have automatically become homogenized into some kind of undifferentiated mass is a concept that has confused as much as it has clarified. Nevertheless, we can discern the emergence of sub-melting pots. Italian immigrants who formerly were fiercely loyal to the villages and provinces from which they emigrated have become Italo-Americans. Hitler's holocaust and the Arab threat to Israel have done much to blur the old distinctions among Jews of German, Russian, and Spanish descent. In the suburbs, second-generation Poles, Italians, and Germans are blending into a common Catholicism, more or less Irish in tone. Protestant groups such as the Germans and Scandinavians have in many areas silently merged with the old native stock, with only a few vestiges such as patronymics, food, and Christmas traditions marking their passing. The black community has absorbed tens of thousands of Jamaicans and other West Indians.

The ethnic and racial revivals of the 1960s were a stunning surprise to many observers, who had never questioned the melting pot theory. Suddenly spokesmen not only for the blacks but also for Italians, Jews, Puerto Ricans, and Poles called for cultural pluralism. To describe our society they advanced new metaphors: *patchwork quilt, salad bowl, mosaic.* Like all metaphors, these terms are handy tools to be used with caution. The concept of cultural pluralism does not explain the subtlety and complexity of acculturation any better than does the term *melting pot.* All we can safely assert is that individuals tend to keep their social identities while sharing common assumptions about democracy, private property, and individual rights.

By this time we can discern a recurrent pattern in New York's demographic history. Each wave of immigrants meets opposition by older residents, who view their influx with fear and distrust. As immigrants invade neighborhoods, old-time residents sell out and move to more desirable districts, usually on the outskirts. They share political power grudgingly and sometimes abandon it altogether. Newcomers have to live in slums where small-time criminals prey on them. Nevertheless many push and shove hard in their efforts to climb out of poverty by a variety of routes— mostly hard work but also sports, crime, entertainment.

A less visible group of newcomers consists of those Americans who come to the Big Apple and other large centers to fulfill their dreams and ambitions. They hope to scale the peaks of entertainment, banking, corporate management, law, scientific research, religious and philanthropic organizations, sports, publishing, art, and many other fields. Equipped with education, skills, and connections (family, academic, corporate), they start their climb far above the poverty line. Some give up after sampling the harsh realities of metropolitan living, which make the slower pace and neighborliness of provincial America appear increasingly attractive. A growing number of middle-echelon managers have dropped out of the scramble for the executive suite in preference to the good life of Des Moines or Nashville, where they can spend more time with their families. Most "make it" in a modest way, bring up their families in the suburbs, and join the vast army of commuters.

In New York State we can observe, perhaps more clearly than anywhere else, endless permutations and combinations of nationality and racial groups. Consider Fiorello La Guardia, son of an Italian father and a Jewish mother. Reared in Arizona, Fiorello moved to New York City and became an Episcopalian.

The population of the Empire State has leveled off and may even decline in coming decades. But we can expect a continuation of the astonishing diversity of peoples as ethnic and racial groups increase their efforts to perpetuate their special characteristics. Although suburbanization will undoubtedly continue, several interesting countermovements have taken place. Some upper-middle-class people are moving back to the inner city and rehabilitating sound structures. Other New Yorkers have moved far into the countryside to enjoy Arcadian pursuits and escape urban problems. And since 1970 a considerable number of blacks have moved back to the South, where jobs have become more plentiful and "the livin' is easy."

New York is not a finished culture; it is one continually coming into being. Talented and hard-working individuals from every land and state will continue to influence the outward appearance and, more important, the inner vitality of New Yorkers.

3 | Provincial New York: Embryonic America

The least English yet the most American of the thirteen colonies, New York illustrated remarkably well Frederick Jackson Turner's perception of the Middle Atlantic region as the microcosm of the America that was to be: "It had a wide mixture of nationalities, a varied society, the mixed town and county system of government, a varied economic life, many religious sects.... It represented that composite nationality which the contemporary United States exhibits.... It was typical of the modern United States."[1] A pluralistic political system, a diversified economy, and a heterogeneous society, all hallmarks of the American experience, emerged from the mixing of peoples, races, and religions along the Hudson. What kept this discordant society together was a combination of outside pressures and the self-interest of its residents.

As time passed, confusion yielded to fusion. The wilderness, the network of waterways, and above all a frontier that frequently burst into open warfare shaped the way of life of New Yorkers. As a result of its geography New York became the "pivot of empire."[2] For a century parties of French *chasseurs* and British redcoats rowed across its lakes and up its rivers, setting up posts along the shores of Lake Ontario, the upper Mohawk, and the passage between Lake Champlain and Lake George. Colonial officials became geopolitical strategists because they knew that control of these waterways meant control of the fur trade and the Indians. Officials in Whitehall realized that the fate of the North American continent rested to a large extent on their ability to secure mastery of Lake Champlain, the Mohawk gateway, and the lower Great Lakes. For this reason they placed four independent companies in New York, the only regular troops stationed in any colony throughout the colonial period.

In 1609, when Samuel de Champlain and Henry Hudson entered this area, two Indian groups were dominant. Algonkians lived along the Hudson, on Long Island, and in western New England and eastern Pennsylvania; Iroquois occupied the region from the Mohawk Valley to the Genesee River. The Iroquois confederacy was composed of five tribes or nations: Mohawk, Oneida, Onondaga, Cayuga, and Seneca. These tribes had arrived about 1300 A.D. from the interior, pushing the Algonkians to the east and south.

Archaelogists have estimated that humans have lived in this region for more than ten thousand years. Pottery and stone, bone, and copper artifacts such as flint points, drills, awls, and fishhooks have been found throughout the region. The Indians learned to fish with bone harpoons and to cultivate and grind corn, the most useful crop for the red and later the white farmers in this area. They learned to cook their food in pots instead of roasting whole game over the open fire. They molded soft clay into pots, which they decorated inside and out with incised patterns and baked hard. After the Indians became farmers as well as hunters, they built huts out of saplings, bark, and hides. Soon small villages (approximately seventy to eighty at any one time) sprang up along streams, but they did not become permanent settlements because the Indians exhausted the game and fishing resources and periodically had to move to new sites.

Like many Indians, the Iroquois developed the so-called longhouse or extended family. Families were grouped into clans, which took the names of animals. Children belonged to the mother's clan. Each of the Five Nations had at least three clans: Bear, Wolf, and Turtle. The clan had ceremonial and political functions—for example, the adoption of captives into the tribe—as well as social functions. Each clan had a governing council, which sent representatives to the tribal council. Women had considerable political power: although membership in the clan councils was limited to men, the members were chosen by the women.

Nature—the rhythm of the seasons, the phases of the moon,

the sun's rising and setting—provided the basic time patterns. Festivals punctuated the seasons. After tapping the sugar maples in March, the woman boiled the sap into sugar. In the spring women planted the corn and other crops, after which the villagers held a planting festival in which they danced, prayed, and smoked tobacco. The Green Corn Festival took place in September, and then came the Harvest Festival. Thereafter the men hunted game for the winter. In February came the Midwinter Festival, the most important of all. Heralds announced the coming of the new year. "Bigheads" wearing large masks and clad in bearskins and corn husks called on the people to follow the tribal customs and rituals. They asked everyone to report any new dreams, which were taken very seriously as omens.

An elaborate creation myth explained the origins of the tribe and reinforced its customs. The Iroquois myth told of a woman who fell from the sky and landed on the back of a great sea turtle. She took the soil scooped from the sea bottom and planted in it some roots. She had a daughter who grew up to be a beautiful maiden. The daughter in turn had twin sons. The left-handed twin killed his mother in childbirth by insisting on being born through her left armpit. Corn, bean, squash, and tobacco sprang up from her body. The right-handed twin became the Great Creator, but he could not prevent his brother from ruling at night.

The Indian myth, like all creation myths, offered an explanation of the origins of the world and the coexistence of good and evil. Each creature and plant performed an honored function. The myth expressed and fortified the self-discipline for which the Iroquois were famed.

Each village, containing ten to fifty families, stood in a clearing. The roofs of the longhouses, 50 to 100 feet long and 20 feet wide, were formed by bent saplings and covered with sheets of elm bark. Holes at intervals permitted smoke to escape. Each nuclear family (father, mother, and children) had its own compartment, which rested on wooden platforms above the damp ground. The adults slept on corn-husk mats, the children in bark-lined bunks.

Each village was a busy place as its inhabitants tried to grow and make everything they needed. While the women cooked, planted, harvested, and made clothing, the men fashioned tools and weapons out of stone, wood, and hides. Bark was shaped to make canoes and baskets. The villages traded products in order to secure items they lacked—dried fish, flints, wampum, tobacco, pelts. Trading increased sharply after white traders offered trinkets, guns, blankets, and rum.

According to legend, Deganawidah, a Huron, was the author of the Great Peace, which developed about 1570 into the Confederacy of the Five Nations. He and Hiawatha, an Onondaga, heartsick over the constant warfare, formulated a code of laws to preserve peace. Fifty sachems, chosen among the village chiefs, were to govern the confederacy. Each nation had one vote, although the Senecas and Mohawks enjoyed the status of older brothers. The confederacy banned war among its members, a restriction generally observed. Theoretically other tribes could decide whether or not to join the league, but a refusal meant swift destruction.

Furs and pelts were the items most valued by the whites, who offered in exchange guns, rum, and woolens. By 1650 the reduction in the supply of fur-bearing animals in western New York and the acquisition of firearms caused the Iroquois to seek control of the region north of the Great Lakes, where beaver were still plentiful. When the Hurons refused to share the trade, their villages were destroyed by the Iroquois. Other tribes, such as the Neutrals and Eries, met the same fate when they harbored Huron refugees.

The coming of the whites had varying impacts upon tribes within the New York area. For some, notably Algonkians in the Hudson Valley, contact with the Dutch and later the English brought the demoralizing effects of rum and disease. The Iroquois, on the other hand, appeared to gain by contact with whites because both the French and the British cultivated their goodwill by granting them gifts and selling them arms. During the 1680s Governor Thomas Dongan aggressively sought British control over the Great Lakes region. The French launched devastating raids on the Senecas in 1687, after which they set up a post at Niagara. When they attacked the Mohawks, the Five

Nations criticized the English for failing to provide protection. In 1701 the confederacy asked the French for a treaty of friendship and agreed to a shadowy recognition of the French king as over-lord. They deeded their claims to the area formerly held by the Hurons and other conquered tribes because they could no longer defend it.

The city officials of Albany regulated most of the province's Indian affairs until the middle of the eighteenth century. To pre-serve their own monopoly of the fur trade, they laid down rules for its regulation. No trader, for example, could invite an Indian with peltry to stay at his house during the trading season—a rule frequently broken by unscrupulous traders. Provincial officials and their associates, such as William Johnson, charged that Al-banians used cheap rum to befuddle their customers. Their con-cern, however, was more for imperial interests than for those of the Indians: they wanted to enlist the tribesmen in the death struggle between Britain and France for control of the Great Lakes and thus of North America. Although primarily interested in making money, Albany officials favored the construction of frontier forts. Defying the protests of several imperial officials, they kept trading with customers in Montreal.

The Iroquois barrier remained in place throughout the colonial period. The confederacy tried to remain neutral as William Johnson made vigorous but only partially successful efforts to convert them to the British side. The Seneca in particular leaned to the French, who sent black-robed Jesuits to live among them.

In the seventeenth century upstate New York's population was tiny, widely dispersed, and cosmopolitan, although the Dutch element predominated. Almost all families earned their livelihood by raising wheat and selling forest products to merchants on Manhattan Island, who sold most of them to the West Indies. Merchants and their close allies among the large landowners occupied the topmost position in the economic pyramid. The spirit of gain permeated all layers of society. Perhaps it was easier to accept differences in religion and nationality in a frankly mate-rialistic culture. Such toleration did not embrace black slaves, but native Americans received some protection from royal officials who recognized their military power. As in most frontier societies, the inhabitants of New York lived in fear—fear of losing their scalps to marauding Indians, their possessions to French raiders, their land to threatening neighbors.

When the British captured New Netherland, they acquired about 8,000 white settlers, perhaps one-third of them non-Dutch. New Netherland had grown very slowly despite the excellent harbor and water route inland. Perhaps the most important reason was that Dutch farmers and city dwellers were unwilling to leave their prosperous and fairly tolerant homeland. In addition, the Dutch West India Company neglected the colony to concentrate its attention on the conquest of Brazil and the sugar isles. Only a few dozen traders could handle all the fur business out of Albany. Moreover, the Algonkian Indians in the Hudson Valley occasionally attacked Dutch farms and even forced the company to erect a wall on lower Manhattan Island (the path that ran beside it was later called Wall Street). The company's authoritarian government under a succession of inept or incompetent governors, as well as the enmity of the neighboring Swedes in the Delaware Valley and New Englanders in Connecticut and on Long Island, discouraged settlers.

These factors and others continued to retard growth after the British conquest of 1664. James, duke of York, had little time to spend on his proprietorship, especially after the quarrel between Parliament and the Stuarts intensified. The frontier was not a safe place to be after France and England went to war in the 1680s.

New York remained predominantly Dutch in population and culture. Of the estimated 14,000 inhabitants in 1690, more than half were Dutch; they were particularly strong in Albany and formed about three-fourths of the population of New York City. But economic and political power in New York City was gradually passing into the hands of upper-class Englishmen. The Dutch citizens of New York became frustrated and sometimes took out their resentment in name-calling. In 1679 William Merritt complained to the mayor of New York that he heard the night watch beating English citizens and shouting, "Slay the English dogs!" Sometimes they rose up in rebellion, as in 1689, when most Dutch citizens rallied to the cause of Jacob Leisler.

Before 1700 New York was an aural culture, a society in which the spoken word dominated. Governors made proclamations and sheriffs read the riot act. In elections men voted orally. Because about half of the adult males and a greater proportion of the women could not read, they listened intently to bells, chimes, town criers, and the calls of watchmen.

One looks long and hard for anything that can be called culture in the frontier society of seventeenth-century New York. The tiny population could not support a newspaper, a concert hall, or a bookstore. A handful of schools did spring up around churches, because some clergymen supplemented their incomes by teaching.

Meanwhile Dutch and other settlers were hammering out a pattern of religious toleration, a result more of expediency than of commitment. Neither Dutch governors nor Dutch clergymen favored toleration for Roman Catholics, Jews, Quakers, or even Lutherans, but the directors of the company took the pragmatic view that persecution was bad for business. But some citizens believed in freedom of worship as a basic human right, a startling heresy in that age. When Governor Stuyvesant tried to expell Quakers in 1657, the Yankees of Flushing, Long Island, issued a statement whose eloquence rings down the centuries: "The law of love, peace and liberty . . . extend[s] to Jews, Turks, and Egyptians. . . . Our desire is not to offend one of his [Jesus'] little ones, in whatsoever form, name or title he appears in, whether Presbyterian, Independent, Baptist or Quaker. . . ."[3]

In 1664 the English granted toleration as one of the conditions of surrender, and the Dutch Reformed church remained undisturbed. Although the majority in a town might establish the public church, other citizens were free to attend other churches or worship privately in their own way.

One reason the Dutch and later the English permitted religious freedom was that religion did not enlist the same degree of commitment in New York as it did in New England. Throughout the colonial period, clergymen bewailed the religious indifference, the breaking of the Sabbath, and the loose morals of residents. Almost every visitor noted the convivial nature of New Yorkers, who tended to frequent the taverns more often than the churches.

Hope of gain occupied the minds of New Yorkers and shaped government policy on all levels. The British Empire had embraced the doctrines of mercantilism since 1651. Parliament imposed navigation acts requiring goods to be carried in British ships, important exports to flow to empire ports, and imports to be bought in England. New Yorkers accepted these imperial regulations without much protest because they received more benefits than losses from membership in the British Empire.

New Yorkers also did everything possible to foster the commerce of the province and metropolis. New York City built new docks and officials established regulations to speed the loading, unloading, and delivery of all cargoes. They licensed cartmen and set the rates they could charge. They sought and secured New York City's right to become the staple port, that is, the official port of entry and of export. In 1680 Governor Edmund Andros assigned the monopoly over the bolting (manufacture) and export the flour which the legislature had granted to the city. Millers in other centers protested this monopoly, but the aldermen of New York insisted that only the city's system of inspection could guarantee the quality of flour exports. In 1694 New York City lost its bolting monopoly. Meanwhile Albany had secured the exclusive right to conduct the fur trade with the Indians.

The Common Council of New York devised regulations for the production and sale of bread, regulations that the bakers grudgingly accepted. It also set up markets where farmers sold meat, eggs, butter, fish, fruit, and vegetables. The city licensed retailers and set the price of liquor in taverns and inns.

City fathers wrestled with problems of crime, fire, streets, trash, and clean water. The greatest threat was fire, and in 1697 aldermen were made responsible for safe chimneys and fireplaces in their wards. Earlier the aldermen had banned slaughterhouses and tanneries from any location within the city. They directed cartmen to carry away rubbish each Saturday and they ordered householders to pave with stones and to keep clean the streets in front of their houses.

If local government functioned inefficiently, imperial controls operated sporadically. Governors faced formidable problems, not the least being inadequate revenues and unruly colonists who objected to high taxes. Yet governors had to provide and support defense forces. Small wonder that governors kept complaining to their superiors that they could not follow instructions to the letter.

Time and distance diluted the absolutism claimed by the Dutch West India Company and the Duke of York. The problems of Peter Stuyvesant, the ablest and most durable Dutch governor, provide a good example of the difficulty of ruling a colony three thousand miles from headquarters. Stuyvesant plunged from one crisis to another, sometimes clashing with the directors in Amsterdam, sometimes quarreling with the colonists. Yankees infiltrated Long Island, acting more like an army of occupation than individuals willing to become Dutch citizens. In 1650, Stuyvesant signed a treaty in Hartford whereby New Netherland gave up its claim to the Connecticut Valley and to territory on Long Island east of a line running south from Oyster Bay. He yielded no land actually occupied by Dutch settlers, and he persuaded the English to accept a border that did check expansionist-minded settlers of Hartford and New Haven for over a decade. When Stuyvesant sought a renewal of this agreement in 1663, he met a contemptuous rebuff.

King Charles II and his ministers conquered New Netherland because they believed Manhattan traders were undermining enforcement of the Navigation Acts. To his brother James, duke of York and Albany, Charles awarded all the land from the Delaware River to the Connecticut River, all of Long Island, parts of Maine, and some islands. The duke wisely shaved off huge chunks of land. In 1665 he awarded New Jersey to Lords Berkeley and Carteret, and he ceded to Connecticut the land that now forms the western half of that state.

In theory the Duke of York had absolute power to levy taxes, regulate trade, and appoint officials; in practice he found it necessary to relax his tight reins. Self-interest, whether asserted by Yankees on Long Island, merchants on Manhattan Island, or Dutch in Albany, confronted every governor. Colonel Richard Nicolls, the first English governor, promulgated the Duke's Laws, a code of regulations designed to placate Long Island towns settled by stiff-necked Yankees. Freeholders received the right, as in New England, to elect a board of overseers and a constable, but the governor kept the power to appoint justices of the peace and to supervise the overseers. Although the Duke's Laws were gradually extended to other counties, variations in local government and laws continued.

By 1680 Governor Edmund Andros faced a tax revolt by Manhattan merchants. Distressed, indeed paralyzed, by the drop in income, the duke called a provincial assembly and sent out a new governor, Thomas Dongan. The delegates drafted a "Charter of Libertyes and Priviledges" that provided for a permanent assembly capable of making laws and levying taxes. This charter granted the vote to freeholders and freemen, freedom of worship, and trial by jury.

Although the duke signed the charter, it did not go into effect. James, as king after 1685, had second thoughts about his empire, and determined to centralize its administration. The new charter, granting New York's assembly more power than that of any other colony, threatened his whole program of consolidation.

James's withdrawal of the charter enraged New Yorkers, who were already smarting from a number of grievances: hard times, monopolies, high taxes, ineffective government. Apprehension mounted to near hysteria when French forces raided western New York and war broke out. Catholic persecution of Huguenots gave rise to rumors of a papist plot in which Governor Dongan— like James II a Roman Catholic—would subvert provincial and Protestant liberties.

New Yorkers' sense of security was further undermined when, in 1688, the dominion of New England took over New York and they became subsidiaries of the hated Yankees. Then citizens heard rumors that a thousand French soldiers and Indian warriors were marching on Albany (actually the attack came a year later, when the French burned Schenectady). Next, James II scurried from his throne, and Governor Andros was jailed by a revolutionary committee in Boston. When New Yorkers learned of Andros's fall in 1689, they lit bonfires and paraded in the streets. Incensed by these demonstrations, Lieutenant Governor Nicholson threatened to burn New York City. This threat led the mob to storm the fort, and power passed into the hands of the militia captains. They appointed Jacob Leisler, one of their members, as their commander in chief.

A figure still shrouded in controversy, Leisler stood for freedom, Protestantism, and the Dutch element. Opposed to him and his followers were the elite merchants and landlords, who pointed the finger at Leisler's demagoguery, hot temper, and erratic behavior. This upheaval took place at a time when France threatened to invade New York. Leisler took vigorous steps to protect the upper Hudson from French attack.

Meanwhile the new monarchs, William III and Mary II, sent out Colonel Henry Sloughter to reassert royal authority. Sloughter surrounded himself with the elite, who vowed revenge on Leisler. When Leisler failed to surrender the fort's keys to his representative, Sloughter charged him with treason. With indecent speed a special commission tried and sentenced Leisler to death, and the sentence was carried out at once. But Leisler dead was almost as divisive as Leisler alive. His followers tried to rehabilitate his memory; his foes curried favor with the new governor.

These stirring events of the 1680s gave New Yorkers many lessons in politics. They debated the merits of representative government, the dangers of mob rule, and the evils of entrenched privilege. Temporarily the easygoing society dedicated to money getting yielded to wartime hysteria and fanaticism.

The period from 1690 to 1720 was a transitional one in which Great Britain and thus New York waged war against France. Hostilities disrupted the economy, discouraged frontier settlement, and heightened social tensions. Among the important internal developments were the rise of the Assembly to authority rivaling that of the governor in lawmaking, the anglicization of institutions and culture, the expansion of the land system, and conflicts between landed and commercial interests.

After 1691 New Yorkers had an elected assembly in which their representatives could defend their interests. Most assemblymen were drawn from the wealthier classes—landlords, merchants, and lawyers who had the time, education, and habits of leadership necessary to engage in politics. The right to vote was based on property but a large number of adult white males, perhaps as many as one-half by 1750, could qualify, although many failed to exercise this privilege.

Power over taxation gave the Assembly leverage over the governors, who had to ask each year for money for defense and salaries. The governors ranged widely in ability; some, such as Robert Hunter, ruled wisely; others, such as Edward Cornbury, lined their pockets and made capricious rulings. To become governor, one had to command influence among English ruling circles, not necessarily administrative ability or character.

Benjamin Fletcher, governor from 1692 to 1697, took bribes in exchange for land grants to insiders and winked at merchants who supplied pirates with goods, a practice as lucrative as it was illegal. Even worse was Edward Cornbury, the grafting nephew of Queen Anne. His scandalous life provided ammunition for the assemblymen, who promptly whittled down the governor's powers. In 1704 the Assembly successfully asserted its right to appoint a treasurer who would receive and pay out public funds.

Anglicization gained headway and the Dutch slowly lost their distinctiveness except in the region around Albany and Kingston. Gradually English institutions and practices penetrated many more aspects of life. The government instituted a new judicial system that rapidly incorporated the principles of the common law. At first few lawyers were present in the colony, but by the middle of the eighteenth century the bar was becoming professionalized. The English procedures by which a person became a freeman (birth, apprenticeship, purchase) took firm root.

In 1693 William Bradford became public printer, a post he held for almost fifty years. Soon he was printing the laws of the province as well as spelling books, the Book of Common Prayer, and other works. Governors Fletcher and Cornbury vigorously promoted the establishment of the Church of England in the counties of New York, Richmond, Queens, and Westchester.

The concentration of many imperial agencies within New York speeded the process of anglicization. The War Office stationed a permanent garrison in New York, and the collector, surveyor, and other officials collected duties and enforced the Navigation Acts. On the frontier Sir William Johnson held the position of superintendent of Indian Affairs after 1756.

Meanwhile New York's land system had evolved somewhat differently from those of other colonies. The Dutch company inaugurated the famous patroon system, whereby an individual who brought more than fifty settlers could secure a huge tract of land. Of the several granted, only one patroonship—Rensselaerswyck—actually survived. During the last two decades of the seventeenth century most of the east bank of the Hudson south of Albany passed into the hands of large landholders. In 1685 Governor Dongan confirmed the title of Van Rensselaer Manor, which covered about 850,000 acres in present-day Albany and Rensselaer counties and another 250,000 acres in northern Columbia County. South of it was Livingston Manor, the domain of Robert Livingston, who manipulated two small tracts into an estate of 160,000 acres. Westchester County included six manors, the three largest—Scarsdale, Cortlandt, and Philipsburgh—containing about 400 square miles. Governor Richard Bellomont complained that his predecessor, Benjamin Fletcher, had placed three-fourths of the province in the hands of ten or eleven men.

If Fletcher was extravagant in his grants, Cornbury was prodigal. The Hardenbergh Patent, for example, contained more than 1.5 million acres and covered most of Ulster, Delaware, Sullivan, and Greene counties. The Kayaderosseras Patent, covering most of Saratoga County, had an acreage variously estimated at from 333,000 to 500,000 acres.

Most landlords preferred to lease rather than sell their lands. No doubt they expected to establish estates comparable to those held by the English nobility. A "durable" or perpetual lease was actually a freehold in perpetuity with certain restraints on alienation and a reservation of perpetual rent. Other leases were for "lives." The tenants on Livingston Manor had leases for two "lives-in-being." After the two persons named in the leases died, the farm reverted to the Livingston family.

The Van Rensselaer perpetual leases provided that when a tenant disposed of his farm, he had to pay one-fourth of the money to the patroon or, in some cases, an extra year's rent. This restriction caused resentment, as it was regarded as an illegal restraint on alienation. This was the view that the courts eventually took. On the eve of the Revolution, Van Rensselaer Manor had about 500 tenants, mostly in the lowland towns along the Hudson. Tenants had seven years of free occupancy before they began paying rent. Thereafter they paid an annual rent of ten bushels of winter wheat per hundred acres, four fat hens, and a day's work with a team of horses or oxen. In addition, the landlord reserved all rights to mines, milling, and water sites.

Tenancy discouraged immigration and encouraged slovenly husbandry. A few landlords, notably the Van Cortlandt family, took vigorous steps to attract settlers. An examination of their rent rolls shows much mobility, which indicates that the tenantry was not an oppressed peasantry tied to the soil. Tenants sold their improvements to new farmers and used the money to find better farms.

Most farmers, however, owned their own farms, usually of 100 to 200 acres. Even in the centers of tenancy many individuals owned their own land.

Only in New York Province did the landed and merchant interests possess roughly equal strength. Although intermarriage blurred the lines between these groups, they often competed with each other. Whereas the landed interests opposed any land tax, merchants fought imposts and duties.

The commercial community included four prominent families who jumped into the political arena. The Philipse, Schuyler, and Van Cortlandt families came from Dutch stock, while the De Lancey family was Huguenot in origin. Although each of these families began in trade, each sought the prestige and profits that might come from land speculation. They favored free trade, economy in government, and restrictions on artisans, who were trying to regulate manufacturing and raise wages.

The descendants of some of the landed families have made their marks in New York and national history. In 1710 Lewis Morris, Jr., moved from New Jersey to New York in order to manage his inherited land. He built up a strong political following by handing out patronage and contracts, and he broadened his political base by offering improved roads and cheap money to farmers, protective duties on imports, and restrictions on peddlers (the latter to please shopkeepers). Robert Livingston cooperated closely with Morris and with Governor Robert Hunter (1710–1720), who agreed to spend public money according to a schedule drawn up by the Assembly. In exchange Hunter received a support bill guaranteeing him revenues for five years. Clearly New Yorkers were mastering the art of politics, to the chagrin of royal governors and the annoyance of London officials.

Eighteenth-century New York exhibited most of the features that had developed earlier. Although the mixed population kept expanding (at an increased rate after 1750), it had hardly disturbed the vast wilderness. The economy, still largely devoted to the production and sale of agricultural products, added manufacturing, which sustained a vigorous, sometimes rambunctious artisan class. The expansion of trade itself created demands for many new products needed by shipowners, city dwellers, and prosperous landholders.[4] Merchants needed casks, ships, sails, and bricks; householders and farmers needed cabinets, furniture, nails, and tools; imported sugar had to be refined, beer brewed, goods carted to warehouses. The greater the population, the greater the opportunities for tavern keepers, shopkeepers, and professional men.

The oligarchy occupied the apex of the political and social pyramid, but artisans and freehold farmers were moving from grumbling deference to open challenge of landlord-merchant domination. Meanwhile threats to the upper Hudson and Mohawk frontier increased, reaching a climax during the French and Indian War. As a result, governors had to devote most of their energies to imperial defense. In exchange for the increases in taxes that the governors requested, assemblymen demanded and got increased control over patronage, expenditures, and policies.

Farming provided the livelihood for most families. Several thousand tenant farmers, an unusual feature of the northern colonies, leased land from great families such as the Van Rensselaers, Livingstons, and De Lanceys. Intermittently tenants expressed their discontent in antirent uprisings, encouraged by Yankee newcomers.

A few hundred elite families sported distinctive clothing, imported house furnishings, and patronized upper-class entertainment. Its members cemented power by arranging marriages among their youth. Whereas in early decades of the century members of the lower classes often climbed into the elite, by the 1760s the barriers had risen much higher. No doubt this limitation on opportunity had something to do with the increasing radicalism of the artisans and shopkeepers in the decade before the Revolution.

The contrast between the style of living of the elite and that of frontier farmers or urban poor was striking. Although no more than 2 percent were actually receiving public assistance in the eighteenth century, many thousands of families lived close to destitution. Their dress, shacks, and household goods, or lack of them, betrayed their poverty.

Most striking of all social developments was the emergence of a powerful middle class of property owners in New York City and in the countryside. It was much easier to become a freehold farmer or a relatively well-paid craftsman in New York than in England or on the Continent. Artisans commanded high wages because of their scarcity. They and freehold farmers had a strong sense of class consciousness, if only because the elite treated them with ill-concealed contempt.

Constitutional practices and political procedures became more sophisticated and firmly grounded. The Assembly tried to handcuff the governors and made good its claim for rights similar to those of the House of Commons. Political parties emerged, reflecting the geographical, economic, and ethnic diversity of the province.

Successful party government required an orderly shift in power from one group to the other, with the group currently out of power becoming a "loyal" opposition. When the Morris faction, called "country," became the formal opposition after 1728, it clashed with the "court" party, clustered around the Philipse family. Both parties drew their leaders from the elite, but as time passed they found it necessary to appeal to a broader public. Petty jealousies, family feuds, and rivalries between localities and ethnic groups also prevented factional lines from hardening.

The Zenger case has won a place in history books as a landmark in the struggle for freedom of the press. Though that claim is an exaggeration, it has an element of truth. In 1732 the newly appointed governor, William Cosby, asked Rip Van Dam to refund half of the salary paid to him during the time he served as acting governor. When Van Dam balked, Cosby brought suit.

Fearing a jury trial, Cosby directed the Supreme Court to make decisions outside the ordinary rules of English common law. When Chief Justice Lewis Morris denounced the order as unconstitutional, Cosby fired Morris, who then waged a vigorous campaign for a seat in the Assembly. Morris won handily and his followers financed the *New York Weekly Journal*, printed by John Peter Zenger. The newspaper called Cosby corrupt and incompetent, a charge that stung because it was true. Incensed, Cosby had Zenger put in jail. When the Morris faction sprang to his defense, Cosby's chief justice disbarred two defense lawyers, a serious error because the Morrisites then imported a Philadelphia lawyer, Andrew Hamilton, the Nestor of the American bar. Hamilton insisted that truth was a proper defense against libel and won the case. Zenger's acquittal was an affirmation of the need for open criticism of executive prerogative. Although the Assembly continued to suppress critical newspapers, editors often criticized governors and officials.

If provincial government functioned with difficulty, imperial controls broke down except in respect to the Navigation Acts. Even in that area the Molasses Act of 1733 was often evaded by New Yorkers who wanted to import cheaper sugar from the French and Spanish islands. The governors faced formidable problems, not the least of which were instructions impossible to follow. Because war threatened even when the guns were silent, governors had to beg for more funds for defense from the Assembly, which exacted its price in concessions. New York's strategic position athwart the water routes to the interior thus continued to shape the lives of New Yorkers.

The opening of King George's War (1744–1748) found a former admiral, George Clinton, sitting in the governor's chair. Upon his arrival, Clinton had struck a bargain with James De Lancey, the chief justice, who dominated the Assembly and had powerful friends in England. In exchange for a bill granting salaries for officials for one year, Clinton agreed to allow greater Assembly control over salaries. The two split, however, over the proper policy to follow toward France. The merchants, and probably the public as well, favored neutrality because they enjoyed a flourishing trade with Montreal and the French West Indies. But

Clinton favored war, and he proposed to lead an expedition against Canada.

Clinton allied himself with William Johnson, the fur trader and landowner, who became famous as the trusted friend of the Mohawks and other members of the Five Nations. Born in Ireland, Johnson came to New York to manage a tract of land owned by his uncle, Vice Admiral Peter Warren, who had married Susannah De Lancey. Johnson soon acquired land for himself and brought in scores of settlers. Once Johnson had set up his store near present-day Johnstown, few tribesmen bothered to go on to Albany. Johnson, like Clinton, favored a vigorous policy against the French. He quarreled with the Assembly because it failed to reimburse him for his expenses in keeping the Iroquois as allies.

In New York as well as in national history, warfare has often tilted the balance between executive and legislative branches. On the one hand, the executive usually asserts power because of foreign danger. On the other hand, governors must make concessions to the legislature in order to secure appropriations for defense. The French and Indian War upset the political balance within New York Province and the British Empire.

In 1754 the British government called a major intercolonial gathering at Albany for the purpose of conciliating the Iroquois. Chief Hendricks Peter spoke bluntly to the delegates: "Look at the French, they are men, they are fortifying everywhere—but we are ashamed to say, you are like women."[5]

The next year Johnson persuaded the Iroquois to side with the British. He led a force of militia that turned back a French army near Ticonderoga. For this victory the king made him a baronet. He was also confirmed in the position of superintendent of Indian affairs in the north.

Before July 1758 the French stung Britain with several defeats, forcing a reshuffle of power within England. William Pitt came into office and revitalized the war effort in England and America. In 1758 General Louis Montcalm smashed a British army that gallantly but foolishly stormed the breastworks at Ticonderoga. Colonel John Bradstreet, however, captured Fort Frontenac (present-day Kingston, Ontario), the key to French communica-

Johnson Hall in Johnstown, built 1762–1763 by Sir William Johnson. New York State Office of Parks and Recreation.

tion with the interior. Soon Fort Duquesne, at the Forks of the Ohio, fell to British attack. The next year the British captured Fort Niagara, long a bone in their throat, and in 1760 Montreal capitulated to a combined force, one army sweeping northeast from Oswego, the other moving north from Lake Champlain.

The war created many problems, including the supplying and quartering of troops, who often clashed with citizens of Albany and New York. The provisioning of the British armies brought prosperity and inflation, but the reduction of spending after 1761 caused prices to fall. The British government grew increasingly critical of New York smugglers and claimed the right to determine how money should be spent.

In war as well as in peace, New Yorkers kept insisting on the rights of the Assembly against the prerogatives of the governors. When imperial claims pinched the nerves of provincial interests, colonial spokesmen reacted quickly. Their protests rang forth in tones familiar to persons who were proud of the Magna Carta, the Bill of Rights, and other English historical documents.

The passions and loyalties that characterized New York politics did not carry over to the religious sphere.[6] Observers charged that New Yorkers lacked piety, and that Mammon and Bacchus had more adherents than Jesus of Nazareth. The large number of churches reflected the heterogeneity of the population. One reckoning gives the number of congregations in 1776 as follows: Dutch Reformed, 81; Presbyterian, 61; Episcopal, 30; Quaker, 26; Lutheran, 22; Baptist, 16; Congregationalist, 5; Moravian, 3; Associate Presbyterian, 2; Covenanter, 2; Methodist, 1; Jewish, 1. The Calvinist churches had a decisive majority that kept increasing because of the influx of New Englanders, Ulster Irish, and Scots.

All denominations faced similar problems, especially a scarcity of clergy. Small congregations with fluctuating membership found it difficult to pay even the meager salaries customary for pastors. Dutch, French, and German churches ran into language problems that disrupted congregations and weakened allegiances. Ritual changes and doctrinal questions led to squabbling and divisions.

Governors Fletcher and Cornbury interpreted the Ministry Act of 1693 to provide for the establishment of the Church of England in New York, Westchester, Queens, and Richmond counties. Despite their pressure and the activities of sixty-odd missionaries sent out by the Society for the Propagation of the Gospel in Foreign Parts, the Anglican church never attracted a tenth of adult New Yorkers. It enrolled most officials and many aristocrats, and to it gravitated ambitious youth from the Dutch and French communities. SPG missionaries and teachers made serious efforts to educate the children of immigrants, blacks, and Indians.

The pietistic and evangelistic fervor in the early eighteenth century, which in America was called the Great Awakening, hardly touched New Yorkers. Perhaps it is true that New Yorkers paid more attention to material than spiritual concerns. Although George Whitefield, the flaming evangelist, attracted audiences of thousands in 1739 and 1740, most New Yorkers quickly sank back into their daily routines.

By the time of the Revolution, the Presbyterian church had become the strongest of the denominations because it attracted most of the Yankee immigrants. The Presbyterians of New York and New Jersey supported the College of New Jersey, later Princeton.

A bitter feud embroiled Anglicans and Presbyterians, and it reached its climax after 1750. The struggle concerned institutional power more than disputes over theology or ritual. When Anglicans sought a charter for King's College, their rivals fought the scheme, urging instead a nondenominational college. Lieutenant Governor James De Lancey, however, rode roughshod over his Presbyterian opponents and secured public money for the new college. Equally controversial was the proposed establishment of an Anglican bishop. The other churches interpreted this proposal as a threat to their liberties, because in England non-Anglicans had the status of second-class citizens. When the Revolution broke out, most Anglican clergymen remained "loyal," while the rebels were sometimes called the "Presbyterian party."

Formal education made little progress and many children never attended a school. They picked up skills and instruction in various places: their homes, the shops of artisans, stores, ships, farms. Boys often became apprentices in the shops of craftsmen, where they mastered each aspect of carpentry, blacksmithing, sailmaking, shoemaking, and scores of other occupations. Some children of the poor did attend a few charity schools set up by the Anglicans, Jews, and Dutch Reformed. The middle class preferred to enroll their children in makeshift schools run by ministers and itinerant schoolmasters. In 1732 the Assembly established a public school in New York City for twenty students. Six years later it closed without much protest. The rich hired tutors to instruct their sons and daughters, and a handful of young men traveled to London for further seasoning in genteel manners. Yale and the College of New Jersey attracted some New Yorkers. King's College graduated five to six students a year between 1758 and 1775.

Culturally, New York lagged behind New England, where the Puritan emphasis on education spawned a vast amount of written material, mostly religious in nature. New York City alone had an upper and middle class wealthy enough to support a college, a library, and newspapers. All of the dozen or so newspapers published before 1769 appeared in New York City. William Bradford published dozens of books, ranging from Bibles to almanacs. Probably the most important book was Cadwallader Colden's *History of the Five Nations*. A few individuals collected libraries, and others joined subscription libraries that imported the latest books from England.

Georgian architecture characterized the homes of the elite. Usually square or rectangular, these houses of brick, stone, or wood had four rooms opening off a central hall. They did not display the yellow tiles and gabled roofs so characteristic of the Dutch style. The Schuyler mansion in Albany is a fine example, its gambrel roof topped with a Chippendale railing. The elite, furnishing their homes according to the latest fashions in London, had paneling and rich hangings in their drawing rooms. Some local cabinetmakers had sufficient skill to copy the chairs and cabinets imported from London. The wall cupboards displayed pewter tankards, stoneware, and assorted china.

The homes of average citizens in the villages, cities, and countryside were comfortable but modest. Peter Kalm in 1750 described in some detail the houses of Albany:

The houses in this town are very neat, and partly built of stones covered with shingles of white pine. Some are slated with tile from Holland, because the clay of this neighborhood is not considered fit for tiles. Most of the houses are built . . . with the gable-end towards the street, except a few, which were recently built in the modern style. A great number of houses are built like those of New Brunswick . . . the gable-end towards the street being of bricks and all the other walls of boards.[7]

The strong tradition of painting that characterized the secular society of the Netherlander cities and countryside was carried over to the Hudson Valley. Portraits and biblical scenes represented to Dutch farmers and burghers evidence of wealth and status as well as aesthetic values. Before 1700 Albany traders employed unknown limners to paint their portraits and to decorate their homes. The limners were honest craftsmen though not masters. After 1749, artists—John Wollaston, Benjamin West, and John Singleton Copley, to cite three of the most prominent—visited and settled in New York City, where customers were willing to pay high prices. West and Copley moved on to distinguished careers in London.

The theater arrived rather late, partly because of official disapproval and clerical opposition, but mostly for lack of support. In 1750 Thomas Kean presented *Richard III*, and shortly thereafter an English troupe gave the seaport its first season of drama. Comedies, operas, concerts, and acrobatic performances titillated New York audiences.

Science had the barest of beginnings. Take away Cadwallader Colden and one has difficulty in finding anyone interested in science. Colden, not an original mind, corresponded with Benjamin Franklin and English men of science. He dabbled in Linnaean botany and in medicine, the field of his training, and was a conduit through which some of the recent discoveries became known. Medical science and public health could do little to check the ordinary diseases: measles, whooping cough, and scarlet fever caused the deaths of a high percentage of children among red and black as well as white families. Tuberculosis was probably the greatest killer among young adults. Epidemics of smallpox, yellow fever, and cholera periodically threw citizens into a panic and led officials to quarantine ships coming in from the West Indies.

Urban growth complicated the old problems of controlling fires, crime, disease, and slaves. Volunteer fire companies, the first organized in 1737, did little to stop fires, some of which became disasters. People wandering about the streets after dark invited attacks by footpads. In the countryside individuals faced danger from animals, drunks, rival claimants for land, and persons disturbed by loneliness, deprivation, and delusions. Constables and sheriffs were unable to cope with the rising incidence of crime. In New York City hundreds of prostitutes and their clients—sailors, soldiers, and civilians—infected each other with venereal disease. City fathers took sporadic measures to control the hogs and livestock that made the average street a filthy quagmire.

New York's supply of public institutions (docks, markets, prisons) was adequate and private agencies supplemented them when necessary. Most important were the taverns, approximately one for every twelve adult males in the seaport. Here one picked up mail, auctioned goods, signed up sailors, and completed business deals.

New York had the largest black population north of Maryland. In the 1730s the Assembly imposed a strict black code, but haphazard enforcement tempered its severity. The blacks formed a subculture of their own, a few skilled slaves enjoying a standard of living well above the grim subsistence level. Some tavern keepers broke the law and sold liquor to blacks, and looked the other way when customers paid with stolen goods. In 1741 citizens of New York City blamed a series of unsolved fires and thefts upon the blacks. When they offered a reward for information, a young girl, spiritual sister of the girls who sparked the witch hangings in Salem a half century earlier, provided lurid details of a black conspiracy to kill all white males and burn the city. The public became hysterical and the authorities burned thirteen blacks, hanged eighteen, and exiled seventy to the West Indies.

Perhaps the greatest threat to provincial unity was the invasion of Yankee squatters who took up land in New York and relied on land titles provided by the officials of Massachusetts and New Hampshire or scattered Indians such as the Wappingers. The landlords, who realized all too well how shaky their titles were, fought back in the courts. In 1766 they were able to get the backing of the governor, who dispatched the militia to Westchester County. Because of landlord power and influence, none of the local lawyers would rush to the defense of the squatters or tenants. New York landlords met a crushing defeat, however, in the Vermont area, where land speculators had the support of their local militia, sometimes called the Green Mountain Boys. The Vermonters under Ethan Allen turned back sheriffs from New York, and the area eventually declared itself the independent state of Vermont in 1777.

Colonial New Yorkers were indeed a "factious people," as Patricia Bonomi has so conclusively shown.[8] The intensity of New York's politics mirrored the diversity of its people, who sought to maximize their personal interests. They reacted to policies as landlords, tenants, merchants, farmers, artisans, Anglicans, Presbyterians, Quakers, Germans, Dutch, New Englanders, Long Islanders, Albanians, frontiersmen, Anglo-Americans. On the eve of the Revolution a visitor complained about hearing nothing but "politics, politics, politics!... Men, women, children, all ranks and professions mad with Politics."[9]

Below the froth of politics several forces were creating a sense of community. Fear of the French and their Indian allies drew New Yorkers of all persuasions together. The process of anglicization provided colonists with a rich tradition of political literature and an arsenal of constitutional precedents. A great web of commercial transactions tied the province with the other mainland colonies, the West Indies, Africa, Europe, and of course Mother England. A watery network linked New York City with New Yorkers on Long Island and along the Hudson River.

Practically all New Yorkers subscribed wholeheartedly to the tenets of materialism. About mid-century William Livingston, able lawyer and leading opponent of the charter to King's College, commented, "Our Neighbors have told us in an insulting Tone, that the Art of getting Money, is the highest Improvement we can pretend to...."[10]

New Yorkers did indeed worship wealth, and it has enlisted many votaries in every subsequent generation. Whatever their origins, colonial New Yorkers placed a premium upon getting and spending.

Many elements considered characteristic of "the American way of life" developed in provincial New York: a diversified economy sharply tinged with commerce; a pluralistic culture that tolerated significant differences in national background, economic status, and religious belief; urbanism with its accompanying cultural institutions. And New York exhibited that dynamic spirit of change—relentless, continuous, even mindless—so characteristic of American society.

4

Revolutionary Cockpit, 1763–1789

"What is the reason that New York must continue to embarrass the Continent?"[1] So queried the irascible John Adams in 1776, when New Yorkers were procrastinating in approving the Declaration of Independence. Well might Adams express exasperation at the confusion of New York politics and the reluctance of its leaders to join the movement for independence. Whereas in 1764–1766 New Yorkers had raised the shrillest outcry against British policies, in the final breach of 1775–1776 they stood at the end of the colonial procession.

No state suffered more severely from the Revolutionary War than New York, or recovered from it more remarkably. The exodus of Loyalists, the disruption of the economy, the invasion and occupation by British armies, and the controversy over New York's relation with a new federal government transferred the laggard province into a commonwealth ready to take off.

The story of how New Yorkers reacted to British laws and regulations is a complex one that still stirs debate among historians. Carl Lotus Becker, writing in 1909, set the terms of the debate in the opening paragraph of *The History of Political Parties in the Province of New York, 1760–1776*: "The American Revolution was the result of two general movements: the contest for home-rule and independence, and the democratization of American politics and society." According to Becker, the aristocracy ruled but was divided into two factions: the Livingstons (lawyers, landlords, and Presbyterians) and the De Lanceys (merchants and Anglicans). The Livingstons lost political control to their rivals in 1769. Merchants and lawyers organized the protests against the Stamp Act by enlisting the aid of craftsmen and others who worked with their hands.

Since 1950 scores of books and articles have modified and amplified Becker's interpretations. Some historians have held that the aristocracy was less powerful and more splintered than Becker found it. Scholars have also claimed that the New York elite—landlords, merchants, lawyers—felt at odds with the existing political order after 1763. The importance of economic rivalry between the colonists and the mother country, a conflict stressed by Charles Beard a half century ago, is upheld by some modern supporters. They have shifted their emphasis, however, to the role of the working class in leading resistance to royal rule. But artisans, like landlords and merchants, often split along ethnic, religious, and economic lines.

Bernard Bailyn and others have reexamined the political theories that radical Whigs advanced in England to challenge the powers of the Stuart kings and Parliament. Whiggish denunciation of unbridled power and blatant corruption found eager listeners among colonists, many of whom believed that the British government was introducing a new tyranny in America. The bumbling and greed of officials encouraged colonial resistance. Michael Kammen describes Cadwallader Colden, the acting or lieutenant governor between 1760 and 1775, as the "unwitting provocateur of the early revolutionary movement in New York."[2] Although an ardent defender of the crown, Colden had the uncanny ability to antagonize almost every faction and influential leader. He challenged the land titles of the elite, affronted merchants whose activities skirted the limits of legality, and questioned the right of judges to hold office except at the pleasure of the king. He even challenged the finality of jury verdicts.

In short, New Yorkers stumbled into revolution for a variety of complicated reasons. We must avoid, if possible, imposing on this decade a preordained pattern in which each event leads inexorably to independence and the establishment of the federal government. Actually confusion and contradictions marked this period in both Great Britain and the colonies, nowhere more so than in New York. Furthermore, episodes overlapped in time, making it difficult to sort out issues and assess their importance. For example, the shrillness of the protest against the Stamp Act was reinforced—how much?—by the anger aroused by the Quartering Act.

The close of the Seven Years' War in 1763 marked the triumph of Great Britain over the French in Europe, India, and North America. Victorious but debt-ridden, Great Britain had to seek more tax revenue as well as to reorganize its creaky imperial structure. At that same time the colonists, who had finally freed themselves of the French menace, were vigorously asserting their rights.

To calm the Indians, London officials issued the Proclamation of 1763, which banned white settlement west of the Appalachian crest. Although the ban did little to stop the westward march of pioneers and speculators, it did make them uneasy. In 1768 Sir William Johnson called a conference at Fort Stanwix which opened up more lands and established the famous line running south from the fort to the Unadilla River, then down to the Susquehanna River before swerving to the west. The Quebec Act (1774) threatened to turn New York's declining share of the fur trade over to Canada. A high duty on rum shipped into Quebec from the American colonies also disturbed many merchants.

Much more pressing was financing the war debt and paying for the 7,500 troops stationed in such frontier posts as Fort Niagara. Any increase in taxes was bound not only to cause trouble but to raise constitutional questions. Did Parliament have the right to levy internal taxes on the colonists? Could Parliament regulate trade for the purpose of taxation? Practically every British official insisted upon Parliament's absolute power over taxation and commerce, although some cautioned against using such powers arbitrarily. The colonists, however, cited precedents in English and colonial history to justify restraints on the authority of the king and Parliament, and eventually a majority swung over to the view that only Americans could tax Americans.

In 1764 Parliament passed the Sugar Act to replace the Molasses Act of 1733, which the government had never vigorously enforced. The Sugar Act prohibited the importation of all rum not of British distillation and placed new duties on the products of the French and Spanish West Indies. Both measures injured New Yorkers, especially those engaged in the manufacture of rum and those in commerce. When the government empowered officials to collect revenue by using admiralty courts in place of jury trials, Manhattan merchants bellowed their protest. The New York Assembly stated that taxation could be imposed only with consent because this principle is "inseparable from the very idea of property."[3] "Liberty and Property" became the slogan of New Yorkers during the next decade.

In March 1765 Parliament tried to raise revenue by requiring stamps on legal documents and newspapers after November 1. At once New Yorkers protested and organized opposition. Militant leaders in Massachusetts and Virginia urged representatives of the other colonies to attend a meeting in New York in October. Although this Stamp Act Congress affirmed its loyalty to the crown and "subordination" to Parliament, it also asserted that no taxes should be imposed on them but with their own consent, or by their representatives.

Tension mounted as militants made fiery speeches and published pamphlets denouncing the hated tax. On October 23 the news that a ship with stamps had arrived spread quickly from one public house to the next. Soon two thousand men had gathered to prevent the landing. Acting Governor Colden placed the stamps in Fort George for safekeeping. Outside, a mob assembled every day, and at night angry men shouted insults at the garrison. These men belonged to a radical group called the Sons of Liberty, whose members urged resistance to Parliamentary taxation. On November 1 a mob seized Colden's carriage, burned it, and hanged him in effigy. Fearful of more violence, Colden delivered the stamps to the mayor of New York and promised to make no effort to enforce the act.

Mob violence and threats by the Sons of Liberty alarmed many merchants. Where would all this talk about popular rights end? The Sons of Liberty were organizing a military corps, which drilled in public. At Christmas their delegates met with Connecticut Sons of Liberty to join forces and to form a "like association" with all colonies. Revolution seemed imminent.

Meanwhile the boycott of British goods cut trade and reduced the profits of merchants in London, Bristol, and other ports. Disturbed and alarmed, they took their complaints to officials in London and pressed Parliament to repeal the stamp tax. This dispute over colonial policy helped bring down the Grenville ministry and the Rockingham Whigs took office. The new cabinet urged repeal of the Stamp Act, but Parliament coupled repeal with a Declaratory Act, staunchly asserting its absolute power to levy taxes.

New Yorkers, however, paid scant attention to the Declaratory Act, so pleased were they with repeal. In New York City, Mayor John Cruger urged the Assembly to erect a statue in honor of William Pitt, who had defended the right of Americans to vote their own taxes. Warned that a statue to Pitt alone would irritate George III, the Assembly perfunctorily agreed to erect one in his honor also. These gestures did not smooth ruffled feelings. King George and his ministers seethed with anger when Americans bragged about forcing their "oppressors" to back down.

General Thomas Gage, the commander in chief of British forces in North America, located his headquarters in New York. The Quartering Act of 1765 required colonial authorities to provide barracks and supplies for British troops, but the Assembly and the Albany magistrates refused to grant all of Gage's requests. Would not compliance be tantamount to acknowledging Parliament's right to tax without their consent? On the other hand, New Yorkers needed British troops to overawe the Iroquois and to maintain law and order, as when Gage sent troops to put down a tenant uprising in Westchester County in 1766. He privately grumbled that the landlords "certainly deserve any losses they may sustain, for it is the work of their own hands. They first sowed the seeds of sedition among the people and taught them to rise in opposition to the laws."[4]

The refusal of the Assembly to obey the Quartering Act shocked William Pitt, recently elevated to earl of Chatham, as well as other English friends of America. As a result Parliament suspended the Assembly in July 1767, an unusual move that threatened the independence of the legislature.

Meanwhile Charles Townshend, the chancellor of the exchequer, decided to raise revenue in America to pay for the army. He placed duties on the importation of glass, paint, lead, paper, and tea, and he earmarked the revenues for the salaries of governors, judges, and other officials, thus lessening the ability of the Assembly to apply pressure on them. Most infuriating of all, customs officials could secure writs of assistance, court orders permitting them to search warehouses for smuggled goods.

New Yorkers became enraged as officials seized ships and made charges of smuggling with indecent haste, greed, and force. When the British government demanded payment in silver, merchants, who found specie difficult to secure, agreed to boycott imports. Meanwhile Townshend ordered the Assembly to stop passing legislation because of its refusal to meet all the requests under the Quartering Act.

By late 1768 a decline in farm prices, the scarcity of money (legal tender, coin, sterling), sagging demand for goods by West Indian planters, and a fall in land values created an economic crisis for merchants, farmers, and craftsmen. When the British government would not approve a new issue of paper money, the Assembly defied Townshend and boycotted British imports.

In the late 1760s the Livingston–De Lancey feud reemerged and polarized New York politics. To embarrass the Livingstons, temporarily the allies of Governor Henry Moore, the De Lanceys condemned the suspension of the Assembly and crusaded against lawyers, prominent in the Livingston camp. Debtors and tenants were quick to side with the De Lanceys. Meanwhile the Livingstons counterattacked and charged Captain James De Lancey with planning to place an Anglican bishop over New Yorkers. By this ploy they hoped to win the support of the majority, who disliked any strengthening of the privileged status of the Church of England.

On December 31, 1768, the Assembly, yielding to mob pressure, declared that it alone had the power to tax. When Governor Moore read this statement, he followed his instructions and sent the legislators home. The next year the De Lanceys won a smashing victory and made a deal with Acting Governor Colden whereby the Assembly would make a partial payment under the Quartering Act if Colden would approve a much-needed currency bill.

Alexander McDougall, the son of a milkman and a member of the Sons of Liberty, secretly published a tract castigating the De Lanceys and Colden as fools and traitors to popular liberties. Infuriated by this attack, Colden and the Assembly majority uncovered the author of the broadside and ordered his arrest for libel. Refusing to pay bail, McDougall was clapped into prison. The Sons of Liberty likened him to another martyr, John Wilkes, whose essay against the king had appeared in issue number 45 of his journal *The North Briton*. A flood of pamphlets appeared, each decorated with "Number 45." On February 14, the forty-fifth day of the year, forty-five men ate with McDougall forty-five pounds of meat from a forty-five-month-old steer. Later forty-five virgins (this figure was challenged) appeared before McDougall to take tea and to sing the Forty-fifth Psalm. The grand jury, which considered only the question of whether McDougall had published the article, indicted him for seditious libel.

In the meantime the British garrison and the citizens had renewed their old quarrel. Soldiers angered workingmen in particular by taking odd jobs at low wages. The Sons of Liberty kept erecting liberty poles, and the soldiers, who understood the symbolism, just as regularly cut them down. When the soldiers hacked down a pole in the turbulent year 1770, three thousand men and children assembled and erected another. Soldiers and workers traded jibes and insults until fighting broke out. In the melee one person was killed on Golden Hill.

By late 1769 the ministry in England had grown weary of the ceaseless bickering in America. Although New York had clearly violated the Quartering Act, the Earl of Hillsborough, secretary of state for the colonies, grudgingly accepted a limited grant as better than none at all and clearly preferable to more wrangling. He even offered to end all duties except the duty on tea. Parliament agreed to allow New York to issue £120,000 in loans that could be used as legal tender for the next fourteen years. Most New Yorkers, weary of agitation, were satisfied by these concessions.

The uneasy calm between 1770 and 1773 was shattered by a combination of factors: the contempt shown by officials in London as well as those in the colonies, colonial success in wringing concessions by extralegal means, the rise of tough new leaders, and the spread of radical ideas.

In the meantime the British East India Company was sliding toward bankruptcy, a calamity that the government wished to avert at all costs. Under the Tea Act of 1773, the Commons granted the company full remission of all duties on tea exported to the colonies except for a three-penny tax per pound in America. Furthermore, the company could sell tea directly through its agents or consignees in America instead of through the usual retail outlets. The Sons of Liberty denounced the monopoly and pointed out that the duty, admittedly small, was still a tax levied without consent. McDougall, Isaac Sears, and John Lamb came back into the limelight and organized protests. The militants threatened company agents, who found it prudent to declare that they would not accept or sell dutied tea.

William Tryon, the new governor, took these threats seriously, and he decided to store the tea in Fort George. When Tryon heard about the Boston Tea Party, he planned to send the tea back to England to avert trouble. A new shipment, however, arrived on the *London* in April 1774, and a band of men disguised as Mohawks boarded the ship and dumped the tea into New York Harbor.

Meanwhile Parliament had rushed through a series of laws known to us as the Intolerable Acts. One closed the port of Boston until the citizens paid for the tea destroyed in the Boston Tea Party. Another changed the government of Massachusetts in such a way as to enlarge the powers of the royal governor and ban town meetings without prior permission. Parliament also authorized the quartering of troops in private homes, a measure sure to alarm New Yorkers, who had the largest number of troops stationed among them. Redcoats had a reputation for hard drinking and rowdy behavior, and few families relished welcoming them into their homes.

The De Lancey faction headed off McDougall and other radicals and nominated most of the fifty-man (later fifty-one) committee that was formed to organize resistance. Meanwhile militants in Massachusetts and several other colonies were calling for an agreement not to import any English goods. In May 1774 the New York Committee of Correspondence approved the call for an intercolonial congress to decide the question of boycotting English goods.

The delegates to the First Continental Congress in Philadelphia declared that each assembly was all-powerful within its own territory, a position more radical than the one favored by the New York delegation. The Congress adopted the Continental Association, an agreement not to import from or export to Britain until American rights were restored. To enforce this ban, each town, county, and city elected a committee, a step that meant the shift of actual power from the older units of government to the revolutionary committees.

From early 1774 until the spring of 1776 two authorities—Assembly and Provincial Congress—jockeyed for power. Local committees that worked with a series of provincial congresses were springing up. The last of these congresses, which met on July 9, 1776, approved the Declaration of Independence and then transformed itself into the Convention of the Representatives of the State of New York.

The Assembly, however, sidetracked the resolution of the First Continental Congress. In fact, the Assembly refused to send delegates to the Second Continental Congress. But the radicals outflanked the moderates by securing control of the Provincial Congress, which immediately appointed delegates to the Continental Congress.

In England George III and his ministers had struck back when they heard of the battle of Lexington. They had pushed through the Prohibitory Act of December 22, 1775, which declared all vessels and cargoes of the rebellious colonies forfeited to the crown, as if they belonged to "open enemies." This act was in effect a declaration of war.

A majority of the delegates to the Second Continental Congress were still hoping for reconciliation, among them John Jay and James Duane of New York, who used every tactic of delay. As English subjects they found it hard to cut the ties with the mother country, the guarantor of stability. New York merchants feared the loss of trading rights within the British Empire as well as protection against pirates and other enemies. Tenant farmers leaned to any opponent of the local landlords, while Robert R. Livingston and other landholders feared attacks upon their property.[5]

The independence movement kept moving forward, however, and by July 2 all except the New York delegation had voted for independence. Finally on July 9 the newly elected Congress of New York formally ratified the famous Declaration.

Military developments in revolutionary New York occupy a prominent role in our national history. Textbooks note that in 1776 Sir William Howe ousted Washington's motley militiamen from New York, which remained under military occupation for seven years. Every author concentrates on the famous campaign of 1777, when General John Burgoyne marched into the upper Hudson Valley and met defeat at Saratoga. Some reference is made to the bloody frontier warfare in which Tories and Indians raided settlements, and Americans in the Clinton-Sullivan expedition attacked Iroquois villages. If New York provided a martyr in Nathan Hale, it also furnished a tragic figure in twenty-three-year-old Jane MacCrae, whom Indians scalped near Fort Edward. Benedict Arnold, who almost delivered West Point to the British, became our symbol of treason.

Although these events are more than familiar, they still provoke debate and even controversy. Did General Howe and his brother, Admiral Richard Howe, fail to crush Washington in 1776 because of inertia, policy, or secret sympathy for Whiggish causes? Did the patriots, including Nathan Hale, deliberately set fire to New York City? Did General Philip Schuyler bungle the defense of the upper Hudson or was he the victim of a cabal of New Englanders intent on replacing him with Horatio Gates?

Some historians continue to attribute the failure of the British strategy of 1777 to the famous "forgotten dispatch" from Germain to Howe. The evidence does not support this claim. Neither Burgoyne nor his superiors in London nor Howe doubted that Burgoyne would reach Albany without assistance from Howe. Furthermore, Germain, in London, also approved of Howe's departure for Philadelphia. Only after Burgoyne faced defeat did he argue that he expected reinforcements from Howe. Slowness in transatlantic communications undoubtedly played its part in the disaster at Saratoga. Throughout the war British officials and generals in the field did not understand the environment in which their troops operated.

The significance of Burgoyne's defeat was as clear to his contemporaries as it is to us. For Americans, it gave a tremendous lift

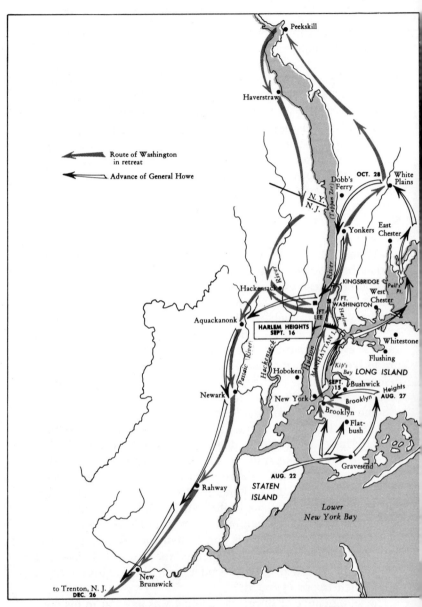

The Revolutionary War in the New York City area, 1776

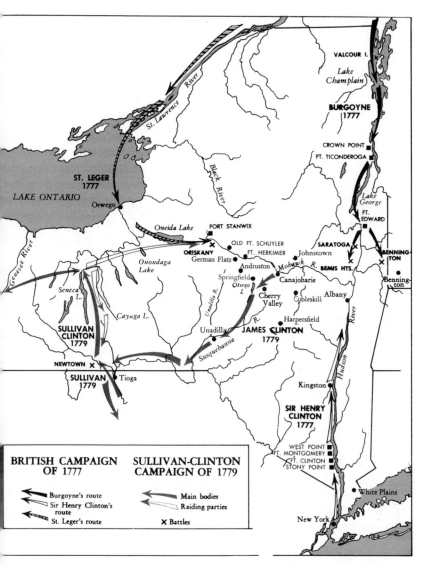

BRITISH CAMPAIGN OF 1777

Burgoyne's route
Sir Henry Clinton's route
St. Leger's route

SULLIVAN-CLINTON CAMPAIGN OF 1779

Main bodies
Raiding parties

X Battles

The Revolutionary War in New York State

as well as assurance of ultimate victory. In Great Britain, this disaster sent shock waves through popular and official circles. The British government made tentative offers to repeal the Intolerable Acts, but these overtures held little attraction for Americans now: independence, not the removal of grievances, had become their goal. To the French, American victory meant eventual British defeat and thus sweet revenge for the loss of Canada and India. The French redoubled aid—supplies and loans—and sent soldiers and ships, which helped guarantee American independence.

Although New York had a sizable number of Loyalists (highest absolutely and second only to Georgia among the states), the British failed to capitalize on them. Repeatedly loyal citizens rallied to the redcoats, who nevertheless withdrew. Thereafter Patriot committees to detect conspiracies punished individuals suspected of favoring the king. No wonder thousands fled to British lines and made the traumatic choice of exile.

A large number of New Yorkers tried to remain neutral, only to find themselves alternately persecuted by partisans of rebellion and agents of the crown. Some, chameleon-like, willingly took oaths of allegiance to any group temporarily in control. A goodly number suffered acute agony because they could not in good conscience make a full commitment to either side. Nevertheless, by 1780 most New Yorkers, however distressed, apathetic, or weary they might be, realized that Great Britain was not able to guarantee their security. That realization played into the hands of the Patriots.

Did a real revolution take place? Or was it only a changing of the guard, a mere severing of imperial ties?

Note that contemporaries in both America and Europe had no doubts that a profound transformation was taking place in the New World. This was especially true in New York State, which experienced the greatest proportionate losses in property, inhabitants, and stability. Military forces occupied New York City while raids destroyed frontier settlements. Parts of New York degenerated into anarchy and civil strife, with Patriot and imperial forces persecuting their enemies. A much higher percentage of residents were expelled from New York than from France, the magnitude of whose revolution finds few skeptics. Incidentally, most émigrés returned to France and recovered their confiscated property; few Loyalists returned to New York or received adequate compensation from either the British or the New York government.

The transformation affected political arrangements, foreign trade, the system of landholding, slavery, the status of the Anglican church, and the structure of society. Out of the crucible of strife emerged a new society that quickly expanded, developed stable institutions, and surged to the forefront among the states.

The Fourth Provincial Congress appointed a committee to draft a state constitution. John Jay took charge and framed a document that compromised the interests of competing groups. The final draft provided for a government quite similar to that of colonial New York. An elected Senate, however, took the place of the appointive Council, the former upper house. The constitution clipped the governor's powers by forcing him to share the veto over legislation with the Council of Revision, consisting of the chancellor and judges of the Supreme Court.

Although a dedicated conservative, Jay took note of the rising democratic spirit. The constitution provided for complete religious toleration as well as separation of church and state. Jay inserted a clause forbidding the slave trade in New York. The vote was extended to almost all adult freemen, a very liberal position for that age. In fact, most white men could vote for assemblymen and about a third could vote for governor and senators.

In June 1777 voters elected George Clinton as their first governor, an office to which he won reelection for six continuous terms and finally, in 1801, after being out of office six years, for a seventh term. Running against him in 1777, Philip Schuyler had argued that although Clinton was able, brave, and virtuous, his "family and connections" did not entitle him to high office. A rough-hewn giant (six feet was unusual in those days), Clinton came from solid farmer stock, and he added to his family holdings by buying thousands of acres of raw lands and by marrying Cornelia Tappen, daughter of a well-to-do Dutch family. Clinton grew up in the Scotch-Irish Presbyterian culture of Ulster

County, where hatred of Stuart kings and Anglican bishops was part of the catechism. Clinton distrusted the landed elite, whose polished ways and formal education made him feel uncomfortable. The common people idolized him because of his plain speech, simple ways, and patriotic fervor. Clinton built up a strong following by appointing friends to office and passing out favors to political allies.

The postwar legislature mirrored the growing diversity of interests and reflected democratic trends. About one-tenth of the legislators still stemmed from elite families, with an equal number aspiring to that status. On the other hand, the number of men who came from common origins or were newcomers rose from two in 1769 to twenty-three in 1785. Clearly the center of gravity among legislators had shifted to the yeoman-artisan middle class. The upheaval reversed at least temporarily the flow of power to the elite. The makeup of the legislature was more similar to that of the early years of the eighteenth century than to that of the three decades before the Revolution.

Two ill-defined groups gradually emerged among the lawmakers. Behind Clinton rallied men eager to smite Tories, keep land taxes low, provide more paper money, and retain power in local hands. The anti-Clinton camp, enlisting majorities in the cities, generally promoted trade and manufacturing and appealed to those who were national or cosmopolitan in outlook. Neither faction, however, developed into a full-blown party with statewide organization and strong discipline.

Clawed by the Lion's Paw, a term angrily used to describe Tories, New Yorkers struck back vengefully. What was more natural than to take out their spite upon local citizens who had declared allegiance to the king or were suspected of secretly favoring the crown? Before long, many rebels insisted that every person who did not aid the Patriot cause was really a partner of the king. Clinton spent most of his first two administrations dealing with military matters and Tory subversion. He led the outcry: Confiscate Tory lands! Root out the traitors!

The peace treaty of 1783 called for the restoration of seized properties and the payment of debts owed to citizens of Great Britain and the states. Clinton wanted to keep former Loyalists from voting, serving as lawyers, and regaining their property. Alexander Hamilton, however, urged reconciliation, arguing that fair treatment would transform Tories into loyal citizens and that compliance with treaty obligations would increase trade with Great Britain, New York's best customer. Privately, Hamilton argued that the votes of former Tories would strengthen conservative forces and property rights. By 1786 a conservative coalition of Hamilton, Schuyler, and the Livingtons captured control of the Assembly and overrode Clinton's objections. Tories won back equal status, including voting rights, and by 1788 two Tories were running for office in New York City.

Destruction during the Revolution disrupted the economy severely. The British government naturally excluded rebellious colonists from special favors in empire ports. Its regulations exacted a heavy price from New York merchants, whose trade had grown up under the sheltering wings of British mercantilism. But New Yorkers showed initiative in increasing trade with France and the Netherlands and even sent ships to China. Clinton had to deal first with inflation, then with sagging farm prices. In 1786 he accepted a bill providing for loans to farmers who submitted their mortgages as collateral. This remedy was a pragmatic solution that helped stimulate economic recovery without upsetting creditors. But Clinton was no radical agrarian encouraging tenants to destroy landlord rights. He turned a stony face to antirenters who challenged land titles and refused to pay rent. He even sent troops against the followers of Daniel Shays when they set up a rallying point within New York. Shays had led an uprising against the tax structure and credit system of Massachusetts. When the Green Mountain Boys in Vermont defied New York authority and rejected the land claims of New Yorkers, Clinton denounced them. Finally, in 1790, he and the legislature decided to recognize the independence of Vermont, in return for the paltry sum of $30,000 as compensation to New York claimants.

The Revolutionary era speeded up reform and promoted a more democratic society. Because many aristocrats had fled, young men from the farmer and artisan classes found it easier to rise to positions of leadership in the army, business, and government. Clinton and Hamilton are excellent examples of young men of modest backgrounds who rose to the top. The confiscation and sale of Tory lands, which ended many large holdings, especially along the east bank of the lower Hudson Valley, increased substantially the number of landowning farmers. The abolition of entail and primogeniture, under which large holdings passed exclusively to the firstborn, further helped break up the aristocratic land system. When Clinton's administrators sold Tory and public lands, they favored his political supporters, most of whom did not belong to the landed grandees. Clinton's following represented the "politics of opportunity" as opposed to the "politics of privilege."

Both Clinton and Jay worked for reform of the criminal code, which listed thirteen crimes as punishable by death; reform was finally achieved under Jay's administration. Both Jay and Clinton favored the end of the slave trade, but Jay alone agitated for the abolition of slavery. Clinton kept silence on this issue because so many of his Dutch neighbors and political allies in Ulster County held slaves.

Most New Yorkers, like most Americans of that period, believed in states' rights. Had they not fought Great Britain because they opposed centralization of power in a distant government? As long as British troops occupied the seaport, the legislature granted to the Continental Congress the right to collect income from duties on imports. Once a peace treaty was signed, legislators refused the 5 percent tariff that Hamilton favored because it would enable Congress to repay the Continental debt. Clinton and the farmers feared that giving up this impost would force New York to impose a land tax. Equally distasteful to Clinton was the prospect of having federal agents operating within his state.

In 1787 Congress called for a new convention to meet at Philadelphia to revise the Articles of Confederation. New York appointed Robert Yates, John Lansing, and Hamilton, the only delegate to favor a strong central government. Hamilton signed the new Constitution, which gave Congress the power to levy taxes, control foreign and interstate commerce, issue currency, and impose imposts.

During the spirited debate over ratification, two camps gradually emerged. The friends of Clinton, or Anti-Federalists, elected forty-six delegates, while the advocates of the Constitution secured only nineteen delegates. Melancton Smith and John Lansing did most of the debating for the Anti-Federalists, partly because Clinton had become president of the convention. The Federalist delegates were an illustrious group, with Hamilton, Jay, Robert R. Livingston, and James Duane among them. Jay became the key man in winning over wavering Anti-Federalists.

Thomas Tredwell, a delegate from Suffolk, observed with considerable accuracy that the ratification struggle was "between navigating and non-navigating individuals." Commercial farmers (a category soon achieved by most pioneers), merchants, and artisans expected a strong central government to open up foreign markets. Holders of public securities saw federal courts as a mighty safeguard to their claims and a federal Congress as a potential friend. Landlords, who had great interest in exports, wanted protection against tenant uprisings.

Anti-Federalists appealed more directly to yeoman farmers, who seldom looked beyond their locality. Passionately devoted to property rights in land, they opposed jobbery in stocks and special privileges to corporations. They had a deep-seated distrust of arbitrary power in some distant government, which they feared would come under the control of elitists.

When the Poughkeepsie meeting opened on July 17, eight states had already ratified the Constitution, and the delegates soon learned that New Hampshire and Virginia had done the same. The knowledge that a federal government would come into existence, thus leaving New York isolated, had a powerful effect upon public opinion and delegates. Acceptance of the Constitution faded as the issue; terms of admission now became the point of debate.

The Anti-Federalists divided into hard-core intransigents and those who could accept ratification with conditions. But conditional ratification provoked more debate. Was it valid? Would the other states and the federal government accept conditions? Finally the New York convention ratified the Constitution in "full confidence" that another federal convention would meet to consider amendments, especially a bill of rights.

Why did enough delegates switch their votes or abstain?

Clearly they were listening to the groundswell of public opinion, and they had to consider the awkward status of New York outside a federal union. Jay kept reassuring delegates that the Federalists would recommend another convention and push for a bill of rights. Meanwhile Hamilton and others were circulating the rumor that southern New York would secede if ratification failed. All these factors drove enough delegates to accept the unthinkable.

Hamilton, Jay, and James Madison wrote a series of scholarly letters explaining the need for a strong central government. Republished as *The Federalist*, these essays analyzed the theory and practice of government so brilliantly that each succeeding generation has profited by studying them. Because of its limited circulation at the time, however, *The Federalist* had little effect upon the outcome.

Ratification not only split the Anti-Federalists at the convention but caused so much bitterness and confusion among their ranks that they lost control of the legislature in the 1789 election. The Federalists were especially strong in the counties surrounding New York City. Although Clinton squeaked through by a narrow margin, the legislature selected two Federalists to represent New York in the United States Senate.

When Great Britain imposed tighter controls after 1763, New York became a battleground, both ideological and military. Its citizens consistently resisted concentration of power in a central government under either the British or the American flag. Who should levy taxes, control trade, regulate currency, and quarter troops? These issues forced colonists to become aware of a degree of collective identity more colonial than British, more American than purely provincial.

In New York the American Revolution brought about a social transformation. The elite found it necessary to share power with the "middling classes," whose new leaders advanced theories of limited government and popular rights. Revolutionary leaders divided the public, which coalesced behind the figures of Clinton and Hamilton. The postwar crisis induced conservatives to seek a stronger central government and a more favorable climate for business enterprise.

The most reluctant to sever the imperial connection and among the last to enter the union, New York actually received the most benefits under the new government. Its pioneers were to develop a new empire west of Albany and its merchants were to capture the bulk of coastal and transatlantic trade. By 1789 Brissot de Warville reported great activity and "rising prosperity" in New York City. This happy turn of events was only just, for had not New York experienced the greatest suffering and upheaval of all the states during the Revolution?

5

The Rise of the Empire State, 1789–1825

No state suffered greater losses in life and property than New York during the Revolutionary War, but New York made an amazing recovery. Within a few years an observer of the Mohawk Valley marveled to find "every house and barn rebuilt, the pastures crowded with cattle, sheep, etc. and the lap of Ceres full."[1]

New York grew faster than the national average in the four decades after 1790. Population quadrupled, from 340,120 to 1,372,812. Whereas in 1785 three out of four citizens lived within ten miles of tidal waters, by 1820 three out of four lived well away from the Hudson River and the Atlantic Ocean. In fact, a majority made their homes west of Rome, a region banned to white settlement before the Revolution.

Dramatic developments both in New York City and upstate powered this amazing growth. Among them were the return of peace and political stability in the 1780s; the insatiable demands of England and France for wheat and ship stores as they grappled for victory between 1793 and 1815; the burgeoning commerce, manufacturing, and finance in New York City; and the conquest of the upstate wilderness by speculators, traders, and farmers. Political leaders vigorously promoted canals and turnpikes, and legislators fostered agricultural improvements and manufacturing. Most important, a spirit of buoyant enterprise animated New Yorkers in almost every walk of life. Merchants scarcely counted their profits before reinvesting in more ships, land, or goods. Every able-bodied member of frontier families pitched in to cut down trees, put up barns, and harvest crops. Communities worked hard to attract turnpikes, secure the county seat, establish academies, and erect churches.

Let us first analyze the effect of these forces on New York City before we examine in some detail their impact upstate. New York's rise to supremacy as a port was spectacular, its growth paralleling that of the rest of the state.

After the Revolution, Manhattan's merchants not only reopened old trade routes to Europe and the West Indies but sought new markets in Latin America and the Far East. Closer to home, tremendous new markets were expanding west of the Hudson, where settlers by the hundreds of thousands were clearing land and growing wheat to ship down the river. Peacetime fostered business recovery, and newcomers, among them many refugees, swarmed to Manhattan. By 1786 the city's population doubled; four years later it exceeded 33,000. Exports soared when the French revolutionaries took up arms against their neighbors and the warring nations sought American foodstuffs. British, French, and Spanish governments opened their West Indian islands to American ships. The value of New York's exports shot up more than tenfold in the fifteen years after 1791. The reexport of foreign goods, especially sugar from the West Indies, accounted for more than half of all exports. Thousands of carters, clerks, ship captains, sailors, and merchants found work handling this commerce. By 1797, Manhattan's merchants were conducting more business than their rivals in Philadelphia. Shortly after Jefferson's election, New York's population surged into top position, never to be challenged by any other American city.

The maritime and mercantile activity of New York City impressed all visitors by whatever route they approached the seaport. New Englanders threaded their way past the rocks and whirlpools of Hells Gate, a narrow channel of the East River. Upstaters and Jerseyites boarded sloops, ferries, and small craft to reach the piers along the Hudson. After 1807 steamboats speeded travel on the waters surrounding Manhattan Island. But the most magnificent view—the Battery on lower Manhattan, a spit of land surrounded by a fringe of masts and wharves—greeted travelers from Europe and southern ports.

British and French interference with American shipping led Jefferson to adopt a policy of economic coercion. His embargo in

December 1807 cut off foreign trade, thus paralyzing shipping and injuring farmers. John Lambert, an Englishman, described in vivid phrases the impact of this measure on the seaport:

> When I arrived at New York in November, the port was filled with shipping, and the wharfs were crowded with commodities of every description. Bales of cotton, wool, and merchandise; barrels of potash, rice, flour, and salt provisions; hogsheads of sugar, chests of tea, puncheons of rum, and pipes of wine ... All was noise and bustle.
>
> But on my return to New York the following April what a contrast was presented to my view ... The coffee-house slip, the wharfs and quays along South Street, presented no longer the hustle and activity that had prevailed there five months before. The port, indeed, was full of shipping; but they were dismantled and laid up. Their decks were cleared, their hatches fastened down, and scarcely a sailor was to be found on board. Not a box, bale, barrel, or package, was to be seen upon the wharfs.[2]

The reopening of trade in the spring of 1809 only partially restored business because under the Nonintercourse Act Congress ordered ships not to enter British or French ports. Thereafter shipowners found their vessels subject to seizure by both French and British frigates. By 1812 the combination of disputes over maritime rights and western issues (the fur trade, Indian control, and land claims) so irritated Congress that it declared war on Britain. Despite several spectacular and heart-warming victories by individual American ships, the British fleet soon formed a screen of ships off Sandy Hook to blockade the harbor.

The peace treaty of December 1814 ushered in a century-long era of remarkable growth and prosperity for New York, which became the entrepôt of North America. In 1815 shipowners rushed to outfit their vessels, to hire crews, and to reestablish trade links with Europe, Latin America, and Asia.

Once again the wharves of Manhattan hummed with activity. The settlers in the Hudson–Mohawk region and central New York poured down a flood of wheat, flour, packed meat, potash, and lumber products. Textiles from New England, coal from Pennsylvania mines after the mid-1820s, tobacco from Virginia, and cotton from the South nourished coastal shipping and trade, centered in New York. The trade in cotton, America's most important export for the next century, was captured by the enterprising shipowners, merchants, and insurers of Manhattan Island. Most vessels carried cotton directly from southern cities to European ports, returning to New York with immigrants, cloth from Lancashire mills, and hardware from Birmingham. They then sailed to southern ports with merchandise for exchange for more cotton.

Meanwhile, by accident, energy, and hard work, New Yorkers were attracting most imports of manufactures. British mill owners and commission merchants, eager to raise cash after Napoleon's fall, dumped their accumulated stocks of textiles on the New York market. New York's auction law, requiring goods put up at auction to be sold at any price, attracted thousands of bargain seekers. Manhattan also attracted the valuable passenger and high-grade merchandise business when promoters in 1818 began packet (scheduled) service to and from Liverpool.

A few hundred men dominated the mercantile life of the seaport. They ran shipping and import houses on South Street, conducted auctions, sold textiles at wholesale on Pearl Street, and borrowed money from Wall Street bankers. Most business firms had their quarters in brick buildings of three to five stories, where customers could inspect items in showrooms, behind which clerks filled out bills of lading and entered orders into ledgers. Nearby was the Tontine Coffee House, a favorite rendezvous where merchants kept up with rumors and completed transactions. Merchants owned about 40 percent of the city's wealth in 1828; in fact, 4 percent of wealth holders held about 60 percent of the total wealth. Most persons who held great wealth or distinguished themselves in the higher ranks of government and business were sons of families who already had status and means. Nevertheless, the burgeoning business world called for more men of talent and energy. Thousands answered the call, including such Yankees as R. H. Macy, such Europeans as John Jacob Astor, and local youth such as Cornelius Vanderbilt.

Importers of raw materials found it necessary and profitable to process products before putting them up for sale. Sugar merchants operated refineries in the New York area, some of them in Brooklyn. Distillers and brewers were hard put to slake the Gargantuan thirst of the sailors, workingmen, and businessmen who

The Tontine Coffee House, northwest corner of Wall and Water streets, New York City, c. 1797. Oil on canvas by Francis Guy. Courtesy of the New-York Historical Society, New York City.

crowded taverns and patronized liquor shops (one for every forty persons). Shipyards sprang up along the East River, and around them clustered hundreds of establishments that made and sold sails, barrels, rope, and ship stores. Sailors and workingmen bought shoes, clothing, and other items made in small shops. The great bulk of manufacturing was carried on in the thousands of shops manned by shoemakers, tanners, cabinetmakers, coopers, sailmakers, blacksmiths, and tailors.

In 1803 the city fathers built their new city hall at the northern edge of the city, near the intersection of Broadway and Chambers and Chatham streets. Population and building kept surging northward at such a rate that by 1820 the city had expanded to 14th Street, placing city hall in the heart of the metropolis. In 1824 alone, Governor De Witt Clinton boasted, the city had acquired another three thousand buildings.

New York City's government could not provide enough services to keep pace with public demands for cleaner streets, protection against crime, and regulation of markets and wharves. Citizens complained that officials did not heed their requests. The governor continued to nominate the chief executive officers—the mayor, recorder, and common clerk—but the State Council of Appointment, a conservative group composed of one senator from each senatorial district, made appointments. In 1821 the new state constitution granted to the common councils of cities the power to appoint their own mayors. Not until 1834 did citizens of New York City receive the right to elect their mayor in annual balloting. This law, however, did not change the practice of selecting mayors from among merchants and lawyers.

The Common Council, an elected body, had adopted many ordinances in colonial days which provided for or regulated police protection, fire prevention, public wells, poor relief, the administration of justice, street construction and repair, health, and the supervision of wharves and ferries. Officials were unable to cope with these problems, however, when population expanded so rapidly. Most councilmen had considerable means, but after 1838 the percentage of wealthy councilmen declined while the number of grocers and artisans on the council rose. No laborer won a place among the lawmakers.

In 1790 New York City was not too clean a town; by 1825 it had become a fairly large and much dirtier city. Carcasses of animals, horse manure, ashes and garbage, pools of stagnant water, and rubble made the streets not only hazardous to traffic but dangerous to health. The public scavengers often failed to collect refuse, leaving the job to the pigs and dogs that rooted among the filth. Aldermen from tenement districts, where the poor prized their all too infrequent meals of pork, hesitated to enforce the laws against hogs in the streets. As late as the early 1830s George Templeton Strong described his city as "one huge pigstye."

The water supply became contaminated by seepage from privies, tanneries, slaughterhouses, and stables. Aaron Burr sidetracked the best chance for securing pure water by turning the Manhattan Company, chartered in 1799 as a water company, into a banking operation—the latter activity was obviously more profitable. Not until 1842 did the water behind the Croton Dam in Westchester County flow into the city and guarantee the people pure water. Fire companies and banks headed a procession from the Battery up Broadway to Union Square, then down the Bowery and back to City Hall in celebration. City dwellers hailed watery plumes from fountains installed in several squares.

The threat of yellow fever hung over the seaport like an avenging angel. The epidemic of 1795 took almost 750 victims, a grisly total that more than tripled three years later. Panic swept the city as thousands fled to the sunny fields of Greenwich Village, Brooklyn Heights, and other rural havens. Yellow fever at last frightened officials into enforcing the sanitation laws—at least in the summertime—and impelled them to provide relief to families whose breadwinners had fallen victim to the dread disease.

Other diseases took a terrible toll, especially among the weak, the young, and the old. Dr. Samuel Mitchill estimated in 1809 that one-third of the children failed to reach their third birthday. If they escaped childhood diseases—scarlet fever, whooping cough, croup, measles, and the like—they then had to run the gantlet of tuberculosis, the greatest killer, especially of young people. Negroes, who occupied the worst tenements, had a death rate about three times that of whites.

Raymond Mohl has indicated in his study *Poverty in New York, 1783–1825* that the destitute poor comprised about one-third of the white population at the opening of the nineteenth century. And Mohl and other observers assert that poverty intensified as the decades rolled by. The state poor laws, public assistance records, the founding of charitable organizations and mutual benefit societies, the growing demands for immigration restriction, all testify to poverty's presence. Visitors avoided certain sections of cities because criminals infested them. There poor families, continually reinforced by waves of immigrants, crowded into tenements, cellars, and boardinghouses. A single room often sheltered several families, while old residences cut up into rooms and apartments housed dozens of inhabitants. Irish and German immigrants sometimes patched together shanties on the outskirts of town.

Another large category was composed of the working poor, those who because of low wages and irregular work could hardly make ends meet. Indentured servants, free blacks, seamstresses, washerwomen, and domestic workers seldom could escape from the cycle of poverty. The "undeserving poor" irritated editors and middle-class moralists, who complained about an army of beggars, prostitutes, drunks, pedlars, and "worthless scum." Poorer citizens kept moving about from one hovel to another and from one town to another, seeking work and a chance to better themselves.

By 1825 New York City had come of age. Its commerce, already first on the American seacoast, soared to new heights as the hinterland surrounding the Great Lakes became tributary to it. New York City had passed beyond the preindustrial stage, although the scale of manufacturing remained small and concentrated in artisan shops. Old urban problems—crime, disease, alcoholism, poverty, water—seemed more unsolvable than ever. Nevertheless, a buoyant spirit swept through the city in 1825, when Governor De Witt Clinton solemnized the "marriage of the waters" by emptying a keg of Erie water into the Atlantic Ocean.

"The American axe! It has made more real and lasting conquests than the sword of any warlike people that ever lived," declared Major Littlepage, a frontier landholder whom James Fenimore Cooper portrayed in his later novels. From his boyhood home in Otsego County, Cooper had ample opportunity to observe the virtues of frontiersmen.

Historians, novelists, and orators have long celebrated the courage, stamina, and resourcefulness of American frontiersmen. The New York frontier was singularly fortunate in its contemporary observers. Crèvecoeur, at his observation post in Orange County, not only described the back country on the eve of the Revolution but also analyzed how the frontier shaped the American character. William Cooper, unhampered by the ideological distortions and romantic notions of his famous son, James Fenimore, wrote a short but classic account appropriately titled *A Guide in the Wilderness, or the History of the First Settlements in the Western Counties of New York, with Useful Instructions to Future Settlers.* In the year of publication, 1810, Cooper regarded Otsego County as a "western" county. Elkanah Watson, a transplanted Yankee who seldom displayed undue modesty, narrated his efforts to bring about agricultural improvements through county fairs and claimed that he had helped create the Erie Canal. Orsamus Turner collected the reminiscences of old settlers in western New York. Foreign travelers described their journeys up the Hudson and across the state to Niagara Falls. More knowledgeable and as interesting were the accounts of Americans who visited the area. Who can resist the perceptive and often censorious comments of Timothy Dwight, president of Yale College, who hailed the fructifying contributions of Yankees on the wild frontier of New York?

Clearing the forest was the main task facing upstaters between 1790 and 1825. During that period they enlarged the amount of improved land more than six times. From dawn to dusk, in summer and winter, frontiersmen spent most of their time felling trees, burning brush, collecting ashes for potash, and building sheds, cabins, and fences.

Making a farm was slow work requiring unremitting toil and endless drudgery. But an optimistic spirit animated upstaters despite their hardships. Were they not assuring a greater income in the future, if not for themselves, at least for their children? Frontiersmen had the satisfaction of seeing their wealth increase in the form of improved lands, fences, barns, and buildings.

Most pioneers, perhaps most townsmen as well, were

speculators at heart. Land values kept rising, although temporary setbacks brought bankruptcy to those who had overextended their holdings and bought on credit. No state offered a more varied or richer supply of land than New York: choice lots on Manhattan; townsites, the dream of every landholder near a cross-road or a lake outlet; loyalist lands; millions of acres of wild lands west and north of Rome, which the state sold or granted on easy terms.

New York State settled its conflicting claims against Massachusetts by ceding to that state all the land west of Seneca Lake. Hard pressed for funds, Massachusetts sold this tract of 6 million acres to Oliver Phelps and Nathaniel Gorham, two legislators. These land jobbers could not raise money to pay for the tract and returned two-thirds of it to Massachusetts. In 1790 they sold the rest, about 1.25 million acres east of the Genesee River, to Robert Morris, a Philadelphia merchant who helped finance the American cause in the Revolution. Morris resold much of this land to Sir William Pulteney and other Englishmen, who sent out Charles Williamson to develop it. By building roads and gristmills and by extending credit, Williamson attracted thousands of settlers.

In 1791 Morris purchased more than 3 million acres west of the Genesee River. Two years later he sold most of this tract to the Holland Land Company, a group of Dutch businessmen in the Netherlands. Their land agent was Joseph Ellicott, who surveyed the tract and subdivided it into lots.

The land companies and speculators used sales methods somewhat similar to those used today. They set up land offices, advertised their lots in other states and in Europe, marked out roads, and selected sites for villages. Most landholders sold their lands to freeholding farmers within a generation. Tenant farming, however, hung on in the mid–Hudson Valley, and even took root in Delaware County, along the upper Mohawk, and in the Genessee Valley. During the 1790s tenant farmers in Columbia County carried on a fierce antirent war against the Livingstons but sheriffs put it down. Not until the 1840s did tenants organize a strong antirent movement that succeeded in destroying the leasehold system in eastern New York.

Dozens of wealthy landholders and their agents moved to the

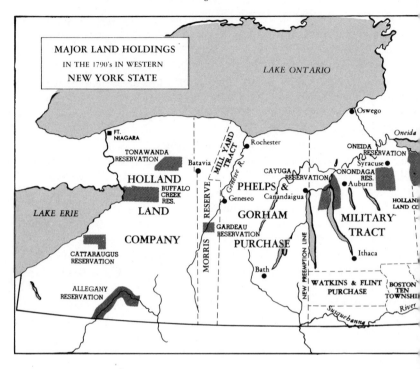

MAJOR LAND HOLDINGS
IN THE 1790's IN WESTERN
NEW YORK STATE

frontier. The names of towns in central, northern, and western
New York bear witness to the founders and owners of large
tracts. William Floyd, a signer of the Declaration of Independence, moved from Long Island to his tract near Rome, in central
New York. Nearby was Steuben, a 16,000-acre tract given to
Baron von Steuben by the state for his services during the Revolution. Zephaniah Platt of Dutchess County settled Plattsburgh
on Lake Champlain. William Cooper from New Jersey left his
name on the village at the base of Otsego Lake, where he established a bastion of Federalism. The Holland Land Company had
representatives on its various tracts: Adam Mappa in Barneveld, a
few miles north of Utica; Jan Lincklaen in Cazenovia; Joseph
Ellicott and relations in Batavia and Maysville. In the Genesee
Valley, James and William Wadsworth founded a lordly estate

that still resounds to the horn, calling red-coated gentry to ride to the hounds. In the north country there were many representatives of the landed gentry, some of them refugees from revolutionary France. David Ogden in 1812 gave up his law practice in New York City and settled near Waddington in St. Lawrence County. The Low family established Lowville, and William Constable erected a fine house in Constableville.

This squirearchy brought cash, agricultural expertise, and political conservatism to the frontier. A considerable number erected Episcopal churches, consciously copying the English gentry with its sense of tradition and good order. These men organized movements for good roads, canals, banks, and local improvements. In short, they were carriers of civilization, genteel manners, and improved farming.

Even before the Revolution agriculture had become thoroughly commercial; New York farmers were more market-oriented than farmers in many other parts of the Northeast. The Hudson River made it easy for most upstaters to send their products to market. Farmers living at a distance from the river drove their livestock to river landings or sleighed their potash, wheat, and furs to storehouses at Albany, Catskill, and numerous landings. Levi Beardsley of Otsego County related how they carried wheat by sleigh to Albany in the 1790s: "I went there with my father on a load of wheat by sleighing. . . . It was a curious sight to observe the immense number of sleighs, on approaching the city; a string a mile long, was no uncommon occurrence in those days, and even more."[3]

Agriculture also received intermittent support and encouragement from the legislature. In 1791 a handful of aristocrats organized the Society for the Promotion of Agriculture, Arts, and Manufactures, which became in 1804 the Society for the Promotion of Useful Arts. The state printed its transactions and provided funds for premiums for domestic manufactures.

The county fair movement under the dynamic leadership of Elkanah Watson stimulated the ordinary farmer to improve his agricultural techniques. Watson urged premiums and prizes for the best crops, animals, and household manufactures. Jesse Buel, publisher of the Albany *Argus*, showed great interest and urged farmers to organize an agricultural society so that they could improve the "wretched husbandry." In 1818 Governor De Witt Clinton recommended to the legislature that it create a board of agriculture that could direct and finance the activities of the county societies. In 1819 the legislature appropriated $10,000 a year to be distributed among the counties in amounts matching the funds raised by local societies.

The county fair movement left a permanent mark upon agriculture in New York. Increased attention was paid to manuring the fields, selecting seeds, and planting fallow crops. Farmers also learned about improved breeds and new machinery. The plowing matches demonstrated quite vividly to onlookers that cast-iron plows were a vast improvement over wooden plows. Because the county fair emphasized improved breeds of sheep and cattle, it speeded the shift toward a more diversified agriculture. The most spectacular development was the introduction of Merino sheep. More significant, however, was the gradual growth of dairying.

The growth of towns along the Hudson in the 1790s is perhaps our most accurate index of the expansion of upstate farming. New towns such as Hudson, Troy, and Lansingburgh and older settlements such as Albany and Catskill enjoyed a mushroom growth. Albany's population was tripled between 1790 and 1810 by the influx of New Englanders. To its warehouses came the wheat of farmers to the west. Albany butchers slaughtered hundreds of cattle and sheep driven from the interior counties. When the ice broke in the spring, fleets of sloops departed, laden with foodstuffs.

Six miles to the north, New England adventurers laid out Troy in 1787, and its enterprising citizens grabbed the major part of the trade with the upper Hudson and western Vermont. Hudson was another New England outpost, established by Nantucket whalers.

The Yankees who settled upstate reconstituted the rural economy of southern New England, which had passed well beyond the stage of bare subsistence. Francis van der Kemp, a Dutch scholar, noted the Yankee passion for improvement. In 1792 he described Whitesborough, the home of Judge Hugh White from Middletown, Connecticut:

> He enjoys now that exquisite gratification of being the creator of his own fortune, and placing all his children in an independent situation. Judge White resided in Connecticut in the year 1785. He made a journey to the western part of this State; made a purchase of the land he now lives on; moved thither in 1786 with his five sons, built a log house and barn; went the next year for his wife and remaining children. . . . In 1788 he constructed a saw and grist mill; possessed in the fourth year all which he wanted for his convenience, ease and comfort in abundance; built in the fifth year a convenient frame house and substantial barn, and is now encircled by a number of respectable families.[4]

Not every settlement enjoyed the good fortune of Hugh White and his neighbors in Whitesborough. The smiling countryside also had its poor and destitute families, living in lonely shacks away from public view. Some pioneer communities experienced a "starving time" before residents had ample supplies of food. William Cooper related that he imported grain in 1789 to relieve a threatened famine on his lands near Otsego Lake. In some cases so many newcomers arrived that they ate up the scanty supply of food. And there were illnesses to contend with: pioneers often suffered from the "shakes" (malaria), dysentery, and tuberculosis. One can go into rural cemeteries today and read weatherbeaten stones telling tragic tales of children taken by disease, women dying in childbirth, and young people stricken by "consumption."

Although foreign trade attracted the most attention in Congress and in the New York press, local markets greatly surpassed foreign markets in importance. Farmers in central and western New York found a stream of consumers flowing past their own doorsteps. Every day in February 1795 five hundred families in sleighs passed through Albany on their way west. Consider their needs for oxen, hay, oats, salt, not to mention shelter and other services. Taverns sprang up every mile or so along the roads to the west. The migrants brought with them varying amounts of cash to lay out for land and supplies.

As important as land agents and landholders in the development of upstate New York were villagers and townsmen. Blake McKelvey made an apt comment when he noted that "settlers trooped in, not as farmers, but as artisans and mechanics, eager to locate in a thriving village."[5]

At first glance we might dismiss a village of five hundred people or a town of one to two thousand as insignificant. Such communities, however, performed many functions, ranging from simple barter to quite sophisticated transactions. Boasting the first land office in the United States, Canandaigua became a center for the Pulteney Associates, a group of English investors. In 1811 John Melish, an English tourist, noted that the village had about 120 "handsome" houses, most of them wood and painted white. An "elegant academy" graced the square, around which also stood a jail and brick courthouse. Visitors could patronize six stores, six taverns, two tanning yards, two distilleries, and six lawyers.

Utica was another bustling community. In 1810 De Witt Clinton described it:

Utica is a flourishing village on the south side of the Mohawk; it arrogates to itself being the capital of the Western District. Twenty-two years ago there was but one house; there are now three hundred, a Presbyterian Church, an Episcopal, a Welsh Presbyterian, and a Welsh Baptist; a Bank, being a branch of the Manhattan Company; a Post Office, the office of the Clerk of the County, and the Clerk of the Supreme Court. . . . Two newspapers are printed here.[6]

All these towns, villages, and country stores were vital links in the expansion of commercial agriculture and a business economy. Here farmers sold and bought goods, sometimes using barter when cash was scarce. Retailers organized a large share of the distribution of imports and locally manufactured goods needed by settlers. In addition they freighted or drove farm products to Hudson River ports. They advanced credit to farmers and small shopkeepers.

Export markets, however, were uncertain, indeed precarious. Farmers had hardly found a market when an embargo, a war, trade restrictions, or a financial panic would disrupt orderly marketing. When prices fell, land values plummeted. Then merchants and farmers who had taken out mortgages and signed contracts in boom times got caught in a credit squeeze.

Throughout this period pioneers turned to lumbering as well as farming in their search for ways to raise money. Farmers cut and dragged out logs during the winter, when there was no work to be done in the fields. If they were unable to float timber to market, they could get cash for potash and pearl ash. Potash could easily bear the cost of transportation because of its high value in relation to its bulk. Thurlow Weed recalled that for the early settlers of Cortland County potash was the "principal, and indeed, only reliance for the purchase of necessaries" from the store.[7]

The rapid expansion of the transportation network—turnpikes and roads, steamboats on lakes and rivers, the Erie Canal with its many feeders, railroads—exposed settlements to all the forces of the market economy. New Yorkers showed resourcefulness and ingenuity in experimenting with a great variety of transport: river boats, arks and rafts, steamboats and canal boats, roads and turnpikes on which traveled vehicles ranging from two-wheeled carts to freight wagons and stagecoaches.

Frontiersmen often used spring freshets to carry their produce down the Delaware, Susquehanna, Genesee, and other river systems. Two men could build an ark in two weeks. These lozenge-shaped vessels drew only two feet of water and were capable of carrying 1,200 bushels of wheat. A crew of four could direct the ark downriver to the port, where they sold the cargo, then broke up the ark into rough timber and sold that, since the ark had no power to enable it to return upstream against the current.

Settlers generally preferred to trade with Albany, from whose warehouses they could secure sugar, tea, and other necessities. Although the Mohawk Valley provided a level route inland, the river had several disadvantages. The great falls at Cohoes sealed the mouth, forcing goods to pass over the sandy plain between Albany and Schenectady. At Little Falls, rapids and cascades formed another barrier. Rifts, sandbars, and shallow water severely restricted the size of boats. In 1792 the legislature accepted Governor George Clinton's recommendation and incorpo-

Voyaging on the Mohawk. From Moses M. Bagg, *Pioneers of Utica* (Utica: Curtiss & Childs, 1877).

rated the Western Inland Lock Navigation Company, which built a mile-long canal at Little Falls and another across the old portage at Rome between the Mohawk and Wood Creek. As a result, boatmen poled boats carrying ten to eleven tons, whereas formerly the largest boats had displaced a mere one and a half tons. These improvements, however, did not guarantee cheap and safe carriage, because accidents, tolls, and low water often interrupted traffic.

Farmers in the Mohawk Valley had always transported most of their produce by sleigh or wagon. The roads were disgraceful, scarcely more than traces through the forest with stumps and roots obstructing passage. Older towns could not afford to keep roads in repair, and highway overseers lacked knowledge as well as funds.

Large landholders such as William Cooper and Charles Williamson in the Genesee Valley demanded state aid for roads to emancipate the western settlements. In 1792 the legislature responded to a flood of petitions from the western districts and earmarked funds for special roads. It authorized a road into the military tract and another to Old Fort Schuyler, the future site of Utica. The Genesee road ran from Utica to Geneva and Canandaigua with scheduled stage and mail service. These primitive roads could not take care of the rapidly expanding traffic.

Frontiersmen, landowners, and aggressive river towns enthusiastically sponsored turnpikes after 1800. The first chartered turnpike company was the Albany and Schenectady (1797), which completed a hard-surfaced road within the next decade. From Schenectady the Mohawk Turnpike and Bridge Company constructed a toll road to Utica, from which the Seneca Road Company struck westward to Canandaigua. Soon this turnpike was extended to Batavia and Black Rock, a neighbor of Buffalo. The Mohawk route had a strong rival in the Great Western Turnpike or Cherry Valley system of turnpikes, which Route 20 follows today.

The Hudson River was the terminus for almost all turnpikes completed before 1807. On the eastern bank of the river the advancing prongs of the turnpike network of New England met roads leading eastward from Greenbush, Hudson, and

Poughkeepsie. Albany, Kingston, Newburgh, and Catskill promoted turnpikes through or around the Catskills to the interior. The Susquehanna Turnpike, which opened in 1801, ran from Catskill to Wattles Ferry on the Unadilla River. Its western extensions permitted migrants to push on to Ithaca and Bath. Newburgh citizens organized the Newburgh and Cochecton Turnpike, which extended on to Ithaca. Mileage increased from 1,500 in 1811 to more than 4,000 in 1821.

Stagecoaches carried businessmen, landowners, and other travelers over the dense ganglia of turnpikes. Foreigners in particular complained about ruts and mudholes that made traveling dangerous as well as uncomfortable. Turnpikes also served farmers and migrants, who complained about high tolls. For each ten miles the average toll was eight cents for each score of horses, cattle, or mules. A horse and rider paid five cents; a wagon with two horses or oxen paid 12½ cents. Wagons with wide rims or thick wheels paid less than those with narrow rims.

Heavily built wagons, drawn by three or four pairs of horses, carried beneath their canvas tops wheat, flour, cheese, potash, and whiskey. Teamsters could hope to average about fifteen to twenty miles a day with a loaded wagon.

Land transportation remained expensive because of turnpike tolls and the cost of maintaining horses and teamsters. Teamsters had trouble fording swollen streams, repairing broken axles and wheels, and crossing swamps. All these factors convinced merchants and farmers in the frontier counties that a canal was necessary. The famous memorial drafted by De Witt Clinton in 1816 cited the need for "cheapness, celerity, certainty, and safety in the transportation of commodities." It went on: "It is calculated that the expense of transporting on a canal, amounts to one cent a ton per mile, or one dollar a ton for one hundred miles; while the usual cost by land conveyance, is one dollar and sixty cents per hundred weight, or thirty-two dollars a ton for the same distance."[8] Political leaders who had grown up in a climate of mercantilism, whether they considered themselves Federalists or Republicans (Clintonians), took a pragmatic attitude toward economic issues, although a few leaders spoke out for laissez faire. They used public funds to reward allies and granted subsidies to enterprises that had widespread public support or powerful private influence.

Alfred Young has analyzed the issues dividing Republicans from Federalists. He finds that a "spirit of reformation" led to the beginnings of state aid for elementary schools and a softening of the rigorous criminal code.[9] In 1790, abolition of slavery failed to pass the Assembly by only one vote, despite the relatively large number of slaveholders. Republicans launched attacks on the Western Inland Lock Navigation Company largely because it was managed by Philip Schuyler, the leading Federalist and an aristocrat to boot. High tolls, poor construction, especially of the locks, and voracious demands for state aid caused followers of George Clinton to attack the company.

Manufacturing also received encouragement by members of most parties. In 1790 the legislature authorized a loan of £200 at 5 percent for three years to any person who would import European craftsmen to make earthenware. Three years later the manufacturers of cotton and linen textiles and of glass received similar favors. The School Fund Act of 1805 set aside 500,000 acres of vacant land for the encouragement of common schools. The income from land sales was available as loans to entrepreneurs. After the Embargo Act began to pinch, the legislature authorized the state to lend up to $450,000 to residents of rural counties. The sums available ranged from $50 to $500, presumably to permit settlers to buy household items such as looms and to acquire breeding sheep. To encourage household manufactures, county courts could award cash prizes for the best cloth submitted.

So numerous were the charter requests that the legislature passed a general incorporation statute in 1811. Manufacturers were freed from lobbying individual charters through the legislature. By granting limited liability the statute also encouraged more people to invest in corporations. The statute enjoyed wide public support as an effective counterweight to British "aggression" and also as a useful method of encouraging both agriculture and manufacturing. Under its provisions a corporation had a life of twenty years and could amass capital up to $100,000.

The postwar collapse of many textile companies, which faced

vigorous British competition, led to additional relief measures. In 1817 legislators exempted from state and local taxation the buildings, inventory, and machinery of all the makers of cloth and thread. Meanwhile Congress rushed through the protective tariff of 1816. The stronger companies survived and textile manufacturing expanded by adopting the power loom.

Manufacturing continued to be almost exclusively confined to the home and shop. The census of 1820 lists fewer than 10,000 persons engaged in manufacturing outside the home. Even in Oneida County, where immigrants from Rhode Island had transplanted the textile industry, fewer than 800 operatives were listed in 1827.

Laborers were gaining freedom and equality in legal status. The apprenticeship system and indentured servitude withered away largely because of immigration and the difficulty of maintaining barriers to employment in a society in which workers were constantly moving about. Most gratifying was the decline of slavery, an outcome urged by Quakers and stimulated by egalitarian impulses let loose by Revolutionary rhetoric. In 1799 the legislature provided that the children of slaves born after July 4, 1799, should eventually acquire complete freedom (females at twenty-five, males at twenty-eight). Another act in 1817 declared that blacks born after July 4, 1799, should become free after July 4, 1827. Emancipation did little to better the economic conditions of most blacks, although by incredible exertions a few acquired some education and managed small businesses, especially in catering.

Before De Witt Clinton formally opened his Grand Western Canal, New Yorkers had developed an economy and society richly deserving the name Empire State. While ship captains were venturing even to China's shores, pioneers were clearing the wilderness, sending vast quantities of wheat to market, and creating a network of villages and towns. New Yorkers for the first time were exploiting their geographical advantages by creating a transportation network, the envy of their rivals in Pennsylvania and Maryland.

In 1815 Hezekiah Niles of *Niles' Review* stressed, as the dominant feature of American national character, "the most universal ambition to get forward."[10] New Yorkers of old stock such as De Witt Clinton embraced the doctrine of progress as avidly as Yankee newcomers who exhibited the full repertoire of Calvinist virtues. New York's transportation revolution galvanized America's economy far beyond the borders of the Empire State. Its greatest achievement, the Erie Canal, became the linchpin of national unity, a tribute to free institutions, and a demonstration of American ingenuity and enterprise.

6

A Burgeoning Economy

Materialism, more vulgarly described as the pursuit of the almighty dollar, characterized the mind-set and life-styles of New Yorkers after as well as before 1825. Persons of New England stock, comprising over half of the population at that date, exemplified the Protestant ethic. In this respect, immigrants differed but slightly, if at all, because most had sailed west to better themselves. Hard-working and frugal, many were quick to show enterprise in starting small businesses. Persons of every ethnic background and nationality—Italians, Scots, Jews, Germans, Greeks, Armenians, Lebanese, Chinese—enthusiastically joined the race for riches.

Rural folk as well as city dwellers regarded money making as essential, occasionally entertaining, and God-ordained. When farmers fed their horses in the church barn between services, they often traded a horse or cow. Homer, a village near Cortland, was the locale of Edward Noyes Westcott's *David Harum*, whose hero was modeled after David Hannum, a local banker and shrewd horse trader, who declared, "Do others or they'll do you—and do 'em first."[1] The father of John D. Rockefeller, who sold rattlesnake oil at upstate fairs, allegedly cheated his sons in order to "bring them up sharp." He succeeded brilliantly. Daniel Drew, a Putnam County drover, fed his cattle salt and then drove them into the river before he took them to the slaughterhouse. A thirst-crazed steer would swallow fifty pounds or more of water. Later Drew applied his talents on Wall Street, where he won fame for "watering the stock."

Most New Yorkers have chased the dollar in order to spend it, not to hide it under the mattress. Of course, there were exceptions; for example, Hetty Green, the eccentric millionaire who stinted herself and her family. Because she refused to pay for medical treatment for her son, he lost his leg. After her death her son spent his inheritance with reckless abandon.

Conviviality has always characterized the lusty transient society that sprang up along the waterfront and canal. In 1895 William Dean Howells declared that nothing was more characteristic of New York City than the "eating and drinking constantly going on in the restaurants and hotels, of every quality, and the innumerable saloons."[2] The philosophy of "easy come, easy go" prevailed. No doubt outlanders opposed a "bailout" for New York City in 1975 partly on the ground that convivial denizens of the metropolis had squandered their substance not only unwisely but in fact prodigally.

In 1833 James Fenimore Cooper returned to New York after seven years in Europe. He felt that society had suffered a great "moral eclipse," that selfishness had shunted aside devotion to truth and character. A "vulgar aristocracy" had turned Manhattan into a "bivouac," a collection of restless transients, who were united only in worshiping the Dollar. Since Cooper's time, Europeans and Americans have rung the changes on this theme.

Upstaters also took as much satisfaction in spending money as in making it. Traders, land barons, and factory owners had hardly made their fortunes before they were erecting mansions and entertaining lavishly. Teamsters and boatmen thronged the taverns; lumbermen blew a season's earnings in saloons in Glens Falls, Utica, and Ogdensburg. Getting and spending were major features of the New York syndrome.

Expectant capitalists in New York created an economy whose productive capacity has surpassed those of all but a handful of foreign nations. During the century and a half following De Witt Clinton's triumphant journey from Buffalo to New York Harbor, the state has almost always led every other in transportation, commerce, finance, corporate headquarters, services, communications, and manufacturing. Lest this statement smack too much of boosterism, let me cite Fernand Braudel's study of the Mediterranean world, which has received universal acclaim. When explaining what Venice meant to the fifteenth and sixteenth centuries, he wrote, "Venice dominated the Interior Sea as New York dominates the western world today."[3]

If one had to single out the most significant factor in New York's remarkable growth, one would probably choose its excellent transportation. The Empire State lay athwart the most lucrative trade routes and its citizens took full advantage of new developments in water, land, and air transport. Cheap transportation facilitated and nourished the conquest of central and western New York. Pioneers and storekeepers had to get products to market if they were to buy land, tools, salt, sugar, and other necessities. Business leaders in each community realized that they had to secure a turnpike, a canal, or a railroad in order to survive and to prosper. They were well aware that taverns and villages along the Cherry Valley Turnpike shriveled after canal cities diverted trade from them.

The Erie Canal captured for New York most of the commerce from the Great Lakes hinterland. Cheap western wheat undercut the wheat from exhausted eastern fields. The canal spawned new cities such as Syracuse and Rochester, and the populations of older cities such as Albany, Utica, and Buffalo skyrocketed. Citizens in other sections clamored for state aid for canals, highways, and later railroads. As a result, the Canal Board of Commissioners constructed a series of feeder canals that linked Clinton's Ditch with Lake Ontario, the Finger Lakes, and the Susquehanna River. Other seaboard states—Pennsylvania, Maryland, and Virginia—tried to build canals to the Ohio River but failed to divert the interior trade from the Erie. Canal mania spread to the Midwest as Ohio, Indiana, and Illinois embarked upon ambitious canal systems.

In 1835 the Erie's smashing success encouraged legislators to begin a program of enlargement that was vigorously supported by Whigs and the Hunker branch of the Democratic party. Engineers increased canal depth from four to seven feet and increased the width from forty to seventy feet. Enlargement, interrupted by panics and the opposition of Barnburner Democrats, was not completed until 1862.

Before 1835 the Erie attracted mostly local traffic; practically no freight originating west of Buffalo passed through the canal.

Lockport on the Erie Canal. This primitive painting of 1832 shows a canal boat with its well-dressed passengers being towed toward the locks. Watercolor by Mary Keys. Munson-Williams-Proctor Institute, Utica, New York.

During the 1840s the Erie lost most of its passenger business and much of its local freight to railroads. The process accelerated during the 1850s as railroads improved their connections and became better organized. Forest products and wheat comprised most cargoes moving east. The Civil War gave the aging canal a boost, but after 1870 it lost more freight to railroads, which had formed large systems with many connections to western cities. The expansion of railroads spelled doom for feeder canals, whose tolls had seldom covered their operating costs. In the 1870s the public voted to keep in operation only the Erie, Oswego, Cayuga, Seneca, Black River, and Champlain canals.

Distressed by the decline—indeed collapse—of the Erie Canal, its supporters struck back at their archrivals, the railroads. In 1882 legislators abolished canal tolls, but this measure did not halt the diversion of traffic to the rails. Railroad arrogance, rate fixing, discrimination, and political corruption led to regulation of railroad rates by New York State and then by the federal government (Interstate Commerce Act of 1887). These actions proved ineffective, and anti-railroad feeling was running so high that in 1903 voters authorized the construction of a barge canal. The Barge Canal, however, did little to drive down railroad rates and attracted minor traffic, mostly oil and gravel.

The Hudson River continued to serve as an artery of commerce. By 1840 more than a hundred steamboats plied the lordly Hudson. Because passengers demanded speed, many captains overtaxed their boilers. The results were sometimes as spectacular as the headlines.

A thriving commerce developed on the Great Lakes. In 1835 a thousand schooners, barks, brigs, and steamboats cleared Buffalo Harbor. During the next half century, lake shipping made many adjustments: a shift from sail to steam, from wooden ships to iron, and the expansion of the "long trades" from the western ports of Lake Superior. After the construction of the Sault Sainte Marie Canal between Lake Superior and Lake Huron, wheat from Duluth and Superior as well as iron ore from the fabulous Mesabi Range passed eastward to the lower lakes. In 1907 Buffalo handled more tonnage than any other lake port, and in general it has continued to do so ever since. Buffalo has imported

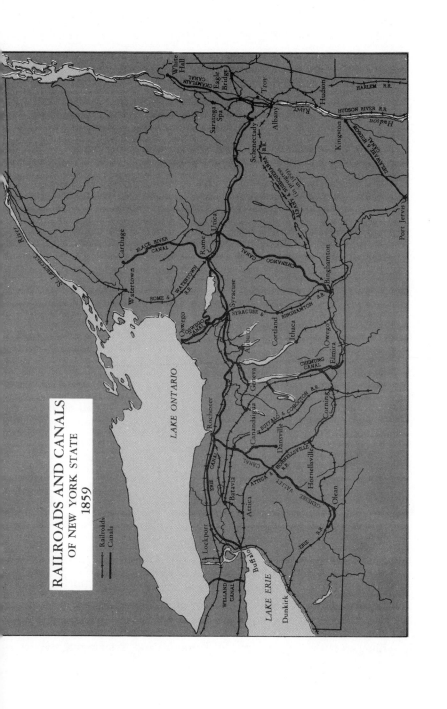

RAILROADS AND CANALS
OF NEW YORK STATE
1859

Railroads
Canals

much more than it has shipped out. Its flour and steel mills have required vast quantities of wheat and iron ore, petroleum and coal.

In 1932 Canada and the United States signed a treaty providing for cooperation in constructing a seaway around the falls of the St. Lawrence River, but railroads, opponents of government spending, and New York City interests checked appropriation of funds for this project. In 1953 Canada announced that it planned to build its own seaway if the United States would not join in the project. As a result, Congress authorized the New York State Power Authority to work with the Canadians in building a channel capable of handling oceangoing vessels and in constructing a plant to generate electricity. Robert Moses took charge of the construction of a twenty-seven-foot channel and three dams that produced about 2 million kilowatts of electricity. Traffic has never lived up to the expectations of seaway champions because of accidents, repairs, crop fluctuations, and changing foreign demand. The development of electricity, however, has proven highly successful in meeting the demands of industries, homes, and public agencies in the northeast. The New York Power Authority built another generating plant near Niagara Falls, utilizing some of the tremendous energy of the Niagara River.

New York Harbor normally handled more than half of the nation's imports and over one-third of the exports, measured by value, during the century following 1815. Wooden sailing vessels remained the chief carriers until the last quarter of the nineteenth century, when iron steamships captured passenger business as well as a growing amount of freight. Steam supplanted sail slowly because ships could not carry enough coal for long voyages until marine engines became more efficient.

Cornelius Vanderbilt, who began his career rowing boats from Staten Island to Manhattan, became a leading shipping magnate. He acquired so many steamboats on the Hudson and adjoining waters, and his sloops and schooners handled so much of the coastal trade, that people began to call him "Commodore," a practice he did nothing to discourage. When thousands of men clamored for quick passage to California and its goldfields, Vanderbilt operated steamships to Panama and Nicaragua, where passengers could disembark, make a short journey overland to the Pacific Ocean, and take another ship for San Francisco. Having made a shipping fortune of more than $20 million by the time he reached sixty years of age, Vanderbilt entered the railroad business and tripled his fortune.

Most ships were tramps, picking up cargo wherever they could. Packets began scheduled service between New York and Liverpool in 1818. By 1845 more than fifty packets cleared New York Harbor for European or cotton ports. The clipper ship, pride of the American merchant marine, represented the greatest achievement of the East River yards. In 1851 the *Flying Cloud* made San Francisco from New York in eighty-nine days, a record never bettered by a sailing vessel. Sag Harbor on Long Island and the city of Hudson, settled by Nantucket fishermen, sent out dozens of whaling ships south to the Antarctic and as far north as the Bering Sea. For most New Yorkers, whaling was less a life of high adventure than one of extreme danger and niggardly earnings. The discovery of oil in Pennsylvania just before the Civil War was to undercut the whaling industry.

The merchant marine declined after 1857 because of the financial panic of that year but especially because of high losses during the Civil War. Confederate raiders captured many ships and drove insurance rates so high that shipowners transferred their vessels to British and other foreign registries. Meanwhile British and German shipping lines were improving steamships, whereas Americans, including such New Yorkers as George Pullman and George Westinghouse, were concentrating on railroad technology.

Each decade the volume of goods passing the Statue of Liberty rose, but tonnage in American bottoms kept declining. In both World War I and World War II, the shortage of tonnage and the immense task of supplying American and allied armies led to frantic construction of ships. When peace returned, the national government sold hundreds of ships to private firms, but they found it difficult to compete with foreign vessels, whose crews were paid substantially less than the crews of American ships.

Hardly had Governor De Witt Clinton opened the Erie Canal when a group of Albany and New York City capitalists chartered the Mohawk & Hudson Railway, running from the capital to Schenectady. In 1831 a tiny locomotive bearing the name of the recently deceased governor pulled three stagecoaches fitted with flanged wheels. Everyone regarded this railroad as an integral part of the waterway system, since its function was to speed passengers to the docks at Schenectady, where they could take canal packets west. For the next twenty years this railroad and its western extension, the Utica & Schenectady, carried only passengers, because the legislature prohibited canal-side railroads from hauling freight. In 1842, when seven short lines between Albany and Buffalo established through train service, passengers deserted the packet boats. Few persons regretted leaving the stifling canal bunks, the low bridges, and the four-mile-an-hour gait of canal horses.

After 1842, when Boston capitalists completed rail connections to East Albany, some Midwest buyers visited Boston mercantile showrooms during the winter months. Fearing a loss of business, Manhattan merchants poured new funds into two small lines poking northward from their city. By 1852 the Hudson River Railroad and the New York & Harlem, the latter following a more inland route, had reached East Albany.

Mixed feelings of envy and fear drove citizens of the southern tier of counties to demand comparable transportation. They flirted with an east–west canal project but sensibly switched to a railroad, for which they secured more than $6 million in state subsidy. In 1851 the New York & Erie reached Dunkirk on Lake Erie, becoming for a brief time the longest continuous line in the world. The Erie Railroad has had a checkered history marked by scandals of such epic proportions that they have served as classic examples of railroad chicanery and corruption. Who has not heard how Daniel Drew and Jay Gould looted the railroad's treasury, watered the stock, and manipulated its securities? The Erie became known as the Scarlet Woman of Wall Street.

In 1851 the legislature lifted all restrictions on freight carriage by railroads paralleling the canal. Two years later Erastus Corning and Dean Richmond consolidated eight short lines from Albany to Buffalo into the New York Central. Promoters in other cities projected and began construction of new lines tapping

Pennsylvania's coal fields and serving the area between the Erie Railroad and the New York Central.

Trackage more than tripled between 1860 and 1900 as communities and their business leaders kept demanding rail service. More than three hundred cities, villages, and towns in thirty-three counties granted almost $37 million to eighty-five railroad companies as subsidies or loans. Unfortunately, some companies failed, leaving cities with debts but no railroad. A Cooperstown paper ruefully commented:

> When our children pay the mortgage
> Father made to haul the load,
> They'll not have to ask the question
> Here's the bond, but where's the road?[4]

The state constitution was amended in 1874 to ban additional public aid, but promoters continued to finance new routes. Two "anthracite" roads, the Lehigh Railroad and its rival, the Delaware, Lackawanna, & Western, pushed westward toward Buffalo. Another coal carrier, the Delaware & Hudson, ran from Pennsylvania through Binghamton and Albany to Montreal.

Throughout the 1870s and 1880s ferocious rate wars erupted between the trunk railroads carrying wheat from Chicago to the seaboard. Unless they could agree on rates, they faced bankruptcy. In 1877 trunk-line railroad officials agreed to permit carriers serving Philadelphia and Baltimore to charge a rate below the Chicago–New York rate. When New York City's merchant exporters heard this news, they howled in rage. They struck back at the New York Central and the Erie railroads by getting the state to investigate them. Spokesmen for the railroads insisted (and the Interstate Commerce Commission later accepted this argument) that Philadelphia and Baltimore needed lower land rates because New York City had cheaper ocean rates to European markets. Since their rivals would cut rates to the bone to get some traffic between Chicago and Liverpool, railroads serving New York City had to grant them a differential.[5]

What canal partisans and legislators could not accomplish to chastise railroad misdeeds, the internal combustion engine could. In this century automobiles, buses, and planes have lured away almost all passengers, and trucks have captured much freight by offering flexible service. Many modern factories have relocated in the countryside, near major highways but sometimes far from railroads. The change from coal to oil, natural gas, and electric power hit railroads very hard. Even the so-called coal roads found Diesel engines more efficient to operate in the yards and over the rails.

The rail network has slowly contracted since World War I as hard-pressed companies have abandoned routes despite the outcries of communities and protests by unions. Some lines collapsed, notably the New York, Ontario & Western, whose rails were sold for scrap. Others merged in order to economize; thus the Erie joined with the Delaware, Lackawanna & Western. The New York Central cut its main line from four tracks to two and eventually merged with its onetime rival, the Pennsylvania. The new company, however, slipped into bankruptcy in 1970. Six years later it became part of Conrail, a quasi-government corporation consisting of seven bankrupt lines in the Northeast.

The larger the cities grew, the greater became the needs of their citizens for fast transportation to carry them to and from work. Carriages took the rich to work and social engagements, but ordinary folk turned to omnibuses and jitneys. In the early 1830s a coach pulled by a horse began to roll down rails on a Manhattan street. A second coach crashed into the first; it was not the last accident on Manhattan streets. By the time of the Civil War, New York City and other centers had thousands of horsecars to carry shoppers and workers. Between 1860 and 1900 the number of passengers drawn by horsecars in New York City (50 million a year) increased more than twelve times. Civic leaders and editors complained about congestion, delays, and pollution.

Promoters kept looking for improved and speedier transportation. When an efficient electric motor was developed in the 1880s, communities rushed to acquire the new streetcar service. By 1900 almost every city with more than 5,000 population had a streetcar system, with lines radiating from "downtown" to the suburbs. Investors poured billions into traction companies, which expanded their systems to include lines to other cities.

Such lines were called interurbans. In 1914 a passenger could travel all the way from Oneonta, south of Little Falls, to Buffalo, and westward to Chicago and beyond.

New York City presented special problems apart from its large population. Vehicles could gain access to Manhattan Island at only a few points, such as the Brooklyn Bridge, the Pennsylvania Railroad's tunnel under the Hudson, and bridges connecting northern Manhattan with the Bronx. With only a few north–south avenues, traffic going uptown and downtown was congested. To speed traffic, promoters built elevated railways. Then people complained about clanging cars and the soot, cinders, and live coals that flew from steam locomotives. The City Council required these trains to adopt electric engines.

In 1900 a private company began to dig the first subway tunnel on Manhattan. Subways provided fast service, and by 1920 various systems had lines to the outskirts of Brooklyn and the Bronx. In 1932 the City of New York opened its own line, and Mayor Fiorello La Guardia urged that the city form one unified subway system. The private companies, which were beginning to lose money, were glad to sell their holdings. The New York City subway system faced many problems after World War II: increasing competition from automobiles and buses, a militant union of transit workers, rising power charges, crime and vandalism, and failure to maintain the properties in good condition. Meanwhile the fare has increased steadily from five cents to fifty cents.

Henry Ford's Model T appeared in 1908 and its popularity soon challenged the trolley. After World War II most traction companies turned from trolleys to buses, a move that did not save them from automobile competition. Bus companies kept losing riders while at the same time their costs kept rising. Many city governments, such as those in Utica and New York City, took over ailing companies that then became a drain on public funds.

Before World War I, ruts, mud, dust, and holes made road travel uncomfortable and hazardous. Town officials had neither the expertise nor the funds to build and repair highways. A good-roads movement got under way, backed by wheelmen's (bicycle riders') and automobile clubs. The state gradually took over the repair of interurban highways, leaving local roads to

Brooklyn Bridge at its completion in 1883. *Harper's Weekly*, May 26, 1883.

town and county care. The state paid for highways with license fees and a tax on gasoline.

During the 1930s federal agencies gave money to the states for unemployment relief, and New York promptly hired thousands to work on new highways. World War II brought construction to a halt, but after the war the remarkable suburban development required more highways and arterials for commuters. Governor Thomas E. Dewey urged the legislature to authorize funds for a superhighway from New York City to Buffalo, with an extension to the Pennsylvania border near Dunkirk, a link to Niagara Falls, and a connection with the Massachusetts Turnpike. In 1956 President Eisenhower and Congress inaugurated a massive highway program under which the federal government financed interstate highways by additional taxes on gasoline and tires. Under this program Route 17 has crossed the western Catskills and the Southern Tier, the Northway has linked Albany with Plattsburgh and Canada, and Route 81, connecting with the Pennsylvania system, has been extended through Binghamton to Syracuse and on to Watertown.

In 1921 New York and New Jersey established the Port of New York Authority in order to provide terminals, manage transportation facilities, and encourage foreign trade. This agency gradually enlarged its operations to cover almost all metropolitan transport: three large airports, bridges such as the George Washington, the Holland and Lincoln tunnels, several piers and truck terminals, and a major bus terminal on Manhattan Island. Reluctantly it accepted responsibility for the rapid transit system (PATH) that runs cars under the Hudson River to New Jersey. The twin towers of the World Trade Center were built and are administered by the Authority. Critics have charged that its officials have favored motor vehicle travel and have neglected subways, bus lines, and commuter railroads.

When rail commuter lines serving Long Island, Connecticut, Westchester, and New Jersey began to collapse because of motor vehicle competition, the governors of New York, New Jersey, and Connecticut cooperated in a rescue operation. In 1968 the New York State Legislature set up the Metropolitan Transportation Authority to aid the ailing Long Island Rail Road and operate the subway system. It operated the world's largest subway system (720 miles of track, 7,000 passenger cars), 4,200 buses, two airports, and the commuter services of several railroads entering New York City. The MTA later took over the Triboro Bridge and Tunnel Authority.

Most travelers flying into and out of this country have used the airports of Greater New York. La Guardia Airport was opened in 1939, when Newark could no longer handle the traffic. Within another decade the Authority built Idlewild (renamed John F. Kennedy) Airport, which now handles most international flights.

In 1945 C. S. Robinson flew a plane from Ithaca to New York. When friends asked for rides, he organized Robinson Airlines, which in 1952 became Mohawk Airlines. Mohawk expanded rapidly, and by 1971 its planes served more than a hundred cities. When a strike caused its collapse, Allegheny Airlines took over its routes, and Allegheny has continued to serve most upstate centers.

Promoters of communications as well as transportation have centered their activities in New York City. Samuel F. B. Morse, who moved to New York, and natives such as Hiram Sibley of Rochester and Ezra Cornell of Ithaca pioneered in building and extending telegraph lines. Cyrus Field, another Yankee immigrant, won the official thanks of Congress for his persistence during the 1860s in laying the Atlantic cable. Merchants in Liverpool were able to find out in an hour or two the price of wheat in Chicago.

A method of sending a message without a wire would save the expense of stringing wires across the countryside and along the streets. In 1895 M. Guglielmo Marconi sent a wireless message for more than a mile, an experiment that became the basis of the radio and television industries. Lee De Forest of New York City helped to make many of the basic discoveries in radio, and New York City became the center of broadcasting. When John D. Rockefeller, Jr., was building Rockefeller Center in the early 1930s, he included Radio City within it. Three major networks set up their headquarters on Manhattan, and producers found sponsors for programs that were carried across the nation. Radio spawned a rival in television, which had a spectacular growth after World War II. Clearly television has rivaled the automobile in social impact. Consider only three areas: political campaigning, professional sports, and education.

Television has revolutionized the motion picture industry, sounding the death knell for thousands of theaters. At the same time television has also become an important customer of Hollywood. New York State has had a particular interest in motion pictures because the major producing companies have made their headquarters here. In 1896 citizens of New York City had the chance of seeing the first motion picture show, which became tremendously popular. Promoters rushed to rent long narrow stores to show short films to customers for a nickel. By World War I the lowly "nickelodeons" were being replaced by great palaces, boasting exotic designs, huge organs, and liveried ushers. Although producers made many early pictures in New York City, on Long Island, and in Ithaca, they soon moved the industry to Southern California, where landscapes of mountains, deserts, and seashore, a warm climate, and almost perpetual sunshine guaranteed excellent conditions for filming.

The motion picture industry depended on photography, an industry of unusual importance in the Empire State. In 1888 George Eastman of Rochester offered a cheap camera with the catchy name Kodak. Sales soared and Eastman became a multimillionaire. He gave his fortune to the University of Rochester Medical College and the Eastman School of Music.

New York has remained the undisputed capital of American finance. Of the forty-five largest commercial banks in the country, nineteen have their headquarters in the metropolis. Bank deposits in New York State are more than double those in California, its closest rival. The state's leadership in insurance is comparable, with Metropolitan, Equitable, and New York Life handling almost one-fourth of all life insurance written. About 70 percent of all shares traded each day are handled by the New York Stock Exchange.

Missouri had its Jesse James; Indiana had its John Dillinger; and New York produced its own bank robber, Willie Sutton of Brooklyn, who also became a folk hero of sorts. When asked why he robbed banks, he declared, "That's where the money is." Although New York State lost thousands of manufacturing plants to other states and dozens of corporate headquarters to Connecticut and Houston in the 1970s, it is still the place where the money is.

In contrast to its financial and commercial supremacy, agriculture in the Empire State dropped from the top rank in 1860 to twenty-fifth place by the mid-1970s. Only 2 percent of New Yorkers still farm, but rural traditions exert much influence upon popular symbols and thought. When New Yorkers make money, they often buy "a place in the country." Thousands have bought up old farms, "winterized" them, and then retired to enjoy bucolic delights.

Although by 1825 pioneers had made clearings and erected barns, cabins, and homes in almost all sections of New York, the forest remained a formidable obstacle for another half century. Children of pioneers had to wield the ax with as much skill as their fathers, and almost as frequently. Because they had neither the time nor the energy to tidy up their clearings, English visitors and some American reformers called their husbandry slovenly. Given the conditions—ample timber and soil resources but a scarcity of capital and labor, as well as the prevailing passion for land speculation—New York farmers made the natural decision to exploit their resources and postpone improvements. Above all else they needed cash in order to pay for their land, stock, and basic equipment. Next they had to provide sound shelter for their families and livestock, often in reverse order. If meanwhile their clearings remained disfigured by girdled trees, logs, and stumps, so what? Decay and another burning or two would eventually get rid of them.

Even while pioneers were still bringing land under cultivation—in fact, as late as 1880—farmers in parts of New York settled earlier were abandoning exhausted fields or turning them into pastures. Other farmers heard the siren call of the cities and took jobs in stores, shops, and factories. An even greater number marched westward to fertile Genesee lands and beyond. By 1860, more than 800,000 New Yorkers (one-fourth of those born in the state as of that date) had resettled in the Old Northwest, where they left their mark on transportation, education, and farming. For example, Stephen M. Babcock, born in Oneida County, taught agricultural chemistry at the University of Wisconsin and developed the Babcock milk test.

Most farmers shifted over to animal husbandry, particularly dairying. The hilly slopes and well-watered pastures of New York were ideal for nourishing sheep and cows. There was a demand for meat and dairy products among mill workers and businessmen in urban centers along the Erie Canal and in New York City. Since 1850, butter, cheese, and milk have brought in over half the income of the state's farmers.

Regional specialization had emerged by mid-century. The wheat region lay west of Syracuse, with its center in the Genesee Valley. Mohawk Valley farmers specialized in raising barley for the breweries being established by German immigrants. Washington County specialized in flax, Otsego and Oneida counties in hops. The Hudson Valley and the Lake Ontario lowland specialized in fruit growing.[6]

During the last third of the nineteenth century, wheat growing dropped sharply because railroad cars and lake vessels brought millions of bushels from the northern plains. The dairy industry, however, kept expanding, ribboning along the tracks of the Erie and other railroads and penetrating the Appalachian highlands, the St. Lawrence Valley, and the Finger Lakes region. Horticulture developed rapidly in the lowlands south of Lake Ontario, whose waters moderated the climate. For the same reason, farmers in the Finger Lakes region and in Chautauqua County grew grapes for wine.

New York farmers adopted agricultural improvements at a comparatively slow pace. For thousands it was easier to move west than to learn new methods. Farmers gradually learned to grow clover and place lime on their fields. They changed from oxen to horses because horses moved faster; they found iron plows turned over a deeper furrow. Jesse Williams, near Rome, developed a cheese factory where skilled managers could produce a uniform and better product. Agricultural papers ran articles urging farmers to rotate their crops, put in tile for drainage, and use manures more carefully.

Most farmers regarded book farming with suspicion, but a determined minority kept urging more education and more research. In 1865 the legislature chartered Cornell University and assigned to it the income from land granted to the state under the Morrill Act for agricultural and mechanical education. Cornell's agricultural department attracted few students before 1888, when Liberty Hyde Bailey began to agitate for improved facilities and more research. In 1904 he persuaded the legislature to make the College of Agriculture a state institution. Thereafter enrollments rose sharply. Earlier, in 1881, the legislature had authorized the creation of the Geneva Agricultural Experiment Station, whose experts in pomology and agricultural sciences made important discoveries.

During the 1930s farm prices sank to disastrous levels. Farmers blocked roads and emptied milk cans to keep milk off the market. The legislature finally stepped in with a milk board that fixed milk prices. Later the federal government set prices for milk in various milksheds.

Although paintings of Grandma Moses and prints of Currier and Ives convey the impression that stability characterized farm life, change—constant, unremitting, ruthless—has marked rural as well as urban life. Since 1880 acreage in farms and improved land has been more than halved. Even more striking has been the decline—over 80 percent—in the number of farmers. The average size of farms has more than doubled and the investment per farm has risen more than tenfold in the last century. Output has greatly increased despite sharp declines in the numbers of operators and farm laborers.

In 1920 the farms of New York had more than 500,000 horses but only 7,500 tractors. The days of old Dobbin, however, were numbered, as farmers bought tractors in order to speed plowing, cultivating, harvesting, and manure spreading. By 1950 few farms had horses.

Since 1900 dairying has changed radically. Farmers used to get up at 4:00 A.M. in an unheated house and warm their hands on the cows' udders. By hand they carried water to cows and milk to the springhouse, where running water could keep it cool. Every day farmers hitched up their teams and took a couple of cans to the creamery, cheese factory, or station. During the 1920s farmers found that they could carry cans on a rack in the back of a Model T Ford. By the 1930s trucks carried milk to market. Meanwhile electricity illuminated barns and provided refrigeration. By the 1960s few farmers took milk to market. Instead, they emptied their machines directly into large tanks, which truckers carried to the creamery.

Electric power has revolutionized rural and urban life. In 1929 fewer than one-third of the farms had power, but New Deal agencies in Washington and the Little New Deal in Albany pushed the use of electricity. During the prosperous years after World War II, wires were strung to almost every farm. Electricity freed farm families from many dirty and laborious tasks. All over the state kitchens were remodeled and filled with gleaming white appliances, and milking machines appeared in barns. Every morning farm families listened to weather and market reports on the radio.

Life in the countryside became increasingly similar to that of millions of New Yorkers who had moved to the suburbs. Farm families watched the same news, entertainment, and sports programs that television stations were beaming to city dwellers. Automobiles, television, national advertising, and consolidated schools blurred the old distinctions between urban, suburban, and rural living.

Conservation of natural resources attracted its most ardent supporters among city dwellers. After the Civil War a handful of citizens became worried about the destruction of forests and water supplies. Among the leaders were Franklin B. Hough and Verplanck Colvin, who urged the legislature to set aside a forest reserve in the Adirondacks and Catskills. When lumbermen slashed timber from state lands in the 1880s, conservationists organized public protests. In 1894 they persuaded delegates to the state constitutional convention to approve the following amendment, described as the "most loved and most hated" clause in New York State's constitution:

The lands of the State, now owned or hereafter acquired, constituting the forest preserve as now fixed by law, shall be forever kept as wild forest lands. They shall not be leased, sold, or exchanged, or be taken by any corporation, public or private, nor shall the timber thereon be sold, removed or destroyed.

The legislature has appropriated funds to buy more land and has taken over tax-delinquent tracts. The Adirondack preserve has grown from 800,000 to more than 2.4 million acres, and the Catskill Park from 50,000 to more than 240,000 acres.

In 1972 the newly formed Adirondack Park Agency adopted a master plan for state-owned land and regulations governing commercial and residential development of the private lands that constitute more than half of the area within the 6-million-acre Adirondack Park. The Office of State Parks and Recreation administers 141 parks with an acreage almost as large as that of all the other state parks combined. Furthermore, New York State has encouraged localities to develop city parks, playgrounds, and historic sites.

The Pure Waters Program received a great stimulus from the Environmental Quality Bond Act of 1972, which authorized another $650 million to improve water resources. More than 200 projects for sewage treatment have received state grants.

By the bicentennial year, the tourist industry was bringing in more than $4 billion to the motels, restaurants, and gas stations of the Empire State. Thousands of conventions each year have met in Manhattan to take advantage of its theaters, restaurants, and fine airport facilities. Niagara Falls and the Thousand Islands have attracted many tourists from outside as well as inside the state.

Although New York lost its leadership in agriculture, it maintained its grasp on first place in manufacturing for well over a century and a half. Its numerous mills, lofts, and factories have employed the greatest number of workers in the widest variety of manufacturing. Nevertheless, smokestacks have not dominated urban centers in New York as conspicuously as they have in most midwestern states.

The Industrial Revolution began to transform New York in a substantial way during the two decades before the Civil War, when Pennsylvania coal freed manufacturers from dependence upon the water wheel, a highly uncertain means of obtaining

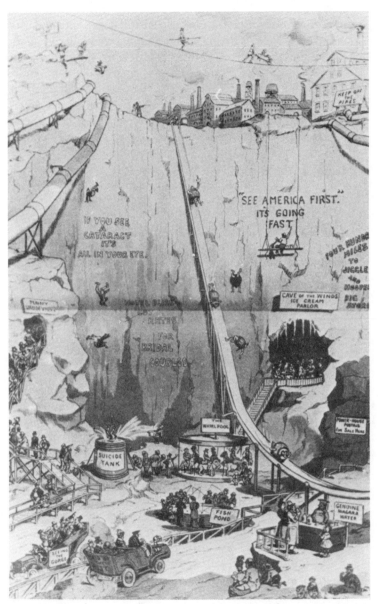

A British view of Niagara Falls as a tourist attraction. *Punch,* 1906.

power. Canal boats brought cheap coal to cities along the Erie Canal and the Hudson River. A national market emerged as the Erie Canal and the railroads linked midwestern farms to the industrial cities of the Northeast. Local urban markets expanded rapidly as immigrants and native-born alike demanded clothing, shoes, stoves, flour, beer, meat products, and many other articles.

Other factors stimulated manufacturing in the Empire State. Labor was plentiful, ranging from unskilled to highly skilled. Native New Yorkers had been brought up on the maxims of *Poor Richard's Almanac* and *McGuffey's Readers*, which preached thrift, industry, and initiative. Horatio Alger settled in New York City and wrote more than a hundred novels dedicated to the proposition that moral earnestness and industry (plus luck) would guarantee young people good fortune. Labor has always shown high productivity in New York. As late as 1973 the Annual Survey of Manufactures found New York well above the national average in value added per worker hour in almost all lines of manufactures.

The greatest pool of capital collected in New York City, whose bankers were able to draw also upon English and German money marts. Occasionally the state and local governments lent money to enterprises and encouraged manufacturing by charters, rights of way, and other forms of assistance.

During the Civil War years industrial expansion was slowed by the draft, short supplies of cotton, a decline in immigration, and inflation. To be sure, woolen factories and rifle makers had to fill tremendous orders. During the last third of the century the pace of industrialization rose sharply despite setbacks during the depressed 1870s and 1890s. By 1900, when the United States had elbowed England and Germany aside for first place, the Empire State accounted for about one-sixth of the national output. Thereafter its share slowly declined because of the rapid growth of manufacturing in midwestern, Pacific, and southern states. In 1974 about 18 million New Yorkers (roughly 8.5 percent of the nation) accounted for less than 8 percent of the nation's employees in manufacturing plants. Nevertheless, the total number of New York's employees remained higher than that of California's until the mid-1970s.[7]

What accounts for the startling loss (about one-third) in manufacturing jobs since the 1950s? Several factors spring to mind. Militant unions drove up labor costs while state social legislation raised business taxes far above the levels of southern states. The national government under Presidents Richard Nixon and Gerald Ford adopted policies, especially in defense spending, that favored the Sunbelt states. The Fantus Company, a locational consulting firm, recently gave New York State the worst rating for "business climate" as measured by taxes, labor laws, size and cost of government, and per capita debt.

New York manufacturing has developed rather distinctive characteristics. First, clothing, printed materials, foodstuffs, and other consumer goods dominated New York manufacturing before World War II. Since then, however, the durable-goods sector has steadily grown until in 1976 its employees equaled in number those in the consumer sector. Second, production units have remained considerably smaller than the national average. No doubt tens of thousands of small clothing and print shops have skewed average size downward. Finally, an unusually high percentage of the work force has been composed of women and immigrants.

For over a century New York City accounted for upward of 60 percent of the state's employment in manufactures. It has remained unique among large cities in the proportion of its total manufacturing employment devoted to small-scale enterprises, which have continued to be largely unstandardized, almost handcraft operations. Small garment firms in midtown Manhattan lofts have repesented the typical unit of New York's industry, in contrast to the vast assembly plants of Detroit, the steel mills of Pittsburgh and Gary, the farm-equipment factories of Chicago. Since 1969 New York City has lost more than 600,000 jobs, mostly in manufacturing. As a result, its share of the state total of persons employed in manufacturing has dropped to about 40 percent. The reasons have received wide publicity: high rents, high taxes, congestion, union regulations, racketeering, and obsolete buildings.

Clearly industry in New York State has had a difficult time, but there are signs of improvement more significant than the tiny gains in manufacturing employment after 1975. Governor Hugh Carey helped found the Coalition of Northeast Governors, dedicated to demonstrating that the Northeast pays much more in taxes to the federal government than it gets back in federal spending. Its demands for increased federal aid for welfare and other costs have been well publicized. The governments of both New York City and New York State have slowed their extravagant spending, primarily because of ultimatums from the banks. Politicians and unions seek to improve the business climate so that firms will not flee from the state.

Our discussion of manufacturing has necessarily overlapped labor's history as well. At the outset, let us note that factory labor constitutes less than one-fourth of the total work force, and that white-collar labor greatly outnumbers blue-collar labor. Services employ more workers than manufacturing, and government employees are almost as numerous. Although most workers have never belonged to trade unions, the unions have played an important role in improving wages and conditions for the rest of the labor force.

Dozens of unions were founded in the 1830s and 1850s, but they had weak leaders and empty treasuries. As a result, they found it difficult to survive long strikes and depressions. In 1886 Samuel Gompers, a Manhattan cigar worker, helped organize the American Federation of Labor as a federation of craft unions. He sought to build strong craft unions that could fight employers on equal terms. His main goal was "more and more, here and now." Gompers fought off Socialist attempts to capture the labor movement, which at this time was coming under Marxist control in most European countries. The AFL made impressive gains after 1897, especially in organizing building trades, metal trades, and teamsters.

The needle trades expanded enormously between 1895 and World War I, and tens of thousands of immigrants, especially Jews from Eastern Europe, found work sewing garments for both men and women. Feeling exploited, workers formed unions and conducted strikes. In 1909 the International Ladies' Garment Workers' Union won a fifty-hour week and a ban on work in the home. The next year the Amalgamated Clothing Workers made similar gains after a long strike. On March 25, 1911, fire swept through the Triangle Shirtwaist Company factory in lower Manhattan, snuffing out the lives of more than a hundred women who were trapped on the upper floors. This tragedy shocked citizens and an outcry was raised for a thorough investigation of working conditions. The special State Factory Investigating Commission made the most comprehensive study of its kind in American history. Two of its members, Alfred E. Smith and Robert F. Wagner, became ardent advocates of labor reform. As a result, legislators banned child labor in tenements and canneries, prohibited night shifts for women, and set a nine-hour day for women workers. Soon they enacted a compulsory accident insurance law as well. It required almost annual amendments, however, in order to plug loopholes. The fight against child labor did not succeed until the legislature passed laws compelling attendance at school.

During World War I a shortage of labor drove wages upward. The AFL, relying on the federal government's support of collective bargaining, organized many plants and doubled its membership. Labor unions suffered many setbacks during the next decade, however, despite the overall prosperity of the period. High profits meant higher salaries for many white- and blue-collar workers, some of whom bought cars and began to send their children to college. Unions lost headway for a variety of reasons: anti-union campaigns by many employers; court decisions declaring several labor laws void; the Red Scare, which gave conservatives a chance to attack union leaders as communists; fights between moderates and left-wing factions; racketeering; and the migration of textile mills and garment shops to other states. The panic of 1929, followed by the disastrous depression of the 1930s, struck a devastating blow to all labor, organized or not.

The New Deal of Franklin D. Roosevelt greatly affected labor conditions within the state. The Wagner Act protected labor's right to organize, with the result that the AFL and the CIO (Committee of Industrial Organizations) recruited many members. The Social Security Act of 1935 and the Fair Labor Standards Act three years later established many safeguards for which labor had struggled for decades: a system of old-age pensions, unemployment insurance, a minimum wage, maximum hours (forty), and a ban on child labor in establishments whose products entered interstate commerce.

Since World War II, New York labor has experienced many changes. The proportion of persons gainfully employed has risen, and the number of women in the work force has expanded dramatically. While the number and percentage of workers in manufacturing have declined, the number of persons employed in service trades, retailing, and government has risen sharply.

Membership in trade unions has fallen off largely because of declining employment in railroads, the needle trades, and factories. To offset this decline, about 900,000 of the million or more civil servants in state and local government have joined associations or unions, many of which have conducted strikes and lobbied vigorously for increased benefits. The Taylor Law of 1967 banned strikes by civil servants but set up a system of employee representation, collective bargaining, and neutral administration. It did not prevent strikes by policemen and teachers, and taxpayers have shown their resentment by voting down many school budgets and turning down referenda calling for additional expenditures by local and state governments. Politicians, however, have found it necessary to make concessions to civil service unions, which provide funds and workers for campaigns.

The economic condition of minorities deserves further elaboration. During World War II and through the Korean war blacks made remarkable gains, if only because of steady employment for most job seekers. Thereafter the picture becomes blurred and the evidence seems contradictory. Actually blacks continued to make impressive gains in the professions, sports, entertainment, business, education, and many other fields. In 1977 the appointment of Clifton R. Wharton, Jr., as head of the State University of New York illustrates the sort of breakthrough achieved by qualified blacks in many fields. Much more significant, however, was the fact that thousands of black families were moving into the middle class each month. Andrew Brimmer, a governor of the Federal Reserve Board, noted that in the 1960s blacks made progress in terms of higher employment, occupational upgrading, and a narrowing of the income gap between blacks and whites.

Since 1970, however, blacks have not kept pace with national trends in employment and income. A Census Bureau report, *The Social and Economic Status of the Black Population in the United States, 1973,* showed that black family income had declined because the number of female-headed families had increased to 34 percent. These national trends were evident also in New York City, which contained about three-fourths of the state's black population. Because both state and metropolis experienced stagnation and indeed lost more than a half-million jobs in the next six years, blacks and Puerto Ricans, who were highly concentrated in the most marginal jobs, bore an exceptional burden. In February 1977 unemployment in New York City exceeded 10 percent—2.5 percent higher than the national figure. Unemployment among blacks has normally been double that among whites, and among black teenagers it has reached 40 percent or more, a tragic and ominous figure.

The Puerto Rican story is similar. Because many Puerto Ricans do not speak English fluently, they have had difficulty securing white-collar jobs in banks, stores, and corporations. The percentage of Puerto Ricans on welfare has generally exceeded that of blacks. On the other hand, a considerable number of second-generation Puerto Ricans have "made it" into the middle class. Meanwhile a wave of legal and also illegal Hispanics from the Dominican Republic and other nations have entered the metropolis, where they have tended to occupy the most dilapidated buildings and find only the most unpleasant jobs.

The record of New York's economy is one of mighty achievements followed by serious decline. For over a century and a half New Yorkers exploited their location and transportation advantages to develop a manufacturing plant and financial institutions second to none among the states. Millions of newcomers from other states and other continents found it possible to acquire modest comforts and status, and a considerable number became rich. Before 1960, per capita income in New York stood very close to the top among the states.

By 1976 personal income still stood about 10 percent higher than the national average.[8] But when the high cost of living, including the highest state and local taxes, is considered, the real per capita income represented the same as that of southerners and slightly less than the national average.[9]

This turn of events sobered and chastened New Yorkers, and they began to show a determination to reverse the downward spiral. They recognized the fact that they would have to work harder, reduce expenditures even on useful programs, and join forces with other northeastern states to change federal policies. Actually New York State offered many advantages, ranging from the greatest pool of investment capital to a better-than-average work force. As late as 1976 it awarded more college degrees than California. New York City remained the destination for many talented outlanders and attracted much capital from Europeans and Arabs who were fearful of political unrest at home.

In 1975 New York's legislators selected the beaver as the state animal. In colonial days, beaver skins constituted an important export and even served as currency on occasion. Perhaps the legislators were subconsciously urging New Yorkers to emulate this sturdy animal, a symbol of industry, skill, and foresight.

7

Mind and Spirit

New York's cultural ascendancy was the offspring of its wealth, tolerance, and close relations with Europe. Every generation saw another group of writers, artists, and creative spirits move to Manhattan, where patrons emerged to support them. New York City became one of the world's major cultural centers but in the process lost some of its special identity. Its intelligentsia came to regard upstate as part of the vast hinterland, somewhat provincial in spirit if not benighted. Upstaters continued to find their roots in the old Yankee tradition, the countryside, and such institutions as the Erie Canal, the small town, the county fair, and religious eccentricities.

Busy harbors, cleared land, crowded canal locks, and bustling cities—such were the most visible signs of achievement in post-Revolutionary New York. New Yorkers also made great progress in building schools and churches, and a talented few were writing books and painting landscapes of considerable distinction.[1] Leaders in business and government recognized that a dynamic society needed victories in mind and spirit matching those in business and public works. Significantly, both Philip Hone, mayor of New York City, and Governor De Witt Clinton were patrons of the arts, advocates of education, and active churchmen.

A glance at artistic and intellectual trends during the first half of the century will reveal how New Yorkers, unabashedly materialistic, mobilized their resources for education and encouraged a cadre of talented writers and artists. The average citizen felt great pride on learning that Washington Irving had won access to the most exalted circles and salons of Europe. In those heady times, New Yorkers believed no summits of endeavor were too high for them to scale.

In 1809 Washington Irving published *Diedrich Knickerbocker's History of New York*, a burlesque in which torpid New Netherland burghers whiled away their days smoking long pipes and swilling immense tankards of ale. After the War of 1812 Irving sailed for Europe, where he studied Spanish history and wrote sketches of English life. His *Sketch Book* (1819) contained "The Legend of Sleepy Hollow" and "Rip van Winkle," two stories that enveloped Hudson Valley landscapes in a nostalgic haze of folklore. His writings won for him the plaudits of Goethe, Heine, Byron, and Sir Walter Scott. Irving's success inspired other writers, who formed what has been called the Knickerbocker school. Among them was James Kirke Paulding, whose books, notably *The Book of St. Nicholas* and *The Dutchman's Fireside*, have left us an authentic picture of the Anglo-Dutch society of colonial New York.

In 1822 James Fenimore Cooper settled in New York City and founded a luncheon club of illuminati who exchanged the latest information about intellectual fashions in Europe and America. Its members included Chancellor James Kent, who was preparing his *Commentaries* on American law; the poet Fitz-Greene Halleck; the painter Asher Durand; Gulian C. Verplanck, who wrote on law and theology; and several other painters and writers. New York City was rapidly supplanting Philadelphia as America's literary center.

Cooper's novels have probably attracted more readers than those of any other New York author. Indeed, some literary historians assert that *The Last of the Mohicans* is, to this day, the most widely read novel ever written in any language. Reared on the shores of Glimmerglass (Otsego Lake), Cooper described the founding and early development of an American village during the 1790s under the beneficent aegis of a man very much like his father, William Cooper. The younger Cooper showed a keen concern for conservation and the division of labor in an infant settlement. Whether civilization or nature should determine men's actions was a question that intrigued Cooper, and he used his novels to express his ardent support for democracy, landlordism, and Americanism, and his antipathy for Yankee culture, antirenters, and Whig newspapers. Although some critics describe his prose as pedestrian and his women characters as unbelievable, none deny his ability to create memorable male characters, such as Natty Bumppo, hero of the *Leatherstocking Tales*. For Europeans, his Indians and pioneers were authentic figures, and his upstate landscape became the authorized version of the New World.

In 1825 William Cullen Bryant, recognized as the foremost poet of his day, deserted his native Berkshires for New York City, where he edited the *Evening Post*. Bryant, a Democrat, favored free trade and labor unions, but later he switched to the Republican party because most Democratic politicians in Washington echoed defenders of slavery. Horace Greeley, another Yankee, arrived and began the *New Yorker*, whose columns contained much literary comment. In 1841 he founded the *New York Tribune*, our first national newspaper. A crusader for reform—temperance, women's rights, free homesteads, public education—Greeley campaigned for protective tariffs, championed Whig and Republican candidates, and opposed slavery in the territories. James Gordon Bennett, a Scot, published the *Herald,* whose columns alternately shocked and titillated readers with sensational stories interlarded with solid news. Bennett scooped the world by sending Henry Stanley to Africa to look for David Livingstone, the Scottish explorer who had dropped from sight.

In 1832, Irving returned to his native New York after seventeen years of exile. Mayor Hone and Chancellor Kent greeted the literary lion at a great public dinner. Irving settled down in his home near Tarrytown. Like Cooper, he deplored the passing of the genteel world of landlords and merchants and the rise of the world of commerce, ruled by the "Almighty Dollar" (his coinage). The following year Cooper returned from seven years in Europe. Almost immediately he became embroiled in disputes with editors whom he accused of defaming his character.

During the 1840s the "valley of the Hudson might almost have been called the literary focus of the country," according to Van Wyck Brooks.[2] At the same time the Hudson River school of painters was reveling in Catskill and Hudson scenes that reached the larger public through the prints of Nathaniel Currier and James Ives.

After the demise of the Knickerbocker school, individual authors emerged, each expressing his unique talent. Herman Melville, an Albany Gansevoort, dealt with themes of man's pride and destiny. Walt Whitman, a son of Long Island's seashore and Brooklyn's streets, also transcended provincial concerns in his *Leaves of Grass*, which made little stir on first publication in 1855.

Most American and foreign artists settled in New York City, where merchants could pay for portraits, the major source of their income. John Trumbull, a student of Benjamin West, set up his studio there and completed several historical projects, perhaps the most famous being *The Declaration of Independence*. In Albany, Ezra Ames limned the features of famous New Yorkers, including the two governors Clinton.

In 1824 Thomas Cole established himself in Greenwich Village and sketched Hudson Valley scenes. Eventually he settled in Catskill, the village just below the legend-haunted Catskill Mountains. There he taught Frederick Church, who built the extraordinary house called Olana, overlooking the Hudson. Meanwhile, in 1826, a group of artists founded the National Academy of Design, with Samuel F. B. Morse as president. Morse, a gifted portrait painter, gradually abandoned painting and by 1832 was experimenting with the idea of an electric telegraph. He finally demonstrated a model successfully a dozen years later. He was encouraged by Joseph Henry, an Albany youth who was doing research in electromagnetism. Henry's findings were basic to the development of the electric motor, generator, dynamo, and transformer.

Growing wealth provided support for architects in various cities. Businessmen, landowners, and political figures constructed impressive buildings to mark their success and add distinction to their cities. They generally followed models fashionable in England and on the Continent.

The Georgian style—the American version was called Federal—prevailed for more than a generation after the Revolution. Philip Hooker almost singlehandedly built Albany, includ-

"Kindred Spirits": William Cullen Bryant and Thomas Cole in the Catskills, as portrayed by Asher B. Durand. New York Public Library.

ing the city hall, the Court of Appeals building, and the old Albany Academy, as well as many churches. Perhaps his most conspicuous legacy is the graceful steeple of the Hamilton College chapel (1828).

Greece and Rome provided not only scores of place names and the core curricula of colleges, but architectual models as well. During the 1820s New Yorkers collected funds to aid Greeks in their rebellion against their Turkish overlords. Asher Benjamin's *Practical Home Carpenter* instructed journeymen in the making of pilasters, pediments, and columns in wood, the great building material of the frontier. Public officials, finding inspiration in Greek democracy and the Roman republic, authorized classical buildings, and bank officials, hoping to convey a feeling of solidity and permanence, kept their money behind classical facades.

The pointed arch, the hallmark of Gothic architecture, was familiar in New York well before the Civil War. St. Patrick's Cathedral, constructed in traditional Gothic style, was opened in 1853. Richard Upjohn applied the Gothic style to several Episcopal churches: Trinity (its third structure) in Manhattan, St. Paul's in Buffalo, Grace Church in Utica. Gothic features were borrowed by many homes and some commercial buildings in the popular Gothic Revival style. Other New Yorkers borrowed Italianate, Flemish, and other features for a style that may generously be described as eclectic. Main Street in many communities presented an ensemble that was strikingly effective and pleasing.

These literary and artistic accomplishments were largely limited to the rich. Still, most New Yorkers—farmers, artisans, small businessmen—made substantial progress in education, religion, and popular culture.

The schools of the Empire State caught up with those of New England in the period after 1825. Under the district law of 1812, citizens organized thousands of schools, with the state matching local funding. Neither state nor local governments provided enough money to build and operate the schools, however, and parents had to pay a fee (usually not large) for each child enrolled. Parents willing to sign a pauper's oath were exempted, but some of them balked at taking it—they had pride even if they lacked cash. Of course, some kept their children home because

St. Paul's Church, an outstanding example of Greek Revival architecture, and the Broadway stages, c. 1830. Courtesy of the New-York Historical Society, New York City.

they needed their help in barns, shops, or stores. Some immigrants suspected that schools were devices to subvert their children. In 1846 more than 46,000 children did not attend school, an unfortunate situation that continued at various levels until compulsory attendance laws early in the twentieth century made truant officers a threat to careless parents and delinquent youngsters.

Workingmen joined forces with reformers and persons of Yankee stock to crusade for free schools. Opposing them were some taxpayers, private schoolmen, and Catholic immigrants who complained that public schools had a Protestant slant (they did). Although by mid-century most citizens favored free schools, legislators, ever wary of taxpayer resistance, did not end the hated rates, or fees, until 1867.

The "little red schoolhouse," celebrated in engravings and idealized in autobiographies, did open doors of opportunity for tens of thousands of youngsters. Many schools had obvious shortcomings: unpainted, shabby structures with no blackboards, maps, or toilets; short terms; incompetent teachers. Teachers had to handle all students of every grade and age, calling them in turn to come forward to recite their memorized lessons. Instruction ranged from excellent to terrible, with most teachers clustered in the "fair" category. The reminiscences of Henry Clarke Wright reveal that instruction in one Otsego County school shifted dramatically from one season to the next. One drunken teacher regularly beat his students with a long whip. Another teacher, however, "was calm, collected, affectionate, but firm and undeviating in her manner. . . . We all loved that teacher, for we felt that she loved us, and that she sought and acted for our good in all she did."[3]

Most children learned to read, write, and do sums in the district schools or in the hundreds of private schools opened by one or two maiden ladies in their homes. A talented few continued their education in the academies that sprang up in larger villages and cities, offering instruction in English literature, modern languages, natural sciences, and such practical subjects as bookkeeping. A few cities took advantage of the law permitting several districts to establish free public high schools. Competition from high schools forced some academies to close; others merged with them. After 1855 academies declined in number until about 1900, when Roman Catholic bishops established many secondary schools to serve the large families of immigrants.

In 1860, only 1,305 students attended "literary" colleges and another 897 enrolled in medical colleges. The major denominations had founded one or more colleges where young men could prepare for the ministry or priesthood. Curricula stressed classical subjects: Greek, Latin, mathematics, rhetoric, and philosophy. Popular demand, however, led Union, Columbia, and Rochester to offer courses in the sciences. At West Point and at Rensselaer Polytechnic Institute in Troy, students could study engineering. Dozens of men received a rough sort of engineering training by surveying the route and designing the locks of the Erie Canal.

Formal education for women lagged far behind that for men, although a few seminaries catered to young ladies of "better" families. Notable among them was Emma Willard Seminary of Troy, founded in 1821 and still in operation. Elmira Female College opened its doors in 1853; a decade later Vassar offered young women a classical education. Coeducation had to wait until Cornell University opened its doors after the Civil War.

Young men who wanted to become lawyers received their training by reading law in attorneys' offices and by attending court. Others became doctors by observing physicians, although several hundred a year attended lectures at medical colleges. Elizabeth Blackwell, the first women physician in this country, had to brave the insults of her fellow students at Geneva (later Hobart) Medical College, from which she was graduated in 1849.

The public's thirst for information about science, literature, and history was met by mechanics' institutes and lyceums, the first of which was organized by Alexander Bryan Johnson, a Utica banker whose studies anticipated many twentieth-century findings in linguistics. These associations collected books and sponsored lectures. The Empire State led other states in libraries; the State Library was established in Albany as early as 1818. When John Jacob Astor died, he left a large part of his estate for a library, which eventually became the nucleus of the New York Public Library.

Closely allied to education were religious developments, as most denominations established schools and colleges. The predominantly Protestant character of New Yorkers was reinforced by the religious revivals of 1825–1826, which swept from Oneida County across the state, into New York City, and ultimately to much of the northern United States. Charles Grandison Finney became the foremost religious figure of the period. A Presbyterian, Finney moved away from the position that human fate is predetermined. He stated, "Genuine faith always results in good works and is itself a good work." Consequently, saving individuals from sin led inevitably to reforming society.

Central and western New York became known as the "Burned-Over District" because a luxuriant growth of sects and cults sprang up after spiritual fires, presumably kindled by the Holy Spirit, swept over the region again and again.[4] Why this region spawned such ardent religious excitement, so many eccentric opinions, and such unconventional behavior still puzzles historians. No doubt many citizens, having survived the backbreaking days of pioneering, had more time to nurture their hopes for a more perfect society in this world, certainly in the next. The speedup of transportation, the expansion of the religious as well as the secular press, and the rising levels of education also contributed to the rapid dissemination of religious and reform information. The rising tensions over states' rights, slavery, and immigration drove many to seek answers in Scripture or the writings of new prophets such as Joseph Smith. Upstaters, largely transplanted Yankees, awaited some sign from the Almighty, which several prophets were quick to supply. Emotionalism reached fever pitch and tens of thousands joined crusades against the Masons, the demon rum, and the slavocracy.

Several new sects flowered in the Burned-Over District. The Perfectionists, led by John Humphrey Noyes, organized the famous Oneida Community, which alternately shocked and fascinated outsiders with its communal sharing of property, women, and children. Near Palmyra, youthful Joseph Smith declared that on a hillside he had discovered golden plates and magic spectacles with which to read them. When Smith's neighbors greeted his prophecies with derision and hostility, he led his tiny band of followers westward to Kirtland, Ohio. His translation of the Book of Mormon is today sacred scripture for some three million members of the Church of Jesus Christ of Latter-Day Saints. The Fox sisters in Hydeville (near Rochester) claimed that they could communicate with the dead. Their followers, called Spiritualists, numbered tens of thousands and included Horace Greeley and later Arthur Conan Doyle. William Miller preached the end of the world upon Christ's second coming—scheduled for March 1844, he said—and by 1843 scores of itinerant preachers were crisscrossing the Empire State, urging people to repent. When life persisted stubbornly after the doleful date, the Adventists redoubled their efforts and eventually formed two new churches.

Fascinating as these sects appeared to their own and later generations, one can exaggerate their importance and forget that New Yorkers overwhelmingly belonged to mainstream denominations. The Methodists, who offered a theology of plenteous grace and assurance that individuals could help themselves win salvation, became the largest Protestant group. Their closest competitors were Baptists, who also relied heavily upon laymen to run their churches. Presbyterians and Congregationalists, whose close alliance in a Plan of Union (1801) came unstuck at mid-century, regarded themselves as the chosen means for bringing learning, culture, and religious sophistication to the frontier. They enrolled most merchants, lawyers, teachers, and substantial farmers, especially those who hailed from New England. Bishop John Hobart found his Protestant Episcopal church suffering from disorganization and a Tory taint. He used traditional values and practices to inspire the members, many of whom came from wealthy urban families.

After 1840 the Roman Catholic church grew rapidly as Ireland's potato blight and social changes in the German states stimulated emigration to America. By 1860 this church had the largest membership in New York City and in several upstate cities. The Catholic influx led to a nativist backlash, especially among workingmen. But nativism faded during the Civil War, when Roman Catholics more than fulfilled their obligations as citizens and soldiers.

Charles G. Finney and his colleagues not only converted hun-

A Methodist camp meeting. *Harper's Weekly*, September 10, 1859.

dreds of thousands but stimulated many reform movements. Upstate became the nursery for humanitarian movements. Among
the reformers were Theodore Weld and Gerrit Smith, who sought
to abolish slavery; Elizabeth Cady Stanton and Susan B. Anthony, persistent fighters for women's rights; and John B. Gough,
a reformed drunkard who enthralled thousands with his lurid
tales of degradation. Finney attracted support from such wealthy
men as the Tappan brothers, silk merchants in New York City,
who gave money for tract societies, manual labor schools, and
colleges.

Reformers had a small but dedicated corps of followers and
could muster support from a much broader group of sympathiz-
ers. Their crusades aroused much opposition, however. Hunker
Democrats were careful to keep on good terms with national
Democratic leaders, mainly southerners. Roman Catholics correctly suspected that many evangelical reformers were also
Papist baiters. Traditionalists in various denominations disap-
proved of any move to turn churches into agents of social reform.
Would not reform split their membership and divert the faithful
from worshiping God? Sometimes opponents engaged in violence. They stoned Weld in Troy, and in 1835 they chased delegates to the first state antislavery convention from its meeting
place in Utica.

Reform spilled over into the political field. Thomas Skidmore of
New York City believed that redistribution of land would cure all
of society's ills. Somewhat later, George Henry Evans organized
the National Reform Association to persuade Congress to grant
free homesteads to actual settlers. The agitation of these men laid
the groundwork for passage of the Homestead Act of 1862.

The reformers prepared American minds for the abolition of
slavery, but their agitation aroused fear and resentment in the
South. When southerners learned that Gerrit Smith and other
New Yorkers had furnished money and supplies to John Brown,
many felt that secession was their only remedy.

New York's lusty and convivial society pursued amusement
with an avidity that New Englanders regarded as unproductive if
not sinful. Theater performances became very popular, although
the righteous, with some justification, deplored theaters as places

of assignation. The second Park Theater in New York, which opened in 1821, could accommodate 2,500; soon the Broadway offered seats to 4,000. Companies of English actors toured the country after their first performances in New York City. Many natives became stagestruck, and some became accomplished actors themselves. Edwin Forrest played Othello in 1826 and many other Shakespearean roles thereafter. In 1849, a Bowery mob—partisans of Forrest—stormed the Astor Place Theatre, where William C. Macready, the great English actor, was appearing. Irish toughs joined with Anglophobe Americans in a riot that took twenty-two lives before troops put it down.

P. T. Barnum, a newcomer from Connecticut, became the greatest showman of his age, perhaps of all time. In 1841 he took over a Manhattan museum, where he displayed General Tom Thumb and other midgets, bearded ladies, trained fleas, and hundreds of other curiosities. Barnum organized a touring circus with elephants, acrobats, and riding acts. During the decades before the Civil War the minstrel show reached great heights of popularity. Christy's Minstrels were favorite performers in New York City.

Sports provided amusement for youngsters and adults. Horse racing, well established before the Revolution, continued to attract crowds. In 1823, more than 50,000 persons thronged the track when Eclipse, the pride of the North, outran Sir Henry, a southern horse, at the Union Course on Long Island.

Baseball evolved out of a variety of games with ball, bat, and bases which youngsters played in city lots and village fields. In 1845 the Knickerbocker Club of New York City published a code of rules for the game for its members, mostly businessmen. Baseball caught on, and during the 1850s workingmen formed teams. The story that Abner Doubleday of Cooperstown invented baseball in 1839 partakes of the fanciful. Upstaters often exaggerated, even created hoaxes. Perhaps the most famous was the Cardiff Giant, a ten-and-a-half-foot figure that a farmer uncovered in his field in 1869. Carved from gypsum and weighing a ton and a half, it was supposedly a petrified man. Some New Yorkers believed the story; others were skeptical from the start. P. T. Barnum took advantage of the public curiosity by sending on tour a figure copied from the original Cardiff Giant.

This brief survey of cultural, educational, religious, and popular pursuits demonstrates that New Yorkers did many other things besides chase dollars. They cultivated both mind and spirit, and they took hedonistic delight in sports, amusements, and the theater.

In 1888 William Dean Howells abandoned Boston for New York, a move that registered the cultural supremacy of Manhattan Island. He commented, "There are lots of interesting young painting and writing fellows, and the place is lordly free, with foreign touches of all kinds all thro' its abounding Americanism; Boston seems of another planet."[5]

New York's cultural ascendancy was due less to the genius of its writers, artists, and dramatists than to its wealth, which sustained talented individuals and attracted free spirits from all over the world. Most large publishing houses had their head offices there. Writers, artists, and musicians made visits to or settled down in metropolitan New York, next to Paris the city most receptive to creative spirits seeking personal freedom and cultural stimulus. There too they found financial support among old families who had cultivated tastes; they sought or endured lionizing by *arrivistes*, who patronized the arts in hopes of winning social acceptance; they welcomed sponsorship by museums and foundations.

Ironically, the more dominant New York City became in the business of culture, the more muted was the song of its native warblers. Melville and Whitman had passed their peak and no new giant rose to express universal themes or to depict the New York way of life. To be sure, dozens of lesser talents ground out formula fiction by the ream in the generation after Appomattox. Mercifully, time has consigned to obscurity the Samantha novels of Marietta Holley of Watertown, the lackluster stories of Horatio Alger, and the Westerns of Edward Zane Judson, who invented and exploited the genre. In the 1870s John Burroughs, who lived in a rustic retreat near Kingston, attracted attention with essays on nature peppered with pleasant homilies on morals and good manners. His books stimulated a growing interest in outdoor life, soon to be embraced by Theodore Roosevelt, himself a prolific writer on history and frontier life.

Thomas F. O'Donnell has observed, "In 1887 the long literary drought that had bedeviled the whole state since the Civil War finally came to an end with the simultaneous appearance of two novels: Henry Cuyler Bunner's *The Story of a New York House* and Harold Frederic's *Seth's Brother's Wife*."[6] Bunner's book analyzed the personality of New York City, a challenge later taken up by dozens of writers. Frederic, a Utican who became London correspondent of the *New York Times*, depicted upstaters realistically. His masterpiece, *The Damnation of Theron Ware*, portrayed the way in which the new ideas spawned by Darwin left their imprint on the minds of clergymen and laymen.

After 1887 the literature of New York City had no closer connection with upstate than with any other region or state. Upstate nourished few great talents, although dozens of earnest souls worked local veins in search of a mother lode. In the north country, Philander Deming wrote stories as harsh as the igneous rocks ribbing the Adirondacks. A few years later, Irving Bacheller penned tales of simple folk in his native St. Lawrence County.

Henry James, a novelist whose works have received critical acclaim and careful analysis, did not exploit New York themes except in *Washington Square* and *The American Scene*. He was more interested in sketching American characters in conflict with European society and traditions. Edith Wharton confined herself to the folkways of Hudson River society, of which she was a charter member. Her novels skillfully dissected emotional conflicts among the elite.

Stephen Crane drew a stark picture of the underside of urban life in his *Maggie: A Girl of the Streets*. Victorian critics gave it no warmer welcome than they extended to Theodore Dreiser's *Sister Carrie*, the story of a sensitive girl who escaped from poverty by becoming the mistress of a rich and powerful man. *An American Tragedy* (1925) continued Dreiser's naturalistic approach, turning into fiction the true story of a young man in Herkimer County who drowned the pregnant sweetheart who stood in the way of his rise in society. The short stories of O. Henry (William Sidney Porter) were gobbled up by the public, who liked the unexpected endings he characteristically gave to his tales of shopgirls, policemen, and clerks.

Newspapers and magazines reached a much wider audience

than books. In 1883 Joseph Pulitzer acquired the *New York World*, which combined sensationalism in news columns with cries for reform in editorials. A dozen years later William Randolph Hearst, a brash young millionaire from San Francisco, bought the *Journal* and promptly waged a campaign to attract more readers than the *World*. He succeeded, but in the process he lowered the standards of journalism by spectacular stories of sex and crime, while his quixotic views on politics and his jingoistic attitudes fanned demagoguery. Meanwhile Adolph Ochs of Chattanooga had bought the ailing *Times*, which he rejuvenated and transformed into a paper noted for coverage and objectivity.

Yellow journalism spilled over into monthly magazines. Samuel McClure established a magazine bearing his name, whose format was followed by *Munsey's, Hearst's International – Cosmopolitan,* and others. Lurid exposés of unclean meat and drugs, railroad skulduggery, and machine politics spurred legislators to reforms.

After the Civil War, New York City attracted artists and sculptors who competed for commissions and attention. The National Academy of Design sought to maintain traditional standards but rebels arose to challenge its authority. Hardly had a new style won grudging acceptance before new rebels emerged. John La Farge, leader of a family whose members became famous in literature, religion, and the arts, exercised his considerable talents in painting, murals, and stained glass. Augustus Saint-Gaudens' masterful statues of General William T. Sherman and Admiral David Farragut set standards of excellence seldom matched by later sculptors. Albert P. Ryder, an eccentric figure, painted wraithlike figures and somber land- and seascapes reflecting his brooding moods.

The "Little Renaissance," which flowered between 1908 and 1917, spread within the artistic community from its center in Greenwich Village.[7] Eager to create an indigenous culture, artists and writers attacked puritanism, assaulted the genteel tradition, and demanded freedom from subservience to European standards. Several artists painted the seamy side of urban life: prizefights, poolrooms, back alleys, and deviants. These realistic painters proudly accepted the label "Ashcan School" which critics pinned on them. In 1913 Arthur B. Davies, a member of this group, organized the International Exhibition of Modern Art at the Sixty-ninth Regiment Armory in New York City. This "Armory Show" featured 1,600 paintings by European and American artists who were experimenting with impressionism, cubism, and other art forms. Alfred Stieglitz's Gallery 291 had earlier presented the works of Rodin, Cézanne, Picasso, and Marin. American art was revolutionized as a result. At the same time, poets and members of little theater groups were experimenting with new forms and techniques.

World War I interrupted the artistic and cultural ferment that had made Manhattan the cultural leader of the nation. As a result of the Little Renaissance, artists and writers of the 1920s enjoyed extraordinarily free atmosphere in which to work. Greenwich Village was to lose its cohesiveness as a community partly because of the departure of leading figures for Paris's Left Bank, partly because of the invasion of bohemians and poseurs of all kinds.

New York City also became the center of the musical world. Europe's outstanding performers usually began and ended their concert tours of the United States in Manhattan. The rising men of trade, finance, and manufacturing, with their wives, threw their support behind the opera, symphony orchestras, and other musical societies. In 1883 the Metropolitan Opera Association began its distinguished performances, relying heavily upon European artists until after World War II. Enrico Caruso began his career at the Met in 1903, and within five years Arturo Toscanini was conducting its orchestra. He later became director of the New York Philharmonic Society.

City growth and business expansion required construction of thousands of office buildings and mansions for the rich. Eclecticism ran riot as architects borrowed from Gothic, Italian, French, and even Moorish styles. Many Victorian homes had mansard roofs decorated with jigsaw ornamentation. Steel, oil, and copper kings commissioned Richard Morris Hunt to design their Fifth Avenue mansions. After the World's Columbian Exposition in Chicago in 1893, classical styles enjoyed a revival. Perhaps the best examples were the Pennsylvania Railroad Station, the Columbia University library, and the State Education Building in

Albany. Henry Hobson Richardson designed the incredibly expensive state capitol, which boasted a million-dollar staircase.

Although skyscrapers were first developed in Chicago by Louis Sullivan, New Yorkers were quick to adopt the new form. In 1894 Sullivan designed Buffalo's Prudential Building; a decade later Frank Lloyd Wright designed the Larkin Building for the lake port. Even before World War I Manhattan had become the home of the skyscraper. Americans took great pride in the Woolworth Building, fifty-seven stories high, which Cass Gilbert designed and completed in 1912.

Frederick Law Olmsted joined with Calvert Vaux in designing Central Park. Olmsted hoped it would become a harmonizing influence, a place where rich and poor, natives and immigrants could come together to enjoy the beauties of nature. With extreme care he had more than 400,000 trees and shrubs planted within the 820 acres. His success brought him commissions from Chicago, Washington, and Boston, as well as Buffalo and Utica.

In 1874 Bishop John H. Vincent organized a summer school for Sunday-school teachers on Chautauqua Lake. A huge success from the start, the program was expanded and attracted thousands of visitors. People could not only study the Bible but learn Greek, attend history lectures, play the piano, and sing oratorios. In 1903 the Redpath Lyceum Bureau organized a traveling "Chautauqua," which sent out speakers, concert groups, and actors to perform in circus tents.

New York's religious complexion was fundamentally altered by the large-scale immigration of Roman Catholics and Jews. Most Roman Catholics settled in cities and found work in factories and construction. They came to dominate the Democratic party and elected many mayors, aldermen, and state legislators. Whereas in Europe workingmen tended to drift away from the church and join Marxist parties and unions, in this country they remained loyal parishioners. Catholics built and maintained an astonishing network of churches, schools, colleges, nursing homes, hospitals, and retreats. They managed to maintain church unity despite rumblings by Germans, Italians, French-Canadians, and Poles about Irish domination of the hierarchy.

Jewish congregations grew rapidly, especially after 1881, when persecution by the Russian government drove thousands into exile. Of the more than one million Jewish immigrants, more than half settled in New York City. Statistics on religious affiliation have always been unreliable and are particularly so in regard to persons of Jewish background, many of whom have chosen not to associate themselves with a synagogue or temple. The Jewish community was divided by the forces of modern science, the Enlightenment, Marxism, and the higher criticism of the Old Testament. Some synagogues became temples when they introduced organs, mixed choirs, family pews, and prayers in English. Russian Jews tended to remain Orthodox in their practices; German Jews tended to join Reform congregations.

Protestant membership kept pace with population growth. The largest denominations were Methodist Episcopal, Baptist, Lutheran, Episcopal, and Presbyterian. Protestants, who had made a good adaptation to rural life, showed less success in meeting the problems of an urbanized and industrialized society. A few showed concern with providing wholesome recreational activities for their members during weekdays. A few church leaders preached the social gospel and searched for remedies for inequalities, slums, and labor exploitation. The most influential prophet was Walter Rauschenbusch, who served as pastor of a small German Baptist church in a Manhattan slum. Later he became a professor at Rochester Theological Seminary, where he urged income and inheritance taxes, old-age pensions, public housing, and minimum wage laws. The social gospel appealed to younger ministers, who gradually swung many laymen from their allegiance to laissez faire.

Because Protestants relied upon the Bible as the ultimate authority, they faced difficulty in adjusting to Darwinism and the new scholarship devoted to analyzing the historical validity of Old and New Testaments. Each generation had its eminent preachers—Henry Ward Beecher, Lyman Abbott, Harry Emerson Fosdick, S. Parkes Cadman—who declared that evolution was part of God's design for his creation. Liberals emphasized divine love rather than the wrath to come.

When the liberals captured Union Theological Seminary and other ministerial training schools, conservatives counterattacked.

In 1895 the Niagara Bible Conference called for acceptance of the Scripture as the "inerrant" word of God and for a return to fundamentals in faith and theology. These "fundamentalists" sent out millions of tracts and sought to expel liberals by heresy trials.

The cultural, educational, and religious life of New York State in the past half century has continued to reflect the movements sweeping Western civilization. New York City has retained its dominant position in theater, ballet, painting, and various forms of artistic endeavor. The metropolis possesses the greatest number of important publishers, museums, foundations, galleries, concert halls, and patrons of art, and aspiring artists and performers still say, "You haven't made it till you've made it in New York."

The United States enjoyed its greatest era of literature in the years between world wars. The rebellion in thought, writing, and art that had emerged before World War I flowered and blossomed. Sinclair Lewis, F. Scott Fitzgerald, Sherwood Anderson, Theodore Dreiser, Willa Cather, Thomas Wolfe, William Faulkner, and Ernest Hemingway wrote novels with great impact, while such poets as T. S. Eliot, Ezra Pound, and Robert Frost revolutionized the writing of poetry. Note that none of these writers hailed from New York State, although most received aid and encouragement from Manhattan publishers. The muses, however, were alive, well, and living in New York State during this period, even if their votaries did not win top rank in every field. Edith Wharton continued to write. Eugene O'Neill became an adopted son and took American drama to heights never before or since reached on this continent. John Dos Passos, who spent much of his life in New York City, wrote *Manhattan Transfer* and other seminal works.

Let us turn from the national literary scene and examine authors who reflected the feelings of New Yorkers more directly or described their traditions and particular neighborhoods. In 1929, Walter Edmonds of Boonville brought out *Rome Haul*, which ushered in the upstate revival. His success opened a floodgate of novels, folklore, and history dealing with the Anglo-French conflicts, the Revolutionary War, the age of pioneering, and the Erie

Canal, the single most fascinating subject for both writers and readers. Edmonds was to set the pace and delimit the dimensions of the revival that followed. His *Drums along the Mohawk*, an artistic and popular success, refought Revolutionary campaigns through the eyes of militiamen. Edmonds concentrated on plain folk, although he later described "quality folk" in *The Boyds of Black River* (1959).

Once Edmonds had demonstrated the potentialities, writers uncovered colorful episodes in almost every section of the state. Frank O. Hough gave "bushwhackers," guerrilla fighters in Westchester County during the Revolution, their place in the historical pantheon. Roger Burlingame found Cazenovia an interesting locale for a family story. Paul Horgan used Rochester as the scene of his novel *Fault of Angels,* and Henry W. Clune's *By His Own Hand* was set in the same city. In 1936 Carl Carmer began his distinguished career as a chronicler of York State with *Listen for a Lonesome Drum*, a fascinating potpourri of folklore and history. His success led him to dig further into regional features in *The Hudson* (1939), *Dark Trees to the Wind* (1955), and *The Tavern Lights Are Burning* (1964). The last volume contains excerpts from a hundred writers, from Dutch times to the present, who have shown "awareness of place" and a feeling for York State character.

Harold Thompson presented a rich collection of ballads, folklore, and *curiosa* under the intriguing title *Body, Boots, & Britches: Folktales, Ballads, and Speech from Country New York.* During the 1940s the flow of regional novels increased, although few attracted national attention. Samuel Hopkins Adams wrote *Canal Town*, the first of several books dealing with canal life and upstate personalities. A national audience took delight in his *Grandfather Stories.* Anne Gertrude Sneller's *A Vanished World* recaptured old rural New York, a peaceful world of family farms, quiet country roads, and small towns.

During the bicentennial year hundreds of localities and organizations tried to put together accounts of their history. Many New Yorkers felt the same need to find roots that took Edmund Wilson back to his ancestral stone house in Talcottville, a tiny hamlet north of Utica. Acclaimed as America's greatest man of letters in this century, Wilson recounted in *Upstate, Records and Recollections of Northern New York* (1971) the changes in the community since his childhood. He stated: "I felt, after many years of absence, that I was visiting a foreign country but a country to which I belonged."

Meanwhile Jewish writers were coming to the fore in metropolitan New York. Abraham Cahan, the founder of the *Jewish Daily Forward*, had written the first important Jewish-American novel, *The Rise of David Levinsky*. Sholem Asch, Isaac Bashevis Singer, and others wrote stories and novels in Yiddish whose full flavor is partially lost in translation. Another gifted writer was Chaim Potok, author of *The Chosen, My Name is Asher Lev*, and other works. After several decades of neglect, critics rediscovered Henry Roth's *Call It Sleep*, a perceptive account of immigrant experience.

The Jewish community also produced a large number of intellectuals who reviewed books for magazines and newspapers, edited journals of opinion such as the *Partisan Review* and *Commentary*, and wrote biographies, histories, and other works of scholarship. Among them were Ludwig Lewisohn, Waldo Frank, George Jean Nathan, Philip Rahv, Alfred Kazin, and Irving Howe. Howe's *World of Our Fathers* (1976) is a brilliant and exhaustive analysis of the way East European Jews made their way into American society.

The black community also produced a considerable number of writers—so many, in fact, that the decade of the 1920s was called the Harlem Renaissance. James Weldon Johnson's poems called for more rights for Negroes. *Along This Way* (1933) is not only his autobiography but a history of Harlem writers. Claude McKay was another significant author. His *Harlem Shadows* voiced his contempt and defiance of discrimination. Langston Hughes, the unofficial poet laureate of Harlem, had a varied career; his poetry not only breathes defiance but celebrates the joys of life.

Ralph Ellison's *Invisible Man* (1952), written in prose both subtle and sinewy, has become a classic because of its insight into human relations. Much more strident are the books of James Baldwin, a black born and reared in New York City who has cried out against injustice. Baldwin was both prophet of the turbulent

1960s and a militant advocate of black awareness. *The Autobiography of Malcolm X*, edited by Alex Haley, described his struggle against poverty and his rage against the white world, which he transcended before his assassination. Haley's *Roots*, which was made into a gripping television miniseries in 1977, represented another major publishing event.

During the 1920s De Witt Wallace and Henry Luce founded two new magazines that became the cornerstones of publishing empires. Wallace began by condensing long articles from various magazines and then publishing the condensations in *The Reader's Digest*. Amazingly popular at home and abroad, this magazine won the largest circulation in the United States and even, in translation, in several foreign countries. Strictly middle-brow, it embodied the hopes of middle-class Americans who believed in success, motherhood, patriotism, dogs, and a sunny attitude toward life.

In 1923 Luce brought out *Time*, the first weekly news magazine, which attracted readers with its crisp and sprightly style. Luce later founded *Fortune* and *Life*, which for more than thirty years portrayed American life and world events in magnificent photographs.

The *American Mercury*, edited by Henry L. Mencken, belabored puritanism, prohibition, and the foibles of middle-class Americans. More permanent was the *New Yorker*, whose witty columns and cartoons comforted its readers that they were more sophisticated than most middle-class boors in the hinterland. Its founder, Harold Ross, announced in the first issue that his weekly was not intended for "the little old lady in Dubuque." Ironically, a majority of its subscribers have always lived outside the metropolis.

In the 1920s newspapers combined because of rising costs and expansionist impulses among publishers. Joseph Patterson, a member of the McCormick clan of Chicago, founded the *Daily News*, a tabloid aimed at office workers and workingmen. Forswearing his early flirtation with socialism, Patterson preached militant patriotism and opposed liberal reforms. The *News* elbowed Hearst's *Daily Mirror* into second place.

During the 1920s Frank Gannett began to create a chain of

newspapers that spread from Utica, Binghamton, Rochester, Albany, Elmira, and Ithaca to small cities throughout the nation. Although he granted his papers much editorial autonomy, they generally supported Republican candidates.

The prosperity following the two world wars encouraged the construction of office buildings on Manhattan Island, headquarters for corporations and banks. The Empire State Building, with 102 floors, ended the first boom. After World War II, Lever House signaled another boom, and corporations competed in finding sites and outdoing each other in size and height. The Seagram and Manufacturers Hanover Trust buildings have an elegance that subsequent crackerbox structures cannot approach. The United Nations Secretariat Building conveys a sense of simplicity and unity quite unlike the frequently jarring debates that take place within it. On lower Manhattan the World Trade Center's twin towers were completed just in time to worsen the glut in office space. Upwards of 78 million square feet of office space was built on Manhattan in the quarter century after 1949. Of course, not all building was commercial. In 1959 the Guggenheim Museum, designed by Frank Lloyd Wright, was opened. Lincoln Center for the Performing Arts contains several interesting buildings, including Philip Johnson's New York State Theater.

No doubt the most ambitious project of these years has been the Empire State Plaza, a governmental and cultural complex in Albany, the apple of former governor Nelson Rockefeller's eye. Thirty state agencies occupy eleven buildings topped by a forty-four-story office tower, tallest structure in the state outside New York City. A splendid State Library–Museum Center and two auditoriums are also included. A cloud of controversy has enveloped this project, whose delays and extravagance severely strained the state budget. Few observers have found this complex an architectural triumph.

Since the Armory Show, painting has witnessed a running battle between realism and abstractionism, the latter scorning exact representation and cherishing experiments in form and color. Each school or tendency has had many skilled practioners. A realist, Edward Hopper painted small-town Main Street scenes

Empire State Plaza, Albany. New York State Office of General Services, Promotion, and Public Affairs.

in sharply contrasting light and shadow. Abstract expressionists won increasing support and many patrons bought their works. Mrs. John D. Rockefeller founded New York City's Museum of Modern Art, which houses a fine collection of works in the newer styles.

Meanwhile the public accorded great popularity to Grandma (Anna Mary) Moses, who took up painting in her retirement years. In her primitives she recalled happy people engaged in everyday work and play in rural Washington County, close to the Vermont line.

The cultural explosion that erupted after World War II brought art to great numbers of New Yorkers. Courses in art and music appreciation proliferated in colleges, evening schools, and art centers. All museums reported ever increasing attendance and politicians even found votes in art. In 1960 Governor Rockefeller and legislators set up the State Council on the Arts, whose annual budget has usually exceeded those for art in all other states combined. Significantly, legislators did not cut the arts budget more severely than other departments during the financial crunch of 1976.

Popular music usually originated in Tin Pan Alley (not a place but a floating group of composers centered in Manhattan's Brill Building), although Nashville surfaced as the country music capital. Before 1960 most popular music heard on radio, television, and on Broadway was composed by musicians living in or near New York City. Who has not hummed snatches from tunes composed by Irving Berlin, Cole Porter, George Gershwin, and Jerome Kern? Who has not marveled at the splendid musical comedies of Richard Rodgers and Oscar Hammerstein II? Meanwhile Louis Armstrong and Duke Ellington were winning friends for jazz all over the world. The big bands of Tommy Dorsey, Benny Goodman, Guy Lombardo, and Cab Calloway set out from New York on their nationwide tours. Although jazz had its origins among New Orleans blacks, it took up residence in New York by the 1930s. Before long, Benny Goodman was giving concerts in Carnegie Hall.

Radio reached the public directly after World War I. WGY, General Electric's station in Schenectady, pioneered in broadcasting. Soon independent stations were banding together in networks that carried programs (most originating in New York studios) across the continent. The three major networks—American, Columbia, and National—had their headquarters on Manhattan Island. Radio has changed many aspects of American life. Political campaigns, for example, were transformed by Franklin D. Roosevelt's fireside chats.

The American dance world has revolved around New York City, where several dance companies offer instruction and present performances. The New York City Ballet makes the New York State Theater in Lincoln Center its home base. Most summers it moves to the Saratoga Performing Arts Center, which it shares with the Philadelphia Symphony Orchestra.

Like culture, the knowledge industry has become one of the most important in the state. If we look specifically at education, we find a tremendous expansion in all aspects, from nursery school to adult programs. Keeping pace with this expansion, school authorities carried out many curricular changes to meet the needs of urban-industrial society. Teachers expanded their methods to utilize audiovisual aids.

Schools in New York have always performed the major function of smoothing the adjustment of children of newcomers. Before World War II, Americanizing the children of immigrants preoccupied many schools in the state. After World War II, teachers found it necessary to meet the needs of children of Puerto Ricans and blacks from the rural South. Business and industry have demanded workers skilled in office and manufacturing techniques, and school programs came to include stenography, typing, machine shop, auto mechanics, and other "practical" subjects.

The district school, a workable unit for a scattered rural population in pre-automobile days, was not as suitable in cities, where districts range from wealthy to poor. In 1911 the legislature encouraged districts to combine, and within a few years most cities had adopted a centralized system. Consolidation of rural schools did not make much progress until Governor Alfred E. Smith in 1925 pushed for state aid for busing and for construction of centralized schools. During the 1930s federal public works programs accelerated the movement by constructing new buildings. Centralized schools offered many advantages: broader and more diversified curricula, auditoriums, cafeterias, laboratories, gymnasiums, and teachers who had special training in subjects ranging from music to home economics.

Before World War I, fewer than one in ten students aged fourteen and above attended high schools. During the prosperous 1920s more parents saw how important education had become in the business world. When the depression made jobs even harder to find, both parents and young people realized the value of a high school diploma. Since World War II the great majority of teenagers have attended high schools.

The postwar baby boom crested about 1960 and then began to decline, slowly at first, then sharply after 1965. In 1972, births totaled only 253,303, and about 100,000 fewer than a decade earlier. School enrollments followed the pattern of births. The number of high school graduates peaked in 1975–1976, then began an inexorable decline. Contraction proved even more painful than expansion. The new schools built and teachers hired in the 1950s and 1960s suddenly found themselves underutilized, and school systems began closing old schools and failing to replace teachers who retired.

The cost of education has greatly outpaced enrollments. Expenditures rose from almost $44 million in 1903–1904 to $563 million in 1950–1951, and then to $7 billion in 1975–1976. Yet state aid to education declined. While the state has been rapidly increasing its expenditures for social services, health, housing, and urban renewal, it has increasingly shifted the educational burden to local districts. During the early 1970s almost half of local school budgets were voted down by taxpayers angry about yearly tax increases.

The citizens of the Empire State have spent more money per capita on education than other states, with mixed results. The much maligned school administrators noted that in 1976 New York State, with 9 percent of the nation's high school students, won 17 percent of the National Merit Scholarship commendations and had 33 percent of the finalists in the Westinghouse Talent Search and Science examinations.[8]

A handful of young people attended colleges and universities before World War I. Only 3,403 degrees were awarded in 1904. Private institutions dominated the academic firmament, with Columbia and Cornell enjoying international reputations for their schools of medicine, law, engineering, architecture, and liberal arts. The state government restricted itself to training teachers in its eleven normal schools and to operating colleges specializing in agriculture and home economics in Ithaca, forestry in Syracuse, and ceramics in Alfred, and several two-year institutes offering agricultural and technical training. New York City opened City College in 1847, and later added many more units that were combined to form City University in 1961.

During the 1920s college enrollments doubled, and they kept on increasing until World War II snatched most of the young men into the armed forces. Hundreds of thousands of veterans took advantage of the GI Bill of Rights, under which they received grants for tuition and subsistence. Because existing institutions could not handle the flood of students, the legislature set up a commission, chaired by Owen D. Young, to study the state's needs for higher education. After much discussion and deliberation, Young issued a report calling for a state university that would take over existing state colleges. It also recommended subventions to communities that established two-year colleges. The State University of New York expanded rapidly, perhaps too rapidly, and by 1976 had a greater number of units (sixty-four), including thirty community colleges and 342,855 full- and part-time students, than California's famous system. Meanwhile New York City's large public system was expanding rapidly. In 1970 City University of New York adopted "open admissions," under which any graduate of a New York City high school could attend a unit of CUNY. The state increased its contribution to CUNY, and at the same time asserted more control. During the financial crunch following 1975 CUNY had to end its tradition of free tuition, cut back on enrollments, and raise its admissions standards. Full-time undergraduates, numbering about 132,000 in 1975, were expected to fall to 105,000 in 1980.

College enrollments broke all records after World War II, with major gains taking place in the public sector. The most remarkable gain occurred in two-year community colleges, whose enrollments jumped tenfold between 1956 and 1975. But private colleges and universities also expanded, at least until 1969. Thereafter rising costs of construction and borrowing discouraged expansion. Moreover, admission officers warned that the available pool of students would decline in the 1980s. Although officials of private and public colleges maintained a public front of harmony, the friends of private colleges complained that low tuition charges in public institutions were undercutting private institutions, some of which were approaching bankruptcy. Legislators increased grants for each bachelor's, master's, and doctor's degree awarded, and also increased the amounts of awards granted to students. In 1976 more than 348,000 students received well over $135 million in scholarships, fellowships, and similar awards.

Graduate education and professional schools expanded rapidly in the 1960s. In 1975, almost 64,000 full-time students were attending graduate schools, and twice that number of part-time students. The majority of these students attended private institutions, which attracted students from all over the world. The most prestigious institutions—Columbia, Cornell, Rochester—boasted faculties well known for their research and publications.

In 1976 New York State ranked first among major states in the proportion of women attending undergraduate and graduate institutions of higher learning. A combination of state and federal programs and vigorous efforts by colleges and universities has also greatly increased the number of students from minority families.[9] In 1975, over 16 percent of the freshmen enrolled were from minority families, a figure that actually exceeds the minority representation among the state's fifteen-to-nineteen-year-olds. This achievement was unmatched by any other state with a sizable minority population. The end of open admissions at CUNY may cause this percentage to decline.

The religious history of New York since the 1920s continues earlier trends and reflects national developments. During the prosperous 1920s many new churches were constructed, especially in the suburbs. Of course, the depression brought hard times for churches.

A remarkable resurgence took place after World War II. The brutalities of war, the Holocaust, and the threat of atomic destruction weakened people's faith in progress and human goodness. No doubt the quest for identity among second-generation immigrants took many New Yorkers back to their religious origins. Thousands more joined churches in order to associate with the "best people" and to become part of suburban society. The baby boom led parents to join churches because they wanted their children to be exposed to religious instruction.

Seeking solace from anxiety and insecurity, many New Yorkers turned to writers and preachers who offered self-confidence and heightened powers through prayer and "positive thinking." Rabbi Joshua Liebman's popular *Peace of Mind* (1946) was followed by Monsignor Fulton J. Sheen's *Peace of Soul*. Norman Vincent Peale, from his Madison Avenue pulpit, preached a doctrine of "positive thinking" and wrote a series of books on it. Even Tin Pan Alley came up with such songs as "I Believe" and "The Man Upstairs."

Orthodoxy, too, had its spokesmen, perhaps the most notable being Billy Graham, who reached thousands with his crusades. The "neo-orthodoxy" of Reinhold Neibuhr and Paul Tillich, both of whom held chairs at Union Theological Seminary, became popular among younger clergymen. Jacques Maritain of France exerted great influence upon Catholics and intellectuals.

By the mid-1960s the religious revival tapered off for several reasons. When clergymen joined the struggle for civil rights and the peace movement, they annoyed many laymen. Young people, at least a good number of them, came to believe that mysticism, astrology, and Oriental magic, not to mention drugs, could lead one to ultimate truth more readily than either science or faith. In 1969, hundreds of thousands of young people assembled in a field at Woodstock (actually nearer Bethel) for a strange meeting that combined aspects of religious exaltation with a drug trip and rock festival. Pentacostalism won thousands of followers, even among traditional Protestants and Roman Catholics. The Jehovah's Witnesses filled Yankee Stadium with their followers.

Roman Catholics experienced a greater upheaval than other groups. Pope John XXIII extended the right hand of reconciliation to other Christian bodies, and convened the first Vatican council in several decades. The council brought about many changes, notably the use of English in liturgy and greater participation in ecumenical activities. Some priests, such as the Berrigan brothers from the Syracuse area, took a leading part in the peace movement and civil rights crusade.

New York's Jewish community dominated Judaism in the state by sheer weight of numbers. During the ethnic revival of the 1960s the Jewish Defense League sprang up. The Holocaust and threats to Israel's existence sent shock waves through Jewish circles, and Jews gave hundreds of millions of dollars to assist their beleaguered coreligionists. An interesting development was the revival of orthodoxy among young Jews, many of whom, like other Americans, sought self-identity.

The cultural patterns. educational progress, and religious development of New Yorkers thus form a rich tapestry of variegated colors and textures. Outsiders have often criticized New Yorkers for their worship of money and success. A fair shot, but New Yorkers have also chased the dollar in order to spend it—for self-improvement and for those less fortunate as well as for good times. They have prized money but they have also cherished values of mind and spirit. Culture and compassion therefore rank with commercialism and conviviality in setting the tone of life for New Yorkers.

8 | *Upstate versus Downstate*

"Statehood for New York City is an idea whose time has come."[1] So stated Bella Abzug, the former Manhattan congresswoman whose large droopy hats are the cartoonists' delight. Her slogan of 1971 had been anticipated two years earlier, when writer Norman Mailer ran for mayor of New York on the platform of cutting ties with Albany. Soon *New York* magazine carried a ballot asking its subscribers to vote for or against the establishment of the metropolis as the fifty-first state. As expected, the results were overwhelmingly favorable. These outcries from New York City were only another illustration of the century-old conflict between the metropolis and the countryside.

Perhaps the classic expression was made by George Washington Plunkitt, the genial "philosopher" of Tammany Hall, who recounted his observations in 1905: "The feeling between this city and the hayseeds that make a livin' by plunderin' it is every bit as bitter as the feelin' between the North and South before the war."[2] He explained the ill feeling and the reason it existed:

The Republican Legislature and Governor run the whole shootin' match. We've got to eat and drink, and have got to choose our time for eatin' and drinkin' to suit them. If they don't feel like takin' a glass of beer on Sunday we must abstain. . . . We've got to regulate our whole lives to suit them. And then we have to pay their taxes to boot.[3]

Upstate—an imprecise term applied to any area within the state, rural or urban, outside the boundaries of New York City, whether east to Montauk Point, north to Rouses Point, or west to Dunkirk—has provided a Republican majority since 1856. The citizens of New York City have voted strongly Democratic since 1800. Nationwide, the Democratic party usually has attracted a majority of city dwellers, especially Roman Catholics, factory workers, and recent immigrants and their children. This generalization has held for cities in such states as Massachusetts, Pennsylvania, Ohio, Michigan, and Illinois.[4] Although upstate cities have populations similar to those of other states, their Democratic vote has been markedly lower. The most plausible explanation for this divergent voting pattern is that many upstaters, though of recent immigrant stock and employed in manufacturing, have thrown their votes to the Republican party as a counterweight to the Democratic majority in the metropolis. At any rate, upstate politicians have campaigned on the platform of keeping state funds out of the hands of Tammany Hall, a tactic that seems to swing thousands of votes. This political feud has undoubtedly kept alive and periodically awakened other issues normally dormant.

Upstaters have found much to criticize about the metropolis: its wasteful habits, its alien character, its wicked people. One upstate delegate to the constitutional convention of 1894 referred to New York City as "a sewer of ignorance and corruption flowing in upon it from foreign lands." Texas-born Stanley Walker, an editor of the *New York Tribune*, in 1935 captured some of the suspicious feelings of New Yorkers north of the Bronx and west of the Hudson. According to Walker, these citizens assume that "every other citizen is either a pickpocket or a sybarite, a con man or a Good-Time Charlie. . . . The City reeks with Jews, Catholics, atheists, communists, nudists, Republicans, Public Enemies, chow dogs, Rolls-Royces, and Heywood Broun."[5] No doubt if Walker were alive today, he would add Puerto Ricans, gays, women's libbers, and blacks. Herbert J. Gans, a distinguished sociologist, observed in 1975 that "New York is . . . America's principal poorhouse, innovator, dissident, creditor, playboy, and stripper, and the rest of the country is reluctant to admit to itself that it uses or needs these things."[6]

A mixture of pride and envy, of alternate fascination and revulsion, has characterized upstaters' attitudes toward their huge neighbor, at once both their ward and their master. This love–hate relationship has been alive and well for more than three centuries.

As early as the administration of Peter Stuyvesant, Yankee

farmers in the towns of Westchester and Long Island protested against the arbitrary rule of the Dutch West India Company in New Amsterdam. Since that time, "upstate hicks" and "city slickers" have disagreed more or less vigorously over issues as varied as the opening of beer parlors on Sunday, the allocation of state funds to the localities, and the inclusion of cows, so Democrats have claimed, in the population figures of upstate counties whenever legislative districts are to be apportioned.

Before 1800, agrarian and commercial interests were the major antagonists. The merchants of Manhattan disagreed with farmers over taxes, trade regulations, and the like. Lieutenant Governor George Clarke observed in 1738 that merchants had tried to get rid of import duties "by laying some tax on lands, but the Country members are too great a Majority against it."[7] The representatives of the farmers favored liberal issues of paper money, which disturbed the merchants and creditors of New York City.

Probably the most interesting quarrel took place in the last quarter of the seventeenth century. In 1679 the governor and council granted to the millers of New York City exclusive right to mill and pack flour and biscuits for export. The purpose was to establish higher standards for New York flour and thereby increase the demand in the West Indies. The country millers were angry about the monopoly granted the millers of Manhattan, and the shipowners of Long Island disliked the requirement that all trade must funnel through New York port. During Leisler's rebellion in 1689 they succeeded in winning the repeal of these monopoly rights. After the rebellion had been put down, the new governor regranted the monopoly, but in 1695 upcountry members pushed through repeal of the measure.

The American Revolution split downstate from upstate. In September 1776 Sir William Howe captured New York City and turned it into a Loyalist stronghold for seven years. As the war dragged on, thousands of Tories from up and down the seaboard and from the interior fled behind British lines. Meanwhile the countryside, with the exceptions of Long Island and parts of Westchester County, swung solidly behind the Continentals. Indian and Tory raids on frontier settlements stiffened upstate resistance to British rule.

The cleavage continued after British troops had departed. Governor George Clinton, hailing from Ulster County and drawing most of his support from farmers, favored drastic measures against Tories. Alexander Hamilton and more conservative whigs defended Loyalists from proscription, partly because of family ties but partly because of fear of agrarian radicalism. After several heated elections the conservatives won this battle and by 1787 had restored Tories to most of their rights as citizens.

Ratification of the Constitution split the state along sectional as well as economic lines. Federalists, relying largely on businessmen and large landlords, were eager to establish a strong central government capable of maintaining American prestige abroad and of preserving property rights at home. George Clinton's followers opposed strong government and feared the power of the aristocracy. Hamilton did not give up the fight after Clinton won a good majority of the delegates to the Poughkeepsie convention. Federalists used the threat of secession to persuade moderate Clintonians not to reject ratification. John Jay wrote to George Washington in 1787: "An idea has taken air that the southern part of the State will at all events, adhere to the Union; and if necessary to that end, seek a separation from the northern."[8]

After 1800 the upstate–downstate conflict became more complex as both sections underwent changes as a result of heavy immigration, the expansion of transportation, and the growth of manufacturing. New York City evolved into the nation's economic capital, dominating finance, foreign trade, and domestic commerce. It also began to supplant Boston in various aspects of the nation's cultural life: publishing, theater, fine arts, music, and writing. The more New York City took on the role of economic and cultural capital for the nation, the less concern it evinced for upstate.

Upstate New York experienced equally revolutionary changes after 1800. By 1900 a majority of upstaters were living in the "industrial streak" fringing the Hudson River and stretching across the state from Albany to Buffalo. Italians, Poles, and other newcomers flooded into the urban centers and made them appear almost as cosmopolitan as New York City itself. Most immi-

Poestenkill, a village near Troy, in 1862. Oil on wood by Joseph Hidley. New York State Historical Association, Cooperstown.

Cohoes textile mill, one of the many that sprang up in New York's river valleys in the late nineteenth century. New York State Office of Parks and Recreation.

grants came from rural sections of Europe and harbored a distrust of metropolitan life.

During the last century and a half, several critical issues have recurrently caused friction: the proper distribution of representation in the legislature, control of the liquor traffic, "home rule" for New York City, allocation of state tax revenues, and state control of the city's finances.

Apportionment has often led to wrangling between various sections of the state. For example, the ultraconservative James Kent, chancellor of the State of New York, in his last-ditch defense of the aristocracy in the constitutional convention of 1821, denounced manhood suffrage as subversive of property rights. In his speech he pointed to New York City: "It is rapidly swelling into an unwieldy population and with the burdensome pauperism, of an European metropolis . . . and in less than a century, that city . . . will govern this state."[9]

Perhaps the clearest example of discrimination came in the constitutional convention of 1894. Elihu Root and other Republican leaders were fearful that the rapid growth of New York City would mean Democratic control of state government. Root devised the formula that no two counties divided by a river (obviously he was referring to Manhattan and Brooklyn) could ever have one-half of the Senate seats. Further, each of the sixty-two counties except Hamilton and Fulton, which shared one seat, was to have at least one member in the Assembly. This system served its purpose: to win Republican control of both houses in most elections until the 1960s.

A delegate from Utica in the 1894 convention got carried away with defiance of New York City:

I tell you, gentlemen, you who represent that great city, that when the time comes, when your streets are filled with those who defy the law, when socialists, when those who believe in no government, are parading your streets, and destroying your property and killing your citizens, then you will cry for help. And to whom? You will then turn your eyes to the green fields of Oneida and Herkimer and Jefferson and St. Lawrence. . . . You will expect us to respond to the call, and we will.[10]

The constitutional convention of 1915 tackled the question of apportionment, on which the delegates were divided. The population upsurge in Queens and the Bronx disturbed many upstaters, who concluded that the restrictive clause in the constitution of 1894 would not prevent New York City from getting a majority. A Republican-controlled committee proposed that Greater New York should never have more than half of the representatives in the legislature. This proposal angered Democratic leaders, including Alfred E. Smith and Robert Wagner. Smith upheld the record of New York City representatives in voting funds for roads, health, education, and canals in upstate counties, even though most state revenues came from the metropolis. Noting the "constitutional majority" enjoyed by Republicans upstate, Smith declared: "I propose to show that every time we danced together, the New York chickens have been stepped on by the upstate donkey." Delegate William Sheehan of New York City hinted that unless the city received fair treatment, its citizens would join a movement to form a separate state.

The 1915 debate did not lead anywhere, since the voters turned down the revisions suggested by the convention. Since 1894 Republicans have retained control of both houses in most elections, although the people have elected several Democratic governors. In 1950, for example, New York City, with a majority of the population, had only 92 legislators, as compared with 114 for upstate.

The Supreme Court settled the question of apportionment by deciding in 1964 that representation in both Senate and Assembly must be on the basis of one man, one vote. As a subject for complaint, discrimination has given way to gerrymandering, the drawing of district lines in such a way as to maximize the number of seats the majority party can carry. Minorities have claimed that politicians have drawn lines so as to minimize the voting impact of blacks, Puerto Ricans, and others. The courts have made some rulings in this area. One court held that districts could be redrawn to permit ethnic minorities to have a chance to elect one of their own members.

Control of liquor has often led to squabbles in the legislature. Since the days of the redoubtable Governor Wouter van Twiller, residents of New York City have earned a reputation for tippling without fear and without restraint. In 1726 Cadwallader Colden attacked excessive drinking as undermining morals and sapping the economy. Alcohol addiction increased in post-Revolutionary years. Some observers estimated there was a "groggery" for every dozen individuals. Illegal liquor shops sprang up along the wharves. A surprisingly large number of taverns fringed roads, turnpikes, and canals. Peddlers hawked whiskey and rum for as little as twenty-five cents a gallon.

The native taste for strong drink was reinforced by the influx of whiskey-drinking Irish and beer-drinking Germans during the 1840s and 1850s. Meanwhile the temperance movement was winning thousands of converts among evangelical Protestants on farms, in villages, and among the urban middle class. By the 1840s it had become a crusade. In 1854 the drys huzzaed when their candidate, Myron Clark, won the governor's office, and the next year the legislature passed a prohibition statute over protests by the mayor and representatives of New York City. One reporter claimed that some German citizens were so enraged that they were forming a military unit to resist enforcement. Tension eased, however, when the Court of Appeals struck down the law.

The legislature rushed through a law that became the basis of liquor regulation for the next forty years. It provided for local option; that is, boards elected by voters in town or county could determine the number of licenses to be issued. The Republicans generally favored few licenses and high fees; Democrats opposed restrictions of any kind.

In 1866 a Republican legislature passed the Metropolitan Excise Act, forbidding retailing of spirits in Kings and New York counties without a license. Provisions for high fees and a ban on Sunday openings of saloons infuriated many Germans, for whom a visit to the beer parlor on Sunday to listen to music and meet friends was a high spot of the week. Democratic politicians charged that New York City was singled out for special treatment and that a Republican-dominated Board of Health had the crucial power to hand out valuable licenses. In 1870 a modification of the excise laws was spirited through the legislature. Governor John T. Hoffman, Tweed's pliant tool, arranged that New York City could fix its own excise rates.

Meanwhile the drys organized a Prohibition party, largely to bludgeon Republicans into respecting their wishes. They kept denouncing not only New York City but upstate centers as well for permitting saloons to remain open on Sunday. The *Lancaster Star* of July 31, 1879, noted that "every saloon in the city [Buffalo] is open from 6 o'clock Sunday morning till 12 at night and the noise of their drunken occupants is forced upon the ear of Christian families on their way to church."

Probably the most famous battle over Sunday closing took place in New York City after Theodore Roosevelt was appointed police commissioner. No prohibitionist, Roosevelt nevertheless insisted on enforcement of the law. He also wanted to end the payment of "protection" money to policemen by saloonkeepers. After many dramatic events that won him nationwide publicity, Roosevelt resigned his office to go to Washington. This struggle stirred up prohibitionists, and Republicans insisted upon Sunday closing as one of their planks in the 1895 campaign.

Rural legislators passed the Raines Law in 1896 in order to cut down consumption of alcoholic beverages and to reduce the political influences of the saloonkeepers, willing servants of Tammany Hall. The law called for high fees, local option, and Sunday closing of taverns, though hotels were permitted to serve liquor with meals on Sunday. In an attempt to meet the hotel requirement, many saloonkeepers took to renting rooms upstairs. In some cases these quarters became brothels, a development that confirmed upstate convictions about the wickedness of New Yorkers.

In the twentieth century, citizens of upstate counties pushed through ratification of the Eighteenth Amendment over the opposition of New York City. During the 1920s citizens of New York City flouted prohibition by patronizing thousands of speakeasies, and rallied behind Alfred E. Smith, who became the symbol of opposition to the dry cause. With their many allies in upstate cities, they approved repeal of the Eighteenth Amendment by a handsome majority.

Gradually the idea of a "Continental Sunday" spread over the state, rippling out from New York City and other large urban centers into the smaller cities and finally into the countryside. No doubt the popularization of automobiles was fully as important as the mores of the metropolis in breaking down the "Puritan Sunday." During the 1920s many small towns held spirited elections on the question of whether police should shut down Sunday baseball and motion pictures. In this century-long struggle over liquor, the traditions of the countryside have yielded to the customs of New York City and its cosmopolitan population, who found many allies in Buffalo and other large centers upstate.

The citizens of New York City have demanded home rule not only in regulating liquor but in governing their own affairs. Almost every generation of city fathers has attacked the legislature and the governor for interfering in municipal affairs and for usurping purely local functions. In 1953 Council President Rudolph Halley accused Governor Thomas E. Dewey of trying to make City Hall into Uncle Tom's Cabin.

The most bitter fight took place in the decade before the Civil War. New York City had fallen into the hands of grafting and bungling officials, and the city charter, by distributing authority to department heads elected by the people, made it difficult to fix responsibility.[11] The mayor found his hands tied. Traction interests contributed to venality by buying franchises for horsecar routes from the Common Council and Board of Aldermen. No doubt city government and its corrupt officials deserved censure from upstaters, although similar troubles in upstate cities and in the legislature took the edge off their charges.

In 1855 the Republican party had emerged and drawn to itself most of the old Whigs and some of the free-soil elements in the Democratic party. The rekindling of the temperance and prohibition crusades drew into Republican ranks upstaters of Yankee stock who believed government should enforce morality upon New Yorkers. Capturing control of the legislature, Republican leaders decided to punish New York City for its sins, not the least of which was its loyalty to the Democratic party. Republicans distrusted the metropolitan population with its strong Irish and German contingents, its increasing number of Roman Catholics under forceful Archbishop John Hughes, its opposition to prohibition, and its opposition to limiting slavery in Kansas and other territories.

The Republicans weakened the political machine of Mayor

Fernando Wood by placing control of police, parks, and other functions under new boards appointed by the governor. In 1857 Central Park was placed under an eleven-man board independent of the mayor, although the city paid its bills. The legislature also created a bipartisan Board of County Supervisors to take over several functions from the Common Council, which was controlled by the Democrats. The supervisors created the Metropolitan Police District of the State of New York for the counties of New York, Kings, Westchester, and Richmond. Five commissioners appointed by the governor exercised full police powers. Again, New York City had to supply the money.

Mayor Wood denounced these proposals and refused to disband his police, nicknamed the Municipals. Governor John King appointed George Walling as head of the Metropolitans, and Walling tried to arrest Wood for failure to obey an order of the governor. Wood replied: "I do not recognize the legality of the service or existence of the Metropolitan Police. I will not submit to arrest . . . or concede that you are an officer at all."[12]

Wood signaled his police guard to throw the intruders out of City Hall, and a pitched battle followed when fifty Metropolitans stormed the building. Badly mauled by Wood's men, the Metropolitans retreated and appealed to General Sandford, commanding officer of the Seventh Regiment. Sandford promptly led his forces to City Hall and forced Wood to agree to a truce. Both forces were to patrol the streets until the Court of Appeals could determine the proper authority.

Citizens were shocked to see members of the rival policy fighting each other on the streets while criminals robbed citizens in broad daylight. A state of near anarchy lasted nearly all summer. On July 4 and 5 two gangs known as the Dead Rabbits and the Bowery Boys rioted. At the height of the riot almost a thousand men were swinging pitchforks and axes and hurling paving stones and brickbats. When the Metropolitans tried to restore order, the rival gangs banded together and drove them back. Finally General Sandford sent in the 8th and 71st Regiments with fixed bayonets.

Wood disbanded the Municipals after the court upheld the governor's power over the police, but he continued to charge

Albany with responsibility for the "demoralized and feeble" state of municipal government. In January 1861 Wood made a dramatic proposal for a "free city." He asserted that New York City should not take part in an assault on "our aggrieved brethren of the slave states." Wood, a supporter of John Breckinridge at the Democratic convention, ardently supported states' rights and bitterly opposed the abolition of slavery. He realized, as did many important merchants, that much of the prosperity of the seaport rested upon its trade with the southern states.

In his amazing message to the Common Council on January 7, Wood recounted the long record of legislative attacks on home rule. He bewailed loss of control over the police, Central Park, the Alms House Department, and the harbor board. "It is, however, folly to disguise the fact that judging from the past, New York may have more cause of apprehension from the aggressive legislature of our own state than from external dangers. . . . Our city occupies the position of a conquered province entirely dependent on the will of a distant, and to our wants and wishes, an indifferent and alien government."[13]

Wood called several conferences of prominent merchants at his residence to discuss strategy, but nothing came of them. The firing on Fort Sumter put a temporary end to "independence" talk on Manhattan Island.

The United States Supreme Court has consistently held that cities are "mere creatures" of the state, with only those powers explicitly granted in their charters. New York State did not grant general powers of local self-government for municipalities until 1913. Not until ten years later did an amendment to the constitution embody home rule protections.

Citizens of New York City have persistently complained that they have contributed more in taxes to the state government, not to mention the federal government, than they have received back in aid. In 1969 the Citizens Budget Committee issued a long and objective report that deplored the "short-changing" argument as basically irrelevant and self-defeating. But what politician could resist this argument, especially when he had to raise local taxes or deny salary increases to city workers? Besides, the charge had validity, especially before 1964, if only because New York City did not have a proportionate share of legislative seats. Two areas where New York City failed to receive a fair deal come readily to mind. Whereas New York City erected and supported a costly university system, New York State was supporting normal schools and later the immense State University of New York without levies on localities. And whereas New York City, like other municipalities, had to take care of its own roads, New York State built many upstate highways and made matching grants to counties and townships for roads.

In the 1930s Mayor Fiorello La Guardia found it easier to se-cure federal funds for roads, hospitals, bridges, and other public works than to secure state money. During the 1960s President Lyndon B. Johnson's war on poverty funneled a good deal of money directly to cities, but this source began to dry up toward the end of the Vietnam war. Presidents Richard Nixon and Gerald Ford tried to reduce the amount of aid to cities and en-dorsed the program of revenue sharing.

Although officials of New York City devoted much of their energies to securing federal funds, they did not diminish their efforts in Albany. Mayor William O'Dwyer stressed "short-changing" in the postwar years. He pointed out that in 1950–1951 New York City provided roughly 60 percent of the state's total revenues but got back less than half in local assistance. Finding this issue a fine political gambit, O'Dwyer encouraged the formation of a committee to study the question. The Haig-Shoup Finance Project concluded that New York City was not the victim of discrimination. The issue did not die, however, for in 1953 City Budget Director Abraham Beame repeated the charge.

In 1959 Mayor Robert Wagner accused the state of "plucking the New York City tax payers at a rate never equalled in the State's history."[14] He claimed (all these statistics are highly sus-pect) that the city provided 55 percent of the state's tax income but received only 38 percent of state aid. Worse still, the legisla-ture rejected his proposal for a tax on off-track betting and stock transfers. In a gesture of defiance, the City Council voted 23 to 1 to set up a committee to weigh secession. Another empty gesture.

Norman Mailer's campaign for the Democratic nomination for

mayor again raised the financial issue in 1969. If New York City became a separate state, it could keep all the tax money it paid to the state and in addition receive a proportional share of federal grants in aid. A careful examination by the Citizens Budget Commission in 1969 showed that the city got back almost as much as its citizens paid to the state, and if current trends continued, New York City would receive more money than it paid to Albany.

Several factors account for the rapid rise in state aid to New York City during the 1970s. The social programs of Governor Rockefeller not only brought in increased state funds but also required the city to match funds for many of these programs. Meanwhile hundreds of thousands of poor people (blacks, Puerto Ricans, West Indians, and others) were moving into the metropolis while thousands of middle-class whites were leaving for the suburbs, eroding the city's tax base and raising costs for social services. Between 1962–1963 and 1972–1973, the expense budget rose from $2.7 billion to $9.4 billion. Whereas in 1962–1963 state and federal funds paid 26.5 percent of the city's expense budget, ten years later they accounted for 46.4 percent. Clearly New York City was becoming increasingly dependent on its outside guarantors. Whenever state or federal authorities changed their policies and cut funds, the city fathers had to make readjustments, sometimes drastic ones. No wonder the United Federation of Teachers of New York City had full-time lobbyists in both Washington and Albany.

Despite his willingness to approve more funds for New York City, Governor Rockefeller became involved in a slashing brawl with Mayor John Lindsay.[15] Patricians and liberal Republicans, both men had considerable abilities but even greater political ambitions. Each hoped that his interest in and remedy for the urban crisis might win him a chance at the White House. When Lindsay denounced Rockefeller for giving in to the demands of the garbage workers in 1968, Rockefeller felt that this attack hurt his quest for the Republican nomination, and retaliated by refusing to endorse Lindsay's bid for reelection the next year. Lindsay in turn endorsed Arthur Goldberg, Rockefeller's Democratic opponent in the gubernatorial campaign of 1970.

Meanwhile Lindsay organized an alliance of the mayors of the six largest cities to lobby for more urban aid. By getting their support, he was able to secure more aid for New York City. When legislative leaders forced cuts in the state budget in 1971, they and Rockefeller cut back on aid to localities despite the outcry of Lindsay and other mayors. Freezing Lindsay out of the negotiations over the tax package for the city, Rockefeller charged him with running his administration in an "inept and extravagant" fashion. Incensed by Rockefeller's hostility, Lindsay countered: "We've been raped, but we're being charged with prostitution."[16] Rockefeller more sedately observed:

In the past, New York City was a very progressive center. It achieved standards in social awareness and competence long before the state did. But the state now has the efficiency and competence and is under less local political pressure than the city. So now we've reversed 100 years of tradition and the state will bring New York City under state regulation and supervision. This is a little traumatic.[17]

Traumatic indeed was the experience of Mayor Beame in 1975, when a huge deficit pushed the municipality to the brink of bankruptcy. The bankers refused to lend the city any more money until officials straightened out its finances, which meant a sharp reduction of city employees.

A combination of factors had brought the metropolis to its knees: the recession of the early 1970s; the loss of more than 400,000 jobs in less than five years; rising costs of welfare and other social services; high salaries won by policemen, firemen, teachers, sanitation workers, and other civil servants; extravagant pensions allowing civil servants to retire after relatively short terms of employment; refusal by the state government, itself in financial straits, to increase grants; lack of confidence in city budgetmaking. In passing we should note that Buffalo and Yonkers were in equally precarious financial plight.

New York City's crisis, however, was preeminently a political one. New forces—the Democratic reform clubs, the school-integration movement, the civil service unions—destroyed the old political balance. Political leaders were unable and unwilling to restrain demands for more services, positions, and salary increases. By 1975 the cumulative short-term debt had risen to

$5.3 billion. In 1965 retirement costs had been $364 million; by 1976 they had reached over $2.3 billion. Annual debt service payments rose fivefold in the same period.

The joyride ended when taxpayers and bondholders declared what in effect was a strike against the city. In May 1975, Republican legislators, who represented primarily the middle-income homeowners of Queens and Staten Island, refused to vote for legislation granting additional taxing authority to the city. The major banks, which had formerly earned handsome commissions floating city bonds, refused to buy any more of them. In fact, they unloaded almost $3 billion of securities, which helped to break the market. Civil service unions organized demonstrations before bank doors and ostentatiously withdrew their funds from the National City Bank. Sanitation men refused to collect garbage and threatened to turn Fun City into Stink City.

The banks faced a dilemma. Unless the city could borrow, it could not redeem its old notes and bonds. If the city defaulted, its securities in bank portfolios would lose their value. Not only were the reputations of bankers at stake (their real estate trusts and foreign loans had also gone sour), but their institutions might face lawsuits by irate bondholders. In 1977 a report by the Security Exchange Commission staff severely criticized bankers and underwriters for "deception" in selling securities to the public.

Faced with bankruptcy, Mayor Beame and bankers appealed to Washington for loans. President Ford's refusal inspired the *New York Daily News* to run its famous headline: "Ford to City: Drop Dead." Finally Ford and Congress relented, but the loan gave the Secretary of the Treasury much power over the city budget.

Ironically the crisis gave bankers, themselves partially to blame, a dominant influence in municipal affairs. Governor Hugh Carey, a former Democratic congressman from Brooklyn, called on four businessmen to devise a scheme to prevent bankruptcy. The committee hammered out a plan for a Municipal Assistance Corporation that would convert up to $3 billion of short-term debt into long-term bonds, secured by sales and stock exchange taxes. "Big Mac," as the agency was called, would also demand cuts in expenditures, dismissal of thousands of employees, and sound accounting procedures.

An Emergency Financial Control Board urged the city to freeze salary increases and to eliminate more than 50,000 employees, almost one-fifth of the labor force. It required drastic cuts in youth services, compensatory higher education, and addiction services, which hired large numbers of blacks and Puerto Ricans. Because of their low participation in voting and lack of seniority, these minorities bore the brunt of staff reduction. Victor Gotbaum, who represented more city workers than any other leader, and Albert Shanker, head of the teachers' union, managed to soften the blows on their membership only by agreeing to invest over $2 billion of their pension funds in city securities.

These moves by Governor Carey and the legislature continued earlier steps taken by Albany officials to whittle down New York City's home rule. The legislature under the prompting of Governor Rockefeller set up an inspector general for social services whose function was to expose laxity and corruption in welfare programs. Rockefeller also appointed a special prosecutor to deal with corruption in the Criminal Justice System in New York's five boroughs. The State Budget Office set up a Program Evaluation Unit to monitor efficiency of officials and effectiveness of various programs. When the City University system's policy of open admissions rapidly increased the cost to the state, which paid half the bill, Rockefeller forced a reorganization of the New York City Board of Higher Education in order to influence its decisions. The board, several of whose members were now appointed by the governor and the Senate, promptly ended the long tradition of free tuition at the City University.

Rockefeller's administration entered several additional areas formerly left to the city, among them mass transit, commuter railroads, middle-income housing, industrial development, public college assistance, hospitals, and nursing home construction. The State Urban Development Corporation enjoyed at the start complete power to enter cities and ignore local regulations as to zoning and building codes. When the UDC proposed putting low-income housing in suburban areas, it stirred up a hornet's nest. As a result the legislature granted to communities a thirty-day grace period during which they could veto such projects.

The process of retrenchment following the crisis of 1975 reduced home rule still further. Federal and state officials scrutinized the city's budget in order to pare expenditures. When Edward Koch won the mayoralty election in 1977 he faced a shortfall of a half-billion dollars in the next fiscal year and the renewed demands of municipal unions whose contracts were coming up for review.

Rural folk and city dwellers in many countries and over many centuries have viewed each other with fear and suspicion. One finds this feud even among fairly homogeneous peoples; the French have witnessed a long struggle between Paris and the provinces. But the sharp differences—racial, religious, cultural, political—between New York City and upstate have aggravated the normal urban–rural cleavages.

Before 1900 New York was a strongly Roman Catholic city while the countryside, villages, and small cities of upstate were strongly Protestant. Subsequently the influx of Jews and later of blacks reduced the proportion of Roman Catholics to a little less than half. At the same time that Catholic influence was declining in New York City, the immigration of Italians, Poles, and other Continental Europeans into upstate centers raised the proportion of Catholics in almost every upstate city to well over half. The concentration of the foreign-born in New York City for well over a century created tensions with citizens of native stock. They differed on many matters: prohibition, Sunday observance, gambling, state aid to parochial schools, politics. The strong allegiance to the Democratic party by metropolitan New Yorkers was matched in intensity by the Republicanism of upstaters, who made loyalty to the GOP a matter of secular faith.

Population changes in the twentieth century have continued to create tension and disagreement. New York City has well over 80 percent of the state's Jews and blacks and over 90 percent of the Spanish-speaking and Oriental peoples. The growing numbers and the distinctive life-styles of these people puzzle, disturb, and occasionally irritate a large number of upstaters, including those who live in fairly large centers. Conversely, the intellectual elites in the big city have tended to treat upstaters as benighted yokels led by small-bore politicians, while the city's blue-collar workers believe that upstaters are unsympathetic to their needs and aspirations.

The dominant trend since the end of World War II has been suburban growth. Thousands of New Yorkers have moved to communities on the cities' fringes from the farms as well as from the inner cities. Industrial plants and shopping centers have followed them. The growth of suburbia leads one to believe that the typical and most influential New Yorker of the future will be neither a hick nor a city slicker but a suburbanite. Perhaps this trend will soften the old conflict between the metropolis and upstate.

9

The Politics of Diversity

The labyrinthine windings of New York politics have baffled outsiders, perplexed citizens, and puzzled participants in every generation. Politics in the Empire State has not only mirrored diverse ethnic, religious, and racial identities but reflected sectional conflicts and economic interests. Testy John Adams once described New York politics as "the devil's own incomprehensibles."[1] Oliver Wolcott, his contemporary who became a Connecticut governor, declared: "After living a dozen years in New York, I don't pretend to comprehend their politics. It is a labyrinth of wheels within wheels, and it is understood only by the managers."[2]

Managers before and since Wolcott would ruefully admit that the fratricidal quarrels that have periodically disrupted parties and shattered political alliances have taxed their understanding. Some quarrels have had tragic consequences, such as Hamilton's feud with Aaron Burr. Others have had elements of opéra bouffe, such as Roscoe Conkling's clash with Chester Arthur. Still others have been petty and nasty displays of temperament, such as Thurlow Weed's knifing of Horace Greeley when the great publisher sought public office.

The Democratic party, claimed by some to be the oldest continuous party in Western civilization, has suffered in particular from bruising infighting. Not the least important reason has been the scramble for spoils: high office and contracts for the rich, secure jobs for the middle class, relief for the poor. Politics, if defined as who gets what, has had many clients in New York. Like sports and crime, politics has provided a ladder of mobility for immigrants pushing and shoving to get ahead of the next group.

Because Democrats have often favored social reforms and attacked vested interests, they have attracted determined—even belligerent—personalities, some of whom have slipped over the line into demagoguery and fanaticism. Democratic publishers and journalists—James Gordon Bennett, Joseph Pulitzer, William Randolph Hearst in his early years—excoriated their opponents in and outside party ranks. Some observers blame "Irish temperament" for heating up Democratic rhetoric. If Irish-Americans were quick to take up cudgels, they also displayed aptitude for kissing and making up. In contrast, Republicans and their predecessors, the Whigs and Federalists, prided themselves on their decorum and civility. Democrats of national standing often bickered and quarreled precisely because the stakes were so high. Grover Cleveland fenced and feuded with Tammany chiefs and with David B. Hill (governor and senator), who in turn knifed Cleveland whenever he could. When he failed to stop Cleveland's renomination for president, Hill allegedly replied to someone who asked whether he was still a Democrat, "I am still a Democrat—very still."[3]

Another titanic fight took place between Al Smith and William Randolph Hearst, whose papers accused Smith of permitting contaminated milk to be sold and thus murdering babies. In 1922 Smith bluntly refused to run on the same ticket with Hearst, whom he branded a ruthless demagogue. The national Democratic party, meeting in Madison Square Garden, had its worst bloodletting in 1924, when Smith's delegates battled for more than a hundred ballots with William McAdoo, spokesman for southern and western Democrats, who opposed wets, Roman Catholics, and aliens. Will Rogers was led to observe, "I belong to no organized party. I am a Democrat." Although President Franklin D. Roosevelt and Governor Herbert H. Lehman temporarily papered over disputes (note Lehman's opposition to Roosevelt's Supreme Court packing bill in 1937), the Democratic party fell back into its contentious ways after World War II. Theodore H. White noted in 1972 that the state organization had collapsed and remained in a state of "dissolution."[4]

Clearly the similarities among the parties and their leaders far exceeded the differences. Horace Greeley, for example, browbeat his fellow Whigs and Republicans as well as Democrats. What politician used more vitriolic language than Republican Roscoe Conkling? On the other hand, who was more of a patrician than Franklin D. Roosevelt or more judicious than Herbert H. Lehman, both Democrats with immense followings?

National and international issues have played more important roles in New York than in most states. In fact, Empire State politics has been national politics writ small, because almost every governor has been regarded as a possible presidential contender. Dennis Brogan correctly declared that the "best springboard for a presidential candidate" was to have been "governor of a large doubtful state, especially the State of New York."[5] Party leaders have undoubtedly looked with favor upon New York contenders because of the state's electoral votes, the largest bloc before California took top place in 1972. If a candidate had New York's delegates in his pocket, he had a headstart, one-sixth to one-seventh of the votes necessary for nomination and election. Admittedly, candidates could win without the Empire State, as was demonstrated by Woodrow Wilson in 1916 and Harry Truman in 1948. Both victories, however, stunned the losing candidates and generated a large literature of explanation.

New Yorkers have occupied the White House for a much longer period than citizens of any other state, although before the Civil War only two New Yorkers—Van Buren and Fillmore—managed to earn this distinction. Even so, the Virginia dynasty (Jefferson, Madison, Monroe) recognized the importance of New York's electoral votes by selecting Aaron Burr, George Clinton, and Daniel D. Tompkins as running mates, and Andrew Jackson picked Martin Van Buren to join him on the 1832 ticket, then anointed him as his successor. Southern Democrats continued to dominate party policies and candidates before secession destroyed their power.

During the last third of the nineteenth century, Democrats almost always selected New Yorkers to head their ticket, whereas Republicans usually selected midwesterners as their standard-bearers. After 1900, however, Republicans turned to the Empire State for their candidates in seven of nineteen elections, matching Democrats in their partiality for New Yorkers. In this century Democratic candidates have come from other states in twelve elections.

New York's period of ascendancy came in the years between 1876 and 1952. During forty-six of those seventy-six years, 1600 Pennsylvania Avenue was occupied by New Yorkers. Even if we assign Eisenhower to Kansas and Nixon to California, we find true-blue New Yorkers (Chester A. Arthur, Grover Cleveland, the two Roosevelts) wielding executive power during almost half of that period. New York's ascendancy passed with World War II. No citizen of New York has won the presidency since Franklin D. Roosevelt in 1944. The last genuine New Yorker to run for president was Thomas E. Dewey in 1948, and he kept stressing his Michigan origins.

Significantly, only one president was born in New York City, and he, Theodore Roosevelt, boasted about his ranching days in South Dakota. Alfred E. Smith adopted "The Sidewalks of New York" as his theme song when he ran for the presidency in 1928, but voters in southern and western states perceived him as a provincial New Yorker. Other New York candidates stressed their small-town beginnings in other states: John W. Davis (West Virginia), Wendell L. Willkie (Indiana), Dwight D. Eisenhower (Texas and Kansas), Thomas E. Dewey (Michigan), Richard M. Nixon (California). Politicians sensed that metropolitan sophistication had less appeal than small-town origins, which after the Civil War replaced the legendary log cabin as the best place from which to hail.

Almost all New York governors have attracted, and few have discouraged, attention as presidential candidates. Newspapers, magazines, radio, and television have given them wide exposure and have sought out their opinions on national issues. New York governors have been expected to voice opinions on such issues as Irish independence, demilitarization of the Sinai peninsula, the Nigerian civil war, détente with Russia, and recognition of Red China. Some candidates for mayor of New York City and governor of the state have hardly announced their candidacy before setting off on the three-I tour (Italy, Ireland, Israel). No doubt future aspirants will make flying trips to Africa and Puerto Rico.

Whereas congressmen from Arkansas, South Carolina, and other states jockey for positions on the House Armed Services Committee and the House Ways and Means Committee, both of which control vast amounts of federal expenditures, downstate congressmen have usually preferred a spot on the Foreign Affairs Committee, where they can gain favorable notice among their constituents by influencing foreign policy. Getting a constituent's relative over or around immigration hurdles is another activity that wins a New York congressman more votes than mastering the details of the defense budget.

During New York City's financial crisis in 1975, New York State congressmen met several times as a group to discuss means of bringing pressure on policy makers to guarantee federal credit so that New York City could refinance its debt. They charged that southern and western states were receiving a much greater share of federal contracts than New York State, which had seen Brooklyn Navy Yard closed and several units phased out at Griffiss Air Force Base in Rome. In 1976 Daniel Patrick Moynihan, who won a seat in the Senate on his pledge to fight for more federal money for the Empire State, sought and won a place on the powerful Senate Finance Committee. In a long position paper in June 1977 he claimed that the federal government took $10.6 billion more out of this state than it put in during the bicentennial year.[6]

Yet in analyzing the effectiveness of New York's government in meeting its citizens' needs we should not let our judgment be unduly influenced by the fiscal crises of the 1970s. From the beginning a welter of crosscurrents has made New York politics turbulent. In the past, historians have interpreted elections and party conflicts mostly in terms of economic advantage. When milk prices sagged, farmers blamed milk dealers. When jobs became scarce, New Yorkers punished the "ins." Because the Democratic party has favored unions, workingmen have usually supported its candidates. Conversely, employers have endorsed Republican leaders, most of whom have opposed labor laws and high taxes. No one can deny that New Yorkers have often voted to protect their pocketbooks, whether in the form of tax levels, social services, state aid to localities, or public works.

More recently historians have begun to explore the cultural milieu, the role of elites, the imagery of political rhetoric, and concern over status and conspiracies. Because of the amazing number of diverse groups that have settled in the Empire State, we should not be surprised to find evidences of what might be called tribalism. Here Irish Catholics clashed with Yankee-Yorker evangelical Protestants; native-born Americans feuded with aliens; small-towners denounced the morals, or rather the lack of them, among metropolitan sophisticates; whites viewed with alarm the influx of blacks; Christians strove to keep their customs, including Sunday observance, from being undermined by freethinkers and Jews. "Land, blood, and religion," to adopt Andrew M. Greeley's phrase, are useful tools for interpreting our politics, provided we do not regard them as a single monolithic instrument.

In any period one cares to consider, one finds ethnic and religious differences creating and shaping political conflict. An analysis of voting in New York City between 1689 and 1710 reveals that the division over Leisler's rebellion was basically a struggle between persons of Dutch and English-Huguenot extraction.[7] Recent studies of colonial New York note "interest" politics, including ethnic rivalries. In the 1760s feuding between Anglicans and Presbyterians foreshadowed the division between loyalists and rebels during the Revolution.

Lee Benson has asserted that "at least since the 1820s, when manhood suffrage became widespread, ethnic and religious differences have tended to be *relatively* the most important sources of political differences."[8] Between 1825 and 1855 Catholic Irish, French-Canadian, German, and French immigrants voted overwhelmingly for Democratic candidates, who had traditionally befriended immigrants. On the other hand, English, Scottish, Welsh, and Ulster Irish immigrants rallied behind Whig candidates, who also attracted almost all blacks and Huguenots. Probably over 90 percent of Catholic voters in this period supported Democrats, whereas Protestants divided fairly evenly.[9] Persons of "puritan" leanings—that is, those in favor of temperance, Sunday observance, book learning, and thrift—tended to become Whigs. They campaigned as the party of law and order and blamed violence on the Irish and other minorities. On the other hand, non-puritans such as those in hard-drinking lumber towns constituted the "highest-ranking Democratic units in their counties."[10]

Ethnic-religious tensions erupted during the 1840s and 1850s because of massive Irish immigration and Catholic attempts to secure public aid for parochial schools. In 1843 nativist work-ingmen and merchants in New York City organized the Ameri-can Republican party. Artisans charged that immigrants were stealing their jobs and forcing wages down. A decade later the Know-Nothing party (officially the American party after 1854) attracted a wide following and in 1856 persuaded former presi-dent Millard Fillmore to run for president on its ticket. The Know-Nothings declined rapidly because slavery, the tran-scendent issue of the time, split this party even as it had fractured the Whigs and divided the Democrats.

The Kansas-Nebraska Act of 1854 ripped the Whig party apart, the bulk of its adherents moving into the new Republican party. Thurlow Weed, William H. Seward, Horace Greeley, and many other former Whigs gained new prominence as Republicans, firm in their opposition to the spread of slavery into western territories. The rekindling of temperance and Sunday observance crusades propelled evangelical Protestants into Republican ranks, for the core of that party lay among Yankee-Yorkers with their stern moralism.

Many Democrats, especially those in New York City, spouted white supremacist doctrines of the most rabid kind. In 1863 Irish workingmen, provoked by an unfair draft law and stimulated by a weekend of heavy drinking, plunged into a rampage of violence in which they lynched Negroes and burned down a "colored" orphanage. What troubled Irish the most was fear of black com-petition, for employers were using Negroes to break strikes.

Ethnocultural friction emerged on several occasions in the decades after Lee's surrender. On July 12, 1871, Protestant and Catholic Irish in New York City engaged in a donnybrook that revived nativist fears of violence. Critics denounced Tammany Hall for trying to prevent Orangemen from holding their annual parade to celebrate the Battle of the Boyne. When Ulstermen insisted on parading, showers of paving blocks rained down on them. Nativists also feared that the Fenians, an Irish revo-lutionary group, was creating a state within the state, for parties of Irishmen had made forays into Canada from Buffalo and St. Albans, Vermont. In 1866 more than 100,000 persons attended a

Fenian rally in Jones Wood in the Yorkville section of New York City. No wonder politicians wooed Irish support in city elections.

Boss William M. Tweed incorporated the immigrant Irish into Tammany Hall. Before the election of 1868 his judges naturalized several thousand new citizens. In fact, the number of registered voters rose by more than 30 percent. Tweed greatly expanded the public payroll and made several grants to community organizations, including religious groups. As a result the city's debt tripled during his last four years. Finally the bankers and creditors rose up in revolt and insisted on the appointment of a reformer, Andrew H. Green, as deputy comptroller with absolute financial authority. The collapse of the Tweed ring led to financial retrenchment and the coming to power of "Honest John" Kelly, in alliance with wealthy Democrats who insisted on economy. Kelly's strength marked victory for the respectable lower-middle-class Irish, who slowly shared the spoils of office with new ethnic groups.

Republicans derided Irish leadership and institutions. "The average Catholic Irishman of the first generation, as presented in this Assembly," Theodore Roosevelt confided to his diary in 1882, "is a low, venal, corrupt and unintelligent brute."[11] One can find even stronger comments in the diary of George Templeton Strong, Manhattan civic leader. Thomas Nast delighted in depicting Irishmen as leering apelike creatures who threatened peace in the community. Irish-Americans were fully aware of nativist attitudes and retaliated in kind.

Irish-Americans, however, captured Tammany Hall and in 1880 put William R. Grace, one of their own, into City Hall. This Hibernian thrust for political power, which was taking place throughout the urban northeast in the 1880s, created a backlash. Grover Cleveland, Buffalo's reform mayor, shrewdly sought battle with Honest John Kelly of Tammany Hall and won every skirmish. He won the governorship on a platform of civil service reform, a device regarded by Irish-Americans as a trick to shut them out of office. Like some blacks in the 1960s, militant Irishmen believed that membership in the "community" was sufficient reason for appointment to office. And they could cite wholesale discrimination against the Irish under White Anglo-Saxon Protestant leadership. When Cleveland refused to appoint prominent Irish-Americans because they were "spoilsmen" (they were), he became the target of verbal brickbats. Cleveland's supporters, however, praised him "for the enemies he has made."

Between 1865 and 1896 neither major party had a solid majority in the nation or state, and New York's electoral votes became a plum to be fought for. Party strategists used many methods to win votes, including "dirty tricks." Democrats gave undercover aid to Prohibitionists, believing that every vote for a "dry" meant one less for a Republican candidate. Republicans tried to detach Irish-Americans from their Democratic moorings by subsidizing Irish-American clubs and supporting Irish nationalists, whom Catholic bishops regarded as rivals for the allegiance of Irish-Americans. They endorsed the Irish National League, which called for Irish home rule and the end of landlordism, and fostered Irish arts and culture. Secretary of State James G. Blaine periodically twisted the British lion's tail in order to win applause and gain some Irish votes.

In 1884, Blaine, running for president, was making headway in attracting Catholic voters when a delegation of Protestant ministers waited on him in New York City. Their leader, the Reverend Samuel Burchard, stated that his followers would not endorse the Democratic party, "whose antecedents have been rum, Romanism, and rebellion." Blaine failed to rebuke Burchard and repudiate this hapless comment, which Irish-Americans regarded as an insult to their faith. Blaine narrowly lost New York and thus the election—possibly for this reason. Roscoe Conkling's hatred of Blaine and Blaine's corrupt association with railroad interests probably lost the candidate even more votes.

Four years later, ethnic and religious animosities again played a part in New York politics. Branding Cleveland as pro-British, Republicans declared that his proposed reduction of tariffs would flood the United States with British goods. Lord Sackville, British minister in Washington, was tricked into writing a letter stating that Great Britain favored Cleveland over Benjamin Harrison. Although Cleveland demanded Sackville's recall, this episode damaged Cleveland, and he lost New York State and reelection.

Recent studies of midwest politics in the 1880s indicate that religious differences, broadly defined, rivaled party loyalty as dominant forces influencing the electorate and had more impact on elections than economic issues or class antagonisms.[12] In New York, tensions between Catholics and their opponents were also mounting. Public aid to parochial schools, for which Bernard McQuaid, bishop of Rochester, had unceasingly agitated for two decades, became the main battlefield.[13] When public officials in large cities with Catholic majorities provided aid (often disguised) for parochial schools, opponents, charging "Romish plots" against public schools, organized the National League for Protection of American Institutions, which attracted such respectable supporters as J. P. Morgan, John D. Rockefeller, and Cornelius Vanderbilt. Since many such leaders had enrolled as Republicans, Catholic publicists charged the Republican party with anti-Catholic bias.

The constitutional convention of 1894 became an arena of conflict between Roman Catholic spokesmen and their opponents. The NLPAI presented a huge petition bearing 40,000 names which demanded a ban on public funds for sectarian institutions. After scores of witnesses had defended the principle of separation of church and state, Frederic R. Coudert, a leading Catholic layman, made a calm and reasoned exposition. Although public aid to parochial schools was simple justice, he insisted, he recognized that "public opinion will not tolerate the diversion of any public monies" from public education.[14] George Bliss, another Catholic speaker, urged continued public support for charitable agencies such as orphanages. He showed that private agencies saved money for taxpayers and claimed that inmates benefited from the compassion they received in institutions watched over by religious groups. The kingmakers at the convention—Elihu Root and Joseph Choate—arranged for a compromise: no public funds for private schools but public aid for charitable agencies. The Republican high command believed the compromise was a reasonable solution, and the history of the next half century or so would seem to validate this judgment. Root and Choate, who feared anarchist threats to order and Populist attacks on the gold standard, knew that they had to placate the 70,000 Roman

Catholics who belonged to their party. Their votes were needed to combat free-silver Democrats, who were swarming behind William Jennings Bryan.

Between 1894 and 1930 northern WASP America dominated politics, law, and government, set standards in the arts and in learning, and provided the basic values for the so-called American way of life. New York, like neighboring Pennsylvania and New England, became almost as solidly Republican as the South was Democratic.

Under Theodore Roosevelt and Woodrow Wilson progressivism challenged plutocracy on one hand and ethnic political machines on the other. Tammany Hall, the prototype of the big-city ethnic machine, naturally received the brunt of Republican moral censure. Progressivism also had its Democratic followers among those worried about overweening corporate power. Boss Charles Murphy, under the tutelage of Alfred E. Smith and Robert Wagner, gradually endorsed various social programs. Meanwhile Al Smith was able to achieve his ambition of becoming governor in 1918.

Republicans sought to undermine Democratic strength by attracting a portion of the immigrant vote. They had little difficulty in winning over such elements as the English, Welsh, Scots, Canadian British, German Lutherans, and Scandinavians. Because Irish-Americans monopolized the Democratic party and told newcomers to start at the bottom and wait their turn, ambitious Jews, Italians, and Slavs drifted toward Republicanism. Manhattan Republicans were willing to give young Fiorello La Guardia the chance to run for Congress in a district overwhelmingly Democratic. To their surprise, La Guardia gained the seat on his second try and, in 1919, won a special election for president of the Board of Aldermen. Republicans in Congress protested pogroms in Russia, and, in 1906, Theodore Roosevelt appointed Oscar Straus of New York as secretary of commerce and labor, the first Jew to hold a cabinet post. Interestingly enough, a large minority of Jewish immigrants supported the Socialist party, and the Yiddish *Daily Forward* preached the class struggle. In 1914, 1916, and 1920 Meyer London won election to Congress by appealing to immigrant socialists.

World War I turned many Germans, Italians, Jews, and Irish Catholics against Wilson's party, partly because of strikes, inflation, and recession, but also because of his failure to win territory and rights for their homelands in the peace treaty. The Republican landslide in 1920 even swept Al Smith out of the governor's chair.

During the 1920s WASPs made their last full-bodied campaign for cultural homogeneity. Disturbed by hyphenated Americans and radical aliens, they launched an "Americanization" campaign while at the same time calling for restrictions on immigration. They tolerated when they did not join the Ku Klux Klan. Worst of all, they rammed prohibition down the throats of their neighbors, many of whom regarded beer, wine, and whiskey as divinely ordained. This full-throated campaign drove more ethnics into the Democratic party, which rallied behind Smith, standard-bearer of the new immigrants. His race for president in 1928 intensified the Protestant–Catholic division that had already split the Democrats in 1924. What was most remarkable was Smith's ability to double the Democratic vote of 1924. Smith corralled a high percentage of German, Jewish, Irish, and Italian voters, who formed a large part of New York's urban population.[15]

Then came the depression, which swept almost every voting group into the Democratic camp. Unemployment, failing banks, low farm prices strained political loyalties and ethnic issues faded into the background. Even Negroes turned Abraham Lincoln's picture to the wall and gave Roosevelt their devotion because of federal job and welfare programs and gestures to civil rights. Thereafter they became the most solid unit in the Roosevelt coalition. In Washington, Albany, and New York City, government became multiethnic.

In 1933 Fiorello La Guardia ran for mayor of New York City on the Republican-Fusion ticket. Italo-Americans deserted their Democratic moorings by the tens of thousands in order to put their "Little Flower" into office.[16] Once again ethnicity displayed its important role in New York history.

The postwar social welfare state suited rather well the Catholic ethnic groups, which formed a large portion of factory labor and

Three outstanding New Yorkers: Franklin D. Roosevelt with Governor Herbert H. Lehman and Mayor Fiorello H. La Guardia, en route to groundbreaking ceremonies for the Brooklyn–Battery Tunnel, October 28, 1940. Franklin D. Roosevelt Library. UPI.

cited papal encyclicals to justify social legislation. Republicans, finding that Democrats had preempted nationalist positions, took up instead the old Democratic slogans of local rights and laissez faire. Desperately in need of a popular issue, they pinned the label of disloyalty upon the Democrats, who were charged with "losing" Eastern Europe and China to godless Communists. In 1952 they picked the war hero Eisenhower to run for president, and he attracted many Americans disturbed by Communist gains, government regulations, and domestic turmoil.

The Republican chieftains in New York State developed a moderate brand of Republicanism, sponsoring a considerable amount of social legislation and welcoming the support of ethnics, blacks, and Jews. In 1945, for example, Republican legislators approved the Ives-Quinn Act, forbidding discrimination in employment. Governor Thomas E. Dewey set in motion the establishment of the State University of New York. No Republican recognized the importance of cultivating ethnics more astutely than Nelson Rockefeller, who made his first of four races for governor in 1958. Newspapers displayed pictures of the smiling heir to the Standard Oil fortune eating blintzes, pizza, chitlins, and grits with extravagant gusto. Aides of Governor Rockefeller admitted that it was a cardinal feature of their strategy to court the votes of Italians, Irish, and Slavs by patronage and by creating jobs in public works. In 1970 Italian-Americans defected en masse from the Democratic ticket, which was headed by four Jews and one black. Although Arthur Goldberg, Democratic candidate for governor, lectured his constituency that ethnic considerations were old-fashioned, many Irish-Americans and Italo-Americans were nursing bruised feelings. In New York City, Democratic "reformers" had ousted prominent Italians and boycotted Irish-Americans while they catered to blacks, Puerto Ricans, and Jews. Reformers repeatedly offended Catholics by advocating abortion and denouncing public aid to parochial schools. When they demanded a police review board, policemen and their friends became incensed. When they urged public housing projects in such white middle-class neighborhoods as Forest Hills, residents organized protests.

In 1960 John F. Kennedy's race for president revived religious voting patterns. The percentage of Roman Catholics who voted Democratic rose considerably over the proportion of those who had done so in the 1950s, when Eisenhower ate into Democratic strength. Despite the pull of religion, however, many upper-middle-class Catholics, especially those in the suburbs, remained tied to their Republican moorings.[17]

In 1963 Nathan Glazer and Patrick Daniel Moynihan published their stimulating study of New York City with the arresting title *Beyond the Melting Pot*. They found that religion and race continued to define the major groups of New York City's society. Glazer quoted at length from a political analysis by pollsters who pretested various candidates of varying religious and ethnic backgrounds in the state race for governor and United States senator in 1962.[18] Because politicians have recently paid close attention to polls in setting up winning state tickets, these population estimates deserve respect, although obviously they are rough approximations.

White Protestant	37%
White Catholic	37%
Jewish	18%
Negro	8%
Irish	9%
English-Scotch	7%
German	16%
Italian	13%

The analysts recommended that the Democratic party nominate a Lehman-type candidate such as Robert Morganthau, a respected lawyer who was United States attorney for the Southern District of New York. Despite their elaborate prognostications, the pollsters and politicians missed their goal by a wide margin, for Morganthau ran poorly. New York City Jews did not vote solidly for Morganthau, as they had been expected to do, confirming other studies that show that Jewish voters tend to be more issue-oriented than others. Well-to-do Jews in Westchester voted strongly for Rockefeller, while working-class Jews in

Brooklyn and the Bronx remained loyal Democrats. Obviously some appeals to ethnicity are really class appeals. Conversely, some conflicts couched in class terms are really ethnocultural.

White Protestants in New York cities can be regarded as a distinct ethnic group largely because they act and feel like a minority. This group has its special occupations, notably banking, corporate administration, education, philanthropy, and law. Its membership circulates within a social milieu of churches, schools, and clubs. Although a majority tend to favor the Republican party and conservative positions, an influential minority, especially those in communications and education, have joined reform movements.

In 1970 Glazer and Moynihan took another look at New York City and discovered significant changes. First of all, Catholic political power had declined precipitously, a finding they attributed to the tendency of dominant groups to split into factions. John F. Kennedy's victory in 1960 helped to end the inferiority complex that Catholics had nursed since Smith's defeat in 1928. Second, the alliance of Jews, blacks, and liberal reformers successfully challenged Irish- and Italian-American control of the Democratic party. This new alliance, however, began to come apart because of explosive black militancy. Although Jewish intellectuals continued to champion black causes, middle-class Jews in civil service jobs became alarmed at "community control" of schools and threats to seniority rights. Nevertheless, many Jews, according to Milton Himmelfarb, will continue to hold the social status of Episcopalians but vote like Puerto Ricans.[19]

In the 1976 presidential campaign ethnic and religious groups in New York shifted a bit. *Mirabile dictu*, blacks voted for a peanut farmer from the Deep South, partly because of dismay at Republican policies but largely because of Carter's ability to win the confidence of Andrew Young and other prominent blacks. Other elements in the old Roosevelt coalition showed some uneasiness about Carter. Sixty-eight percent of Jews supported him, a large drop from the 83 percent that supported Humphrey in 1968.[20] Carter also ran behind other Democrats, especially in Catholic districts, where voters could not easily relate to a "born-again" Baptist.

The 1977 race for mayor of New York City degenerated into another rivalry among ethnic, religious, and racial candidates. Percy Sutton, borough president of Manhattan, at first sought to appeal beyond his base among blacks, but his candidacy met little support. Edward Koch, Abraham Beame, and Bella Abzug split most of the Jewish vote in the Democratic primary. On July 31 the *New York Times* endorsed Mario Cuomo in an editorial significantly headed "Mr. Cuomo, to End the Tribalism." The editorial stated that Cuomo could heal the deep ethnic, religious, and economic divisions in the city. Despite this support, Cuomo lost to Koch.

What conclusions can one draw from this hasty survey of two centuries of politics? Most obvious is the persistence of the two-party system despite the amazing diversity of interests. In every decade disgruntled factions have defected from one or both parties because of feuds, principle, or charismatic leadership. Most defectors have returned to the fold, however, because hope of victory and spoils has outweighed distaste for rivals within the party. Dislike of a common enemy has often driven quarreling factions back into an uneasy coalition.

Second, ethnocultural factors have emerged in every generation and shaped platforms and strategies. Issues of race, religion, and ethnicity seem to have had more impact than strictly economic ones, although few issues have been purely economic or ethnic. Nativists, for example, hated the pope, but they also feared threats to their jobs by aliens. Who can assign the precise weight to each factor for each individual?

On the whole, Democrats from the time of George Clinton have attracted immigrants, ethnic minorities, and the common people. The party platforms have attacked economic privilege, corporations, and speculative growth. Opposing them have been the Republicans, who inherited most of their principles from Whigs and Federalists. Republican spokesmen have held producers in high regard and viewed with suspicion those who wish to regulate business enterprise. They have thought of themselves as the host culture and have guarded old traditions as though they were the Holy Grail. Their perception of an ideal society is one of orderliness, good taste, self-control, and respect for authority, all of which the old Yankee-Yorker stock had cherished.

The aristocratic class not only left scores of impressive mansions throughout New York State but provided a large proportion of political candidates. In every generation members of established families have sought high office while others have displayed a keen sense of civic responsibility. When young Theodore Roosevelt was taunted by some rich friends who wanted to know why he, a Harvard graduate, should sully his hands by engaging in ward politics, he countered that he wished to become a member of the ruling class.

Unlike the English aristocracy, the American social elite was not hereditary and "never developed a definite function or identity."[21] No one understood clearly who belonged to it or how one secured admission, but tenants and aproned artisans were ready to challenge it. When a democratic groundswell forced the landed gentry to court voters after 1760, voters became less deferential. During the Revolution a large number of aristocrats followed the king and lost their land. Meanwhile yeomen and artisans increased their representation in the Assembly as the percentage of senators drawn from prominent families fell.[22]

In 1777 George Clinton, who came from a family of farmers in Ulster County, defeated Philip Schuyler, candidate of the aristocracy. Schuyler disdainfully observed to John Jay that Clinton's family and connections did not entitle him to the office. Fully aware of his shortcomings in education and genteel manners, Clinton fought hard to keep aristocrats out of office. In 1789, when he urged Rufus King, a newcomer from Massachusetts, to accept Anti-Federalist support for a seat in the United States Senate, Clinton noted that "all the great opulent families were united in one confederacy."[23] Clinton planned to keep a "constant eye" on this group.

After the Revolution the well-to-do and influential families in New York City organized many benevolent societies in order to cope with the problems of rapid growth. These societies treated the sick, set up schools for poor children, aided widows and the elderly, housed orphans, fed debtors, and established savings banks. The same class—in fact, many of the same people—that ran humanitarian agencies also provided mayors and aldermen. Until the 1830s wealthy men dominated the New York Common Council.

Subsequently members of the city elite gradually lost their dominant position among officialdom, partly because tough ward heelers were mobilizing the votes of the foreign-born. At the same time patricians were moving uptown to more fashionable homes, farther and farther from the poorer neighborhoods. As a result the old alliance between political and humanitarian elites weakened, and many spokesmen of the old families became critics of government and officials.

In Albany a Dutch merchant patriciate grew up, somewhat similar to that of the medieval Netherlands, where, in Alice P. Kenney's words, "neither the individual nor the mass, but the local community, was the significant entity."[24] After the Revolution Yankees swarmed into Albany and transformed it into a Yankee city. Newcomers from Massachusetts—Elkanah Watson as a young entrepreneur, Benjamin Knower as a hatter's apprentice, Ezra Ames as a portrait painter—climbed from plebeian status to that of bank president. Before long manufacturers sprang up, generally from the merchant class. A notable example was Erastus Corning, a hardware merchant who subsequently became head of the New York Central Railroad. By 1842 a local paper could comment, ". . . in no other place in the Union is this aristocratical feeling carried to such an extent. . . . We have aristocrats here without number."[25] In other upstate centers and throughout the countryside one can find similar examples of individuals with aristocratic pretensions.

Dixon Ryan Fox, in his book on the decline of the New York aristocracy, assumed that George Clinton's Republican party evolved into Martin Van Buren's Bucktails (Albany Regency) and subsequently into Jackson's Democratic party.[26] Furthermore, the elite began as Federalists, moved behind De Witt Clinton's branch of the Republican party, and later joined the Whig party. Fox's schematization, however, does not hold up on close scrutiny, for one can find persons from established families at every point of the political spectrum and within both major parties. An early exception to Fox's rule was Robert R. Livingston, who cast his lot with George Clinton and Jefferson. After 1800 factions scattered voters in every direction. A considerable number of "high-minded" Federalists spurned De Witt Clinton;

several former Federalists, including a son (James) of Alexander Hamilton, became staunch supporters of Jackson and Van Buren.

In America, as in England, landed wealth tended to view trade and manufacturing with suspicion, if not disdain. James Fenimore Cooper, whose father had built a Federalist bastion on Otsego Lake, became a Democrat but wrote screeds against antirenters. In the preface to *The Chainbearer*, one of three antirent novels, Cooper wrote: "The column of society must have its capital as well as its base. . . . In New York the great landlords long have, and still do, in a social sense, occupy the place of the capital."

Many members of New York landed families gravitated to the Democratic party, which seemed more sympathetic to their interests. In the 1830s followers of Van Buren protected the Holland Land Company from purchasers who were refusing to pay up their mortgages. When Governor Silas Wright sent troops to Delaware County to put down an antirent uprising, tenant farmers endorsed Whig candidate John Young, who promptly pardoned antirenters whom the courts had convicted.

Meanwhile persons engaged in trade and manufacturing were amassing fortunes much greater than those of the landed grandees. During the 1830s and 1840s an overwhelming percentage of the very richest men in New York favored Whig principles.[27] Daniel Dewey Barnard of Albany was a good example of the upstate patrician. He believed that aristocratic families with a stake in society should make the decisions for that society. He had little patience with such Whigs as William Seward and Thurlow Weed, whom he accused of pandering to the masses. The rise of the Republican party enraged him because he regarded it as a threat to the Union and a nest of abolitionists. Nevertheless, during and after the Civil War the bulk of industrialists and merchants gradually drifted into the Republican party, which in turn endorsed a protective tariff, sound banking, and few regulations of business.

After the Civil War conservatives adopted wholeheartedly the theories of social Darwinism as popularized by Herbert Spencer. They frankly admitted the jungle character of the economic struggle but justified it on the ground that Nature had decreed that the fittest should survive by the process of "natural selection." In the fall of 1882 Spencer made his memorable visit to this country and American notables gave him a splendid banquet at Delmonico's. His ardent disciple Andrew Carnegie preached the gospel of wealth, declaring it was a disgrace for rich men to die rich. He urged them to contribute their fortunes to humanitarian purposes.

Although one associates wealth with aristocracy, the two were and are not identical. Old families in New York regarded newcomers as parvenus, who needed a probationary period before acceptance into the inner purlieus of society. No doubt the most notable example was the Vanderbilt family, whose founder, Commodore Vanderbilt, retained the rough speech and manners of his sailing days. In 1883 Mrs. William K. Vanderbilt announced plans for an elaborate ball. Miss Caroline Astor wished to attend, but Mrs. Astor had not yet placed her stamp of approval on the Vanderbilt clan. Miss Astor received her invitation after Mrs. Astor summoned her carriage and left her card at the Vanderbilt home. The Vanderbilts had finally "arrived."

Aristocrats, however, have not necessarily opposed changes and reforms. Franklin D. Roosevelt and Averell Harriman, both liberal Democrats, came from families of great wealth and status. Among Republican governors, Theodore Roosevelt and Nelson Rockefeller took positions more "progressive" than those of most other Republicans.

One can cite several notable conservatives among Republican leaders since 1900: Nicholas Murray Butler, Elihu Root, Henry L. Stimson, James W. Wadsworth. Butler, who made Columbia into one of the world's great universities, became an elder statesman among Republicans. Root and Stimson were eminent lawyers who served both as secretary of war and secretary of state. Each won international recognition as a man of great ability, sterling character, and dedicated patriotism. James W. Wadsworth was the scion of a family that has held thousands of acres of lush Genesee Valley farmland since the 1790s. When Hitler threatened American security, Congressman Wadsworth defied the prevailing isolationist temper among Republican politicians and sponsored the draft law of 1940.

The wealthy class has provided not only liberals and conservatives but civic-minded leaders primarily interested in improving the structure and operation of government. Some have devoted their lives to philanthropy; the hard work and wealth of John D. Rockefeller, Jr., stood behind dozens of civic improvements in New York City, the nation, and the world. Abram Hewitt, ironmaster, married Peter Cooper's daughter, and both men gave away millions for educational purposes. Who has not heard of Lincoln's speech at the Cooper Union in 1860? In 1976 a handsome new museum opened in Carnegie's Fifth Avenue mansion to display the treasures of the Cooper and Hewitt collections of textiles and decorative arts.

Perhaps the finest example of civic leadership was provided by Andrew Green, a law partner of Samuel Tilden. Green protected Central Park from Tweed's rapacity and helped expand New York City's park system. He promoted the Brooklyn Bridge and brought about the union of the Astor and Lenox Foundations with the New York Public Library. For years he agitated for the creation of Greater New York, which finally came about in 1898.

The aristocratic tradition in politics was also exemplified in the career of Robert Moses, autocratic and controversial power broker, the greatest builder in world history. An idealistic Yale and Oxford graduate, Moses found his plans for civic improvement ignored or blocked by Tammany chieftains. When Governor Smith asked him for aid in reorganizing the sprawling state government, Moses accepted. Soon he became director of the State Parks Council and Long Island State Park Commission. He opened up western Long Island, the preserve of millionaire estates, by constructing Jones Beach and connecting parkways. In 1934 Mayor La Guardia appointed Moses park commissioner of New York City. As chairman of the Triboro Bridge and Tunnel Authority, Moses built bridges, highways, and the Coliseum. Political leaders turned to Moses because "he got things done" and also because he took care that they and their associates participated in contracts, fees, and commissions. Robert Caro, his critical biographer, estimates that Moses personally conceived and carried through public works costing $27 billion.[28]

The spoils system has rivaled the role of aristocrats in both importance and antiquity. As we have seen, the chief qualifica-

tion for officeholding in colonial days was influence in England
and access to the governor. Independence did not end the practice of rewarding friends and punishing enemies. Governor
George Clinton, with the help of his nephew, De Witt Clinton,
who served as his secretary, rewarded his friends with favors,
while Alexander Hamilton was doing the same thing in the federal government. The classic statement came from Governor
William Marcy: "To the victor belong the spoils of the enemy."
Occasionally favors escalated into outright bribery and graft,
especially after corporations sprang up and sought charters on
favorable terms.

Corruption in New York has certainly attracted more national
attention than that in other states, largely because New York
State has offered bigger prizes and conducted more spectacular
investigations. Because Manhattan's customhouse supervised
over half of the nation's imports, Chester Arthur, Roscoe Conkling, and many others sought to control it. They padded the rolls
with "no show" party faithful, and importers paid kickbacks in
return for favorable or false rulings on weight and valuations of
goods. Upstate, grafters battened on the canal system, seeking
lucrative contracts for repair and maintenance. Traction interests
and utilities bribed officials for franchises and rights of way.
Sometimes legislators blackmailed businessmen by threatening
investigations and harmful regulations.

The Republican legislature, hoping to win kudos and embarrass its foes, periodically investigated Tammany Hall; two of the
most publicized probes were the Lexow investigation of prostitution and police graft in 1892–1893 and Judge Samuel Seabury's
investigation of municipal governments, which led to Mayor
James Walker's resignation in 1932. By earning a reputation as a
fighter against graft, a politician won not only fame but a chance
for higher office. Samuel Tilden, who broke the canal ring, and
Grover Cleveland, who defied spoilsmen, received Democratic
nominations for governor and president. After Charles Evans
Hughes exposed fraud in the gas utilities and insurance companies, he received Republican nominations for governor and
president. Tom Dewey, youthful racket buster, won the governorship and ran twice for president.

Cartoon comment by Thomas Nast on corruption in New York City politics. The corpulent figure at the left represents Boss Tweed. *Harper's Weekly*, August 19, 1871.

Tammany Hall, whether defined narrowly as the Democratic headquarters on Manhattan Island or more broadly as the party in the five boroughs, became the symbol of machine rule and corruption. Whereas in most large cities, notably Philadelphia, Chicago, and Boston, reformers seldom broke the grip of boss rule, they often defeated Tammany and elected so-called reform mayors. But while reformers have periodically tossed the rascals out of office, the spoilsmen have managed to return in the next election.

In 1870 Boss Tweed came under attack, and the next year a citizen committee uncovered kickbacks, bogus contracts, and padded budgets. These revelations of thievery shocked even a cynical public, and William Havemeyer was swept into office. Although he made improvements in streets, schools, and public health, Havemeyer failed to win public confidence. Meanwhile Tammany acquired a new boss, Honest John Kelly. Top Tammany chieftains became millionaires by engaging in "politics for revenue only" and understanding the metaphysics of "honest graft," such as buying up land just before the city announced its decision to build a bridge or put through a street there.

When the Democrats lost momentum in New York County in the late 1880s, the City Reform Club rose up to challenge Tammany. It enlisted a handful of elite young men who appeared in full-dress suits and sported canes, hardly the attire to win mass support. It was only one of several organizations that preached more efficient methods in municipal government.

Richard Croker, Tammany's boss after 1886, looted the public treasury without arousing much uproar, but when an investigation showed that police were shaking down prostitutes, a majority of voters elected William L. Strong as mayor in 1894. As Strong's police commissioner, Theodore Roosevelt tried to end police graft and enforced the law requiring saloons to close on Sunday, infuriating German voters. In 1897 Tammany regained the mayoralty with a minority of votes because Republicans refused to combine with the Citizens' Union on a joint candidate for mayor.

Four years later the Republicans agreed to support Seth Low, the candidate of the Citizens' Union. Low, president of Columbia University, was able and hard-working, but he could not keep his supporters united. While his business supporters were primarily interested in lower taxes, some of his "progressive" allies promised to outdo the machine in providing costly social services.

In 1905 William Randolph Hearst threw a scare into Boss Charles Murphy by running on the ticket of the Municipal Ownership League. He filled the columns of his *New York Journal* with sensational charges against Tammany sachems, whose scandals had shocked even New York's jaded citizenry. Using every trick, including an army of repeaters, Murphy defeated Hearst and elected George B. McClellan, son of the Civil War general and a Princeton graduate, who added dignity and independence to the office of mayor. In the next election Murphy accepted William Gaynor, an eccentric but popular Brooklyn judge who refused to take orders and championed civil service and court reforms. Murphy himself realized the necessity of offering social and labor reforms if his party was to keep popular support.

In 1913 a group of high-powered citizens organized a fusion ticket headed by John Purroy Mitchel, an independent Democrat, who had exposed graft in public offices. Mitchel cleaned up the fire and police departments, the latter tied to criminal elements. Honest, efficient, and energetic, Mitchel preferred to relax with society people instead of common folk. An ardent advocate of American intervention in 1917, Mitchel became the target of German and anti-British Irish voters. He lost his office in 1917 and his life the next year in an aviation training accident.

Tammany defeated Mitchel with red-haired John F. Hylan, but Tammany leaders and Governor Alfred E. Smith soon tired of him. Essentially an inept bumbler, Hylan was replaced by James A. Walker, the dapper and debonair playboy who seemed to embody the gay twenties. "Jimmy" spent most evenings at nightclubs while his associates padded city payrolls and made corrupt deals with racketeers. The depression stripped the glamour from his administration, however, and it collapsed in a welter of investigations. When Walker resigned under fire, voters rallied behind Fiorello La Guardia, who for the next dozen years amused them with his antics and won their respect and affection. Students of American government usually describe the "Little Flower" as one of the best mayors in New York City history.[29] The qualities that differentiated him from his reform predecessors were his human touch and his ability to win reelection.

In 1945 William O'Dwyer recovered City Hall for the Democrats, but he had to resign in 1950 when his name became linked with underworld figures. His successor, Vincent R. Impelletteri (1950–1953), was more of an ethnic accident than a serious figure. He, too, ran as a so-called independent against Tammany Hall.

Mayor Robert F. Wagner, Jr. (1954–1965), shared the keen social consciousness of his father, the New Deal senator and champion of labor unions. He showed considerable ability in conciliating warring groups at a time when the social fabric seemed to be unraveling. Wagner gradually moved away from his ties to borough bosses and in his last election ran as an antiboss candidate.

In 1965 John Vliet Lindsay, an Ivy League patrician, won office as a liberal Republican with the support of independent Democrats. Lindsay had style and helped to pacify militant blacks during the turbulent 1960s by walking the streets of Harlem in shirt sleeves. Although his performance did not match his rhetoric, he did manage to attract enough votes among blacks, Puerto Ricans, and white liberals to win a second term. During his administration New York City slipped into financial straits because of costly social programs, excessive concessions to subway workers and other civil servants, and budgetary manipulations. During the period 1966–1971 expenditures for higher education rose 251 percent, welfare 225 percent, and hospitals 123 percent. In 1973 Abraham Beame, a longtime Democrat, took office only to sink into a financial quagmire. After 1975 both state and federal officials forced New York City to make deep budget cuts and to lay off tens of thousands of employees.

Tammany Hall did not control City Hall much more than half the time after 1900. Old-style politicians (Hylan, Walker, Beame, O'Dwyer, Impelletteri) held the top office for about twenty-five years while so-called reformers (Low, Mitchel, La Guardia, Lindsay) held it for about the same length of time.

How effective were the reformers? They threw out flagrant

boodlers and introduced many improvements in both the structure and the operation of municipal departments. With the exception of La Guardia, reform mayors seldom won reelection and old-style politicians returned. Changes brought about by reformers, however—civil service, secret ballot, and the like—were usually retained. In 1960 Wallace S. Sayre and Herbert Kaufman addressed themselves to a question that has often been asked: Is New York City governable? They found that city leaders had shown remarkable ability in preserving a nice balance between change and stability. In 1965 they posed another rhetorical question in their introduction to the paperback edition of their book: "What other large American City is as democratically and as well governed?"[30]

It is tempting to chortle at this favorable judgment by eminent professors of public administration at Columbia and Yale. What they could not foresee were the startling social changes of the next decade, which disrupted almost all large cities so drastically that the phrase "the crisis of the cities" has become part of our vocabulary. New York City became the prime example of urban breakdown, although Newark had achieved that distinction earlier. The flight of over a million white citizens from New York meant a decrease in tax revenues, while their replacement by a million or so blacks and people of Hispanic descent increased welfare costs. In 1975 12 percent of the population was on welfare, at a cost of over $2 billion a year. Black militancy led officials to initiate expensive programs in housing, education, and welfare, all forcing taxes up. Although population declined slightly in the 1960s, the ranks of public employees rose by about 100,000. At the same time Lyndon Johnson's administration began its war on poverty and dangled matching grants before city officials, who did not dare turn them down although the grants forced the city to increase its budget and enlarge its bureaucracy. Civil servants suddenly became militant, joining unions and striking for higher salaries and fringe benefits. Bus drivers who worked an eight-hour day demanded and received pay for eleven hours.

Companies moved out of New York City, thus reducing the tax base and creating more unemployment. Of the nearly 200 of the nation's top 1,000 corporations that had their headquarters in the metropolis in 1965, about 40 percent had moved elsewhere a decade later.[31] Thousands of small companies also vanished, expecially in the garment industry. More than 600,000 jobs disappeared after 1969. Why? Businessmen complained about rising interest rates, crime, congestion, soaring fuel costs, and high taxes. Whereas Connecticut has no income tax, New York State exacts up to 15 percent of personal income—over 50 percent more than the average of other states. And New York City imposed its own wage tax on top of the state income tax.

The spring of 1978 brought new hope to New Yorkers. Employment figures headed up while the stock market registered great volume. The London *Economist* ran an article on March 31 entitled "Where Next, New York?" Noting the flood of foreign capital sweeping into New York City, which had 130 foreign banks, it predicted that New York City would become the great world capital of finance.

No analysis of New York City's troubles was more devastating than that made in 1977 by Jack Newfield and Paul Dubrul in their exposé of the techniques of the power brokers—unions, Mafia, public utilities, and clubhouse politicians—who form the "permanent government" of New York City.[32] Large banks and real estate developers as well as such public authorities as the Port Authority of New York have extorted privileges and lucrative concessions for insiders.

This focus on mismanagement and legal graft in New York City is not meant to imply that officials in upstate cities have been markedly more honest and effective. The government of Albany, for example, has remained almost a textbook case of machine politics old style. The O'Connell machine, which held power for forty years, supplanted the equally powerful Republican machine of William Barnes, who had inherited the mantle from Thurlow Weed, wizard of the lobby. Recurrent scandals have punctuated the politics of Buffalo, where ethnic groups have scrambled for the best position at the public trough.

The election of Samuel Tilden as governor in 1874 ended an era of flamboyant corruption at the state level. But influence did not cease to play its role. No one has put it better than Elihu Root in his speech to the constitutional convention of 1915:

Then Mr. Platt ruled the state; for nigh upon twenty years he ruled it. It was not the governor; it was not the legislature; it was not any elected officers; it was Mr. Platt and his lieutenants. It makes no difference what name you give, whether you call it Fenton or Conkling or Cornell or Arthur or Platt, or by the names of the men now living. The rule of the state during the greater part of the forty years of my acquaintance with the state government has not been any man authorized by the constitution or by the law. . . .[33]

Root was referring to Boss Thomas Collier Platt, the so-called Easy Boss of the Republican party, who held undisputed sway over the Republican organization from about 1889 to 1901.

In each decade one can find scandals: the canal ring in the 1880s, waste of canal funds in the 1890s, promiscuous lobbying by gas and insurance companies in the 1900s, impeachment of Governor William Sulzer in 1913 for falsifying reports on campaign expenditures, lobbying by the utilities in the 1920s and 1930s. After World War II, developers, contractors, and unions luxuriated in lucrative contracts when New York State and its independent agencies spent billions on huge projects: the Albany Mall, campuses of the State University, Power Authority projects, state housing, and transportation agencies. One investigation revealed shocking fraud in the construction and administration of nursing homes whose sponsors had allies in Albany.

George Washington Plunkitt, self-appointed sage of Tammany Hall, expatiated on the differences between honest and dishonest graft. The latter was the dirty business of protecting criminals, prostitutes, and gamblers. The more fastidious politicians used their knowledge of future state action to buy up land where roads or bridges were to be built, or became open or secret partners in contracting firms, which then had the inside track when government contracts were awarded. In 1977 Newfield and Dubrul provided us with another definition of influence and graft: "Legal graft is the disguised quid pro quo. I'll get you a nursing home license, and you hire my law firm. I'll get you a ninety-nine-year lease from the city, and you give my friend some insurance. I'll make you a judge, but your two brothers each have to contribute $7500 to the party by purchasing tables at our dinners."[34]

Investigations have uncovered similar methods in New Jersey,

New Orleans, Chicago, Philadelphia, and Maryland. Perhaps in New York City the system has been more sophisticated.

The diversity of interests and contentiousness of New York politics has spawned many "third" and other parties, not to mention scores of bolts by disgruntled factions. After 1826, popular indignation over the alleged abduction of William Morgan for exposing the secrets of Freemasons led to a violent upheaval among farmers in western New York against village and urban "aristocrats," who tended to be Masons. Like most third parties, the Anti-Masonic party had a short life, but it brought to the fore Thurlow Weed, William Seward, and Millard Fillmore, who later helped organize the Whig party.

In 1829 a Working Men's party rose up in New York City and spread to other cities. It demanded free public education and the end of jailing for debt. It had hardly begun before its leaders quarreled and flew off in several directions.

Immigration led native-born workingmen, bigoted Protestants, and old-stock citizens to organize so-called American parties. The slavery issue also caused the formation of new parties. Thus in 1840 abolitionists organized the Liberty party, but it attracted very few votes. Eight years later some New Yorkers, fearful that slavery would become rooted in territories taken from Mexico, swung behind the Wilmot Proviso, which stated that "neither slavery nor involuntary servitude shall ever exist in any part" of these territories. They organized the Free Soil party, whose standard-bearer was former president Van Buren. Most Free Soilers were militant or "Barnburner" Democrats, who felt that pro-southern elements controlled their party. Others were "Conscience Whigs," who agonized over the extension of slavery. Free Soilers garnered more votes in 1848 than regular Democrats, throwing the governorship and White House into Whig hands.

The most successful third party was the Republican, which, as we have seen, became the haven of New Yorkers opposed to the extension of slavery in the territories. In 1856 nativists organized the Native American (Know-Nothing) ticket, with Millard Fillmore at its head. Only the Republican party, however, became permanent. Gradually it attracted a large following outside New York City. In the last half of the nineteenth century both Republican and Democratic parties commanded intense loyalty among their followers. The percentage of potential voters who actually went to the polls was greater in those years than at any time in the twentieth century.

Despite party loyalty, rivalries split both major parties on occasions. In 1884 the Mugwumps—that is, Republicans who could not stomach Blaine's corruption—supported Cleveland for president. Similarly Gold Democrats, who could not swallow William Jennings Bryan's views on free silver, ran a separate candidate, John Palmer. In 1912 Theodore Roosevelt's defection to the Bull Moose party split the Republican vote, permitting the Democrats to capture the governorship as well as the presidency.

During World War I the Socialist party attracted many Jews, pacifists, and anti-British supporters. Five Socialists who won seats in the Assembly were expelled by old-time politicians in both parties, who claimed they were unpatriotic and revolutionary. The Socialist assemblymen ran again in 1920 and won reelection, and once again were expelled. This violation of democratic and civil liberties was roundly criticized by Governor Alfred E. Smith, Charles Evans Hughes, and many other prominent figures, as well as by most newspapers.

Third parties have played an exceptionally important role since New Deal days. In 1936 a group of union leaders, particularly David Dubinsky of the International Ladies' Garment Workers' Union and Sidney Hillman of the Amalgamated Clothing Workers Union, organized the American Labor party. Their aim was to give citizens a chance to vote for Roosevelt's New Deal without pulling down the Democratic lever. The next year this party provided the margin of victory for La Guardia as mayor and Dewey as district attorney of Manhattan, both of whom ran as Republicans. When the ALP eventually fell under Communist domination, pudgy David Dubinsky formed the Liberal party, which was both anticommunist and anti-Tammany. In 1944 the combined votes of the ALP and the Liberal party provided the winning margin for Franklin Roosevelt's victory in New York State. In general the Liberal party has endorsed Democratic candidates, although it has backed a few Republicans. The Liberal vote was decisive in the election of Lehman for senator in 1950, Harriman for governor in 1954, Kennedy for president in 1960, and Lindsay for mayor in 1965 and 1969. Critics have charged that the Liberal party became the personal vehicle of its head, Alex Rose, and that its leadership became more interested in patronage than in reform.

In 1962 a group of Republicans organized the Conservative party to exert pressure on Governor Rockefeller, who had greatly increased state activities, expenditures, and taxes. In 1966 the Conservatives garnered more votes than the Liberals, thus winning the coveted third line on the ballot. Four years later they ran James L. Buckley for senator. His total (37 percent of votes cast) was enough to defeat not only the Democratic candidate but also Charles Goodell, the Republican senator who had attacked Nixon's war policy in Vietnam. The Conservatives opposed tax increases, police review boards, school busing, and withdrawal from Vietnam. Whereas about seven out of every ten Liberal party members lived in New York City, about three of every four Conservative voters lived outside the metropolis.

The political history of the Empire State is strewn with defunct third parties. Such organizations tend to vanish once the issue that brought them into being has disappeared. Quite often they break up into factions that drift back to regular parties. At times party chieftains have undoubtedly felt great relief when a quarrelsome faction has stalked off. Who could ever satisfy all the demands of prohibitionists, abolitionists, or the various Marxist factions? When a tight election comes along (and most New York elections have been close), politicians maneuver and shilly-shally to win a third-party endorsement or at least siphon off some of its votes.

Easygoing, materialistic, and nonideological, most New Yorkers have supported Republicans or Democrats because they want to back a winner who can give them some loaves and fishes. Hoping to broaden their appeal, both parties have normally pursued policies of moderation. When they see a third party attracting a large number of voters, they make a gesture to them and sometimes approve a modified version of their demands. The more votes a third party draws, the greater the chance that major parties will steal their most popular planks.

How effective has New York government proved in meeting the needs and encouraging the hopes of its citizens? At the outset we must concede that one cannot run or operate government solely in terms of cost-effectiveness. Parties and governments too must recognize various groups and give their members a feeling that they belong to a community of equals. Occasionally it is more important to massage the bruised feelings of Irish-Americans or the black community than it is to find the best technician to run a cabinet post. Lord Melbourne defended the Order of the Garter, which was awarded to favorites "with no damned nonsense about merit." Governors and legislators have long known that if they expect to get their programs enacted into law, they must build a road, a dam, or perhaps a fish hatchery in the district of an influential politician. In short, the legislative and administrative process involves a great deal of logrolling and backscratching among diverse elements.

Since World War I, most observers have given fairly high marks to New York administration. Governor Smith attracted nationwide attention and approval by combining 187 boards, agencies, and divisions into 19 departments and by establishing an executive budget. As late as the 1970s Jimmy Carter and other governors were seeking to achieve similar goals in their states. Franklin D. Roosevelt and Herbert H. Lehman continued to expand services in education, prisons, mental health, and highways. Thomas E. Dewey earned a reputation as an effective administrator. When the American Commonwealth Series on state governments came out in the 1950s, Lynton K. Caldwell declared that New York's government "is among the best that an imperfect world provides."[35] In 1972 Neal R. Peirce, a careful researcher and shrewd observer, declared that New York "set the pace for all other states."[36]

Political scientists have attempted to assign precise scores for effectiveness in state administration. On one index measuring professionalism in legislative performance, New York stood third.[37] Jack Walter's study of the willingness of states to adopt innovations, using eighty-eight different items, placed New York at the top of the list, followed by Massachusetts and California.[38]

However authoritative these testimonials to the effectiveness of state government may sound, are they not offset by financial mismanagement? Clearly the fiscal troubles of the state as well as of the metropolis have tarnished the reputations of state and city administrators. Put simply, New York State and New York City have spent too much money and piled up too much debt. The state debt rose from $912 million in 1959 to over $3.4 billion in late 1973.[39]

The Empire State slipped down the slippery slopes toward insolvency for the best of motives: to meet citizen needs. At first Governor Rockefeller and the legislature followed constitutional requirements and submitted to the voters several bond issues, the proceeds of which were intended to clean up pollution in rivers, buy parkland, and aid mass transportation. These goals were sound and state budgets could manage the additional debt service without much difficulty.

A compulsive builder, Rockefeller also pushed elaborate improvements in education, housing, transportation, arts, and welfare. When he raised taxes on income, gasoline, liquor, and corporations, conservative Republicans became incensed. In 1971 he and the legislators submitted a constitutional amendment asking the voters to approve a $2.5 billion bond issue for transportation improvements. New Yorkers rejected it by a wide margin.

Rockefeller thereupon turned to a technique of financing already used by Robert Moses and recommended by that eminent legal authority, John Mitchell, whereby semiautonomous agencies issue bonds, whose interest and repayment are guaranteed by tolls, fees, user charges, and the "moral authority" of New York State. In contrast, regular bonds are guaranteed by the "full faith and credit" of New York State. By using this device, Rockefeller was able to skirt the constitution and even the legislature. The Housing Finance Agency, the State Dormitory Authority, the Urban Development Corporation, and other agencies piled up another $6.7 billion in debt. As a result, New York State's spending climbed more swiftly in the 1960s than the average spending for all states, and its debt also rose more quickly.[40] By January 1, 1977, state debt per capita approached $500; local debt per capita was even higher.

Not until Rockefeller left office in 1973 did the financial

crunch strike New York. When the Urban Development Corporation defaulted, its collapse not only undermined other "moral authority" bonds but impaired confidence in regular state securities. Meanwhile New York City, as we have seen, tottered on the brink of insolvency, threatening to pull the state down with it. The banking community, itself guilty of lending money too freely to real estate companies, the governments of underdeveloped nations, and New York City, refused to refinance bond issues.

Governor Hugh Carey, ideological heir to New Deal social programs, had to slash state programs and force Mayor Beame to cut New York City's budget. When Carey submitted his budget in January 1976, he called for the first reduction in state departments and agencies since 1941-1942.[41] He told the legislators that the days of wine and roses were over.

New York State politics illustrates well the strengths and weaknesses of democracy. On the one hand, the system has produced officials of unquestioned integrity such as Grover Cleveland and Herbert H. Lehman. On the other hand, voters have placed in office such rogues as Roscoe Conkling and incompetents too numerous to list. At times officials have climbed pinnacles of constructive achievement, as when they authorized the Erie Canal. At times they have sunk to depths of depravity, as when they "purchased" a new charter for New York City (in 1870) and expelled Socialist assemblymen (after World War I).

We are told that people get the kind of government they deserve. New Yorkers have often failed to rise above petty ethnic, religious, sectional, and class interests. They have applauded charlatans who offered more services and at the same time promised to cut taxes. They have sometimes expected too much from state and local governments. A story often repeated by politicians goes like this: After a politician had listed all the favors he had done for a voter, the latter replied, "But what have you done for me lately?" Every generation of New Yorkers has provided leaders of integrity, imagination, and compassion. Some have been patricians; many have come up from the "middling" classes.

If New Yorkers have been a factious people, they have also been an accommodating people. It has been no small achievement to make the thousands of adjustments, informal as well as formal, whereby New Yorkers have brought about a considerable measure of social peace and justice in a setting of relentless change and unequaled diversity.

Suggestions for Further Reading

The literature on New York and its history is voluminous and is constantly growing. The most comprehensive bibliography is found in David M. Ellis, James A. Frost, Harold C. Syrett, and Harry J. Carman, *A History of New York State* (Ithaca: Cornell University Press, 1967), which also presents the best overview. Still useful is Alexander C. Flick, ed., *History of the State of New York*, 10 vols. (New York: Columbia University Press, 1933–1937). Important chapters on resources, regions, and cities are found in John H. Thompson, ed., *Geography of New York State* (Syracuse: Syracuse University Press, 1966). The Federal Writers' Project of the Works Progress Administration sponsored two valuable guidebooks in the American Guide Series: *New York: A Guide to the Empire State* (New York: Oxford University Press, 1940) and *New York City Guide* (New York: Oxford University Press, 1939).

William A. Ritchie, *The Archaelogy of New York State* (Garden City, N.Y.: Natural History Press, 1965), integrates the complicated story of prehistory and the Indian past. Anthony F. C. Wallace, *The Death and Rebirth of the Seneca* (New York: Knopf, 1970), is brilliant. Equally valuable is Barbara Graymont, *The Iroquois in the American Revolution* (Syracuse: Syracuse University Press, 1972).

Another classic is Jared van Wagenen, Jr., *The Golden Age of Homespun* (1953, repr. New York: Hill & Wang, 1963). Ronald E. Shaw, *Erie Water West: A History of the Erie Canal, 1792–1854* (Lexington: University of Kentucky Press, 1966), is a prize-winning survey. Written for a wide audience and lavishly illustrated is Ralph K. Andrist, *The Erie Canal* (New York:

American Heritage, 1964). One can trace educational developments in an excellent monograph by Carl F. Kaestle, *The Evolution of an Urban School System: New York City, 1750-1850* (Cambridge: Harvard University Press, 1973).

Ira Rosenwaike, *Population History of New York City* (Syracuse: Syracuse University Press, 1972), is a useful compilation. The literature on black Americans is endless. Edgar G. McManus, *A History of Negro Slavery in New York* (Syracuse: Syracuse University Press, 1966), and Seth M. Scheiner, *Negro Mecca: A History of the Negro in New York City, 1865-1920* (New York: New York University Press, 1965), are standard accounts. The important role played by Jews in the garment industry, unions, and cultural developments is perceptively explored in Irving Howe, *World of Our Fathers: The Journey of the Eastern European Jews to America and the Life They Found and Made* (New York: Harcourt Brace Jovanovich, 1976). See also Moses Richin, *The Promised City: New York's Jews, 1870-1914* (Cambridge: Harvard University Press, 1962).

Recent studies of colonial New York have superseded earlier works and provide bibliographies. See Michael Kammen, *Colonial New York: A History* (New York: Charles Scribner's Sons, 1975); Patricia A. Bonomi, *A Factious People: Politics and Society in Colonial New York* (New York: Columbia University Press, 1971); and Alice P. Kenney, *Stubborn for Liberty: The Dutch in New York* (Syracuse: Syracuse University Press, 1975).

The best introduction to the history of New York City is Milton M. Klein, ed., *New York: The Centennial Years, 1676-1976* (Port Washington, N.Y.: Kennikat Press, 1976). Each of the six essays has an excellent bibliography. More popular and well illustrated is Susan Elizabeth Lyman, *The Story of New York* (New York: Crown, 1964). Alexander B. Callow, Jr., *The Tweed Ring* (New York: Oxford University Press, 1965), is the standard account. Charles Garrett, *The La Guardia Years: Machine and Reform Politics in New York City* (New Brunswick, N.J.: Rutgers University Press, 1961), examines New York City during a crucial era. Blake McKelvey has summarized his four-volume history of Rochester in *Rochester on the Genesee: The Growth of a City* (Syracuse: Syracuse University Press, 1973).

Widely available and useful is Alexander C. Flick, *The American Revolution in New York: Its Political, Social, and Economic Significance* (1926, repr. Port Washington, N.Y.: Ira J. Friedman, 1967). For works dealing with events and personalities of the Revolution, see the bibliography *New York in the American Revolution*, comp. Milton M. Klein (Albany: New York State American Revolution Bicentennial Commission, 1974). An exhaustive study is Alfred F. Young, *The Democratic Republicans of New York: The Origins, 1763–1797* (Chapel Hill: University of North Carolina Press, 1967).

The tangled history of New York politics is best approached through biographies. There are good ones of George Clinton, Robert Livingston, John Jay, Silas Wright, William H. Seward, Thurlow Weed, Samuel Tilden, Grover Cleveland, Herbert H. Lehman, Theodore Roosevelt, David Hill, and Franklin D. Roosevelt. The only comprehensive study of politics is De Alva S. Alexander, *A Political History of the State of New York*, 4 vols. (1906–1923, repr. Port Washington, N.Y.: Kennikat Press, 1969). A seminal monograph that has changed national and state historiography is Lee Benson, *The Concept of Jacksonian Democracy: New York as a Test Case* (Princeton: Princeton University Press, 1961). James C. Mohr, *The Radical Republicans and Reform in New York during Reconstruction* (Ithaca: Cornell University Press, 1973), explores the interplay between state and metropolitan politics.

Ulysses Prentiss Hedrick, *A History of Agriculture in the State of New York* (1933, repr. New York: Hill & Wang, 1966), covers a much broader range of social and economic topics than its title indicates.

Marshall B. Davidson, *New York: A Pictorial History* (New York: Charles Scribner's Sons, 1977), includes 750 pictures showing life in both metropolis and upstate. Davidson has succeeded in marrying text and illustrations to provide a rich source of visual documentation, invaluable for an understanding of the state's history.

Notes

1. The New York Character

1. Bayrd Still, "The Personality of New York City," *New York Folklore Quarterly* 14 (Summer 1958):83–92; Allan Nevins, "The Golden Thread in the History of New York," *New-York Historical Society Quarterly* 39 (January 1955):5–22.

2. Paul de Rousiers, *American Life*, trans. A. J. Herbertson (New York: Firmin-Didot, 1910), pp. 242–244.

3. Milton M. Klein, ed., *New York: The Centennial Years, 1676–1976* (Port Washington, N.Y.: Kennikat Press, 1976), p. 184.

4. Quoted in ibid., p. 185.

5. Quoted in Robert Neil Mathis, "Gazaway Bugg Lamar: A Southern Businessman and Confidant in New York City," *New York History* 56 (July 1975):310.

6. Quoted in Thomas S. Cummings, *Historic Annals of the National Academy of Design* ... (New York: G. W. Childs, 1865), pp. 11–17.

7. *Here Is New York* (New York: Harper, 1949), pp. 27–28.

8. John H. Thompson, ed., *The Geography of New York State* (Syracuse: Syracuse University Press, 1966), p. 371.

9. Harold W. Blodgett and Scully Bradley, eds., *Leaves of Grass: Comprehensive Reader's Edition* (New York: New York University Press, 1965), p. 507.

10. Quoted in Joe McCarthy, *New England* (New York: Time-Life Library of America, 1967), p. 6.

11. (New York: W. Sloane Associates, 1949), p. 3.

2. The Peoples of New York

1. Michel Guillaume St. Jean de Crèvecoeur, *Letters from an American Farmer* (New York: Everymans Library, n.d.), p. 43.

2. Quoted in Oscar Handlin, ed., *Immigration as a Factor in American History* (Englewood Cliffs, N.J.: Prentice-Hall, 1959), p. 150.

3. Quoted in Bayrd Still, *Mirror for Gotham: New York as Seen by Contemporaries from Dutch Days to the Present* (New York: New York University Press, 1956), p. 22.

4. Adolph B. Benson, ed., *The America of 1750: Peter Kalm's Travels in North America*, 2 vols. (New York: Dover Publications, 1937), vol. 1, p. 346.

5. Quoted in Alf Evers, *The Catskills: From Wilderness to Woodstock* (New York: Doubleday, 1972), p. 283.

6. *Travels in New-England and New-York*, 4 vols. (New Haven: T. Dwight, 1821–1822), vol. 4, p. 11.

7. Original journal, E. 48, Elkanah Watson Papers, New York State Library, Albany.

8. John R. G. Hassard, *Life of the Most Reverend John Hughes, D.D., First Archbishop of New York* (New York: Appleton, 1866), p. 276.

9. Quoted in Michael Kammen, *A Nation of Nations* (Nashville: American Association for State and Local History, 1975), p. 11.

10. *The Passing of the Great Race*, 3d ed. (New York: Charles Scribner's Sons, 1944), pp. 88–89.

11. *Sunday Times Magazine* (London), 4 March 1973.

3. Provincial New York: Embryonic America

1. "The Significance of the Frontier in American History," in *American Historical Association Annual Report ... for the Year 1893* (Washington: Government Printing Office, 1894), p. 220.

2. Milton M. Klein, "New York in the American Colonies: A New Look," in *Aspects of Early New York Society and Politics*, ed. Jacob Judd and Irwin Polishook (Tarrytown: Sleepy Hollow Restorations, 1974), p. 26.

3. Edmund Bailey O'Callaghan, ed., *Documents Relative to the Colonial History of the State of New-York*, 15 vols. (Albany: Weed, Parsons, 1856–1887), vol. 14, pp. 402–403.

4. Ibid., vol. 5, pp. 685–688.

5. Edmund Bailey O'Callaghan et al., *Documentary History of the State of New-York*, 4 Yols. (Albany: Weed, Parsons, 1849–1851), vol. 2, p. 581.

6. No one should miss the new insights found in Michael Kammen, *Colonial New York: A History* (New York: Charles Scribner's Sons, 1975).

7. Adolph B. Benson, ed., *The America of 1750: Peter Kalm's Travels in North America*, 2 vols. (New York: Dover Publications, 1937), vol. 1, p. 341.

8. Patricia U. Bonomi, *A Factious People: Politics and Society in Colonial New York* (New York: Columbia University Press, 1971), pp. 229–278.

9. Quoted in Klein, "New York in the American Colonies," p. 28.

10. Milton M. Klein, ed., *The Independent Reflector* (Cambridge: Harvard University Press, 1963), p. 33.

4. Revolutionary Cockpit, 1763–1789

1. John Adams to Samuel H. Parsons, June 22, 1776, in *The Works of John Adams*, ed. Charles F. Adams, 10 vols. (Boston: Little, Brown, 1850–1856), vol. 9, p. 407.

2. Michael Kammen, *Colonial New York: A History* (New York: Charles Scribner's Sons, 1975), p. 346.

3. Quoted in ibid., p. 351.

4. Quoted in Merrill Jensen, *The Founding of a Nation: A History of the American Revolution, 1763–1776* (New York: Oxford University Press, 1968), p. 212.

5. Kammen, *Colonial New York*, p. 368.

5. The Rise of the Empire State, 1789–1825

I am indebted to Wendell Tripp, editor of *New York History*, for permission to use portions of my article "The Rise of the Empire State, 1783–1825," *New York History* 56 (January 1975):5–28.

1. Edmund Bailey O'Callaghan et al., *Documentary History of the State of New-York*, 4 vols. (Albany: Weed, Parsons, 1849–1851), vol. 2, p. 1105.

2. *Travels through Canada, and the United States of North America, in the Years 1806, 1807 & 1808*, 2 vols. (London: C. Cradock and W. Jay, 1814), vol. 2, pp. 64–65.

3. Louis C. Jones, ed., *Growing Up in the Cooper Country: Boyhood Recollections of the New York Frontier* (Syracuse: Syracuse University Press, 1965), pp. 75–76.

4. Diary entry quoted in Harry F. Jackson, *Scholar in the Wilderness: Francis Adrian van der Kemp* (Syracuse: Syracuse University Press, 1963), pp. 84–85.

5. *Rochester, the Water-Power City: 1812–1854* (Cambridge: Harvard University Press, 1945), p. 49.

6. William W. Campbell, *The Life and Writings of De Witt Clinton* (New York: Baker & Scribner, 1849), pp. 49–50.

7. H. Perry Smith, *History of Cortland County* (Syracuse: D. Mason & Co., 1885), p. 353.

8. Tacitus [De Witt Clinton], *The Canal Policy of the State of New-York: Delineated in a Letter to Robert Troup, Esquire* (Albany: E. and E. Hosford, 1821), p. 29.

9. *The Democratic Republicans of New York: The Origins, 1763–1797* (Chapel Hill: University of North Carolina Press), pp. 518–545.

10. Quoted in George Rogers Taylor, *The Transportation Revolution: 1815–1860* (New York: Holt, Rinehart & Winston, 1951), p. 4.

6. A Burgeoning Economy

1. American Guide Series, *New York: A Guide to the Empire State* (New York: Oxford University Press, 1940), p. 528.

2. *Impressions and Experiences* (New York: Harper, 1896), p. 271.

3. Quoted in Daniel Patrick Moynihan, *The Federal Government and the Economy of New York State*, rev. ed. (Washington, D.C.: Government Printing Office, 1977), p. 31.

4. Quoted in Harry H. Pierce, *Railroads of New York: A Study of Government Aid, 1826–1875* (Cambridge: Harvard University Press, 1953), p. 57.

5. For more details, see my article "New York and the Western Trade, 1850–1910," *New York History* 33 (October 1952):379–405.

6. An excellent account of New York State's agricultural heyday may be found in Paul Wallace Gates, "Agricultural Change in New York State, 1850–1890," *New York History* 50 (April 1969):115–142.

7. Many current economic data are presented in monthly and annual reports of the New York State Department of Commerce. Since 1967 the Division of the Budget has published a statistical yearbook that provides information on population, employment, education, public health, and natural resources.

8. *New York Times*, 4 January 1976.

9. "The Future of the Northeast," *Empire State Report* 2 (October–November 1976):344, 349.

7. Mind and Spirit

1. Readers can find more detailed summaries of cultural developments and an extensive bibliography in David M. Ellis, James A. Frost, Harold C. Syrett, and Harry J. Carman, *A History of New York State* (Ithaca: Cornell University Press, 1967).

2. *The World of Washington Irving* (New York: E. P. Dutton & Co., 1944), p. 459.

3. Louis C. Jones, ed., *Growing Up in the Cooper Country: Boyhood Recollections of the New York Frontier* (Syracuse: Syracuse University Press, 1963), p. 130.

4. The best survey is Whitney Cross, *The Burned-over District: The Social and Intellectual History of Enthusiastic Religion in Western New York, 1800–1850* (Ithaca: Cornell University Press, 1950).

5. Mildred Howells, ed., *Life and Letters of William Dean Howells*, 2 vols. (New York: Doubleday, Doran, 1928), vol. 1, p. 413.

6. Robert J. Rayback, ed., *Richards Atlas of New York State* (Phoenix, N.Y.: Frank E. Richards, 1957–1959), p. 57. I am indebted to Dr. O'Donnell for many insights. The best account of literary developments in New York State is his text accompanying three literary maps in *Richards Atlas*.

7. Arthur Frank Wertheim, *The New York Little Renaissance: Iconoclasm, Modernism, and Nationalism in American Culture, 1908–1917* (New York: New York University Press, 1976).

8. *New York Times*, 10 April 1977.

9. *The Regents Statewide Plan for the Development of Post-Secondary Education, 1976* (Albany: State Education Department, 1976), p. 12.

8. Upstate versus Downstate

I am indebted to James J. Heslin, director of the New-York Historical Society, for permission to use material from my article "'Upstate Hicks' versus 'City Slickers,'" *New-York Historical Society Quarterly* 43 (April 1959): 202–219.

1. Quoted in *Wall Street Journal*, 23 July 1971.

2. William L. Riordan, *Plunkitt of Tammany Hall* (New York: Alfred A. Knopf, 1948), p. 86.

3. Ibid., p. 27.

4. Ralph A. Straetz and Frank J. Munger, *New York Politics* (New York: New York University Press, 1960), p. 40.

5. "New York: The 49th State," *American Mercury*, December 1935, pp. 476–477.

6. *New York Times*, 19 September 1975.

7. Edmund Bailey O'Callaghan, ed., *Documents Relative to the Colonial History of the State of New-York*, 15 vols. (Albany: Weed, Parsons, 1856–1887), vol. 6, p. 116.

8. H. P. Johnston, ed., *Correspondence and Public Papers of John Jay . . . , 1763–1826*, 4 vols. (New York: G. P. Putnam's Sons, 1890–1893), vol. 2, p. 334.

9. Nathaniel H. Carter and William L. Stone, rep., *Reports of the Proceedings and Debates of the Convention of 1821 . . .* (Albany: E. and E. Hosford, 1821), p. 219.

10. Quoted in Walter Dean Burnham, "Democracy and the Court," *Commonweal* 80 (July 24, 1964):500.

11. The best account is found in Samuel A. Pleasants, *Fernando Wood of New York* (New York: Columbia University Press, 1948), pp. 66–83.

12. Geroge W. Walling, *Recollections of a New York Chief of Police* (New York: Caxton Book Concern, 1887), p. 57.

13. "Communication from His Honor the Mayor Fernando Wood Transmitted," *Documents of the Board of Aldermen of the City of New York* 28, pt. 1 (New York, 1862).

14. *New York Times*, 18 March 1953.

15. For more details on the Rockefeller–Lindsay feud, see Neal R. Peirce, *The Megastates of America: People, Politics, and Power in the Ten Great States* (New York: Norton, 1972), pp. 88–97.

16. Quoted in ibid., p. 95.

17. Ibid.

9. The Politics of Diversity

The title is borrowed from Milton M. Klein's *The Politics of Diversity: Essays in the History of Colonial New York* (Port Washington, N.Y.: Kennikat Press, 1974).

1. Quoted in Michael Kammen, *Colonial New York: A History* (New York: Charles Scribner's Sons, 1975), p. 341.

2. Quoted in De Alva Alexander, *Political History of the State of New York*, 3 vols. (New York: Henry Holt, 1906), vol. 1, p. iii.

3. For Hill's partisan activities, see Herbert J. Bass, *"I Am a Democrat": The Political Career of David Bennett Hill* (Syracuse: Syracuse University Press, 1971).

4. *The Making of the President, 1972* (New York: Bantam Books, 1973), p. 172.

5. *Politics in America* (New York: Harper & Row, 1954), p. 200.

6. *New York Times*, 27 June 1977.

7. Thomas J. Archdeacon, *New York City, 1664–1710: Conquest and Change* (Ithaca: Cornell University Press, 1976), p. 155.

8. *The Concept of Jacksonian Democracy: New York as a Test Case* (Princeton: Princeton University Press, 1961), p. 165.

9. Ibid., p. 187.

10. Ibid., p. 204.

11. Elting E. Morison and John M. Blum, eds., *The Letters of Theodore Roosevelt*, 8 vols. (Cambridge: Harvard University Press, 1951), vol. 2, p. 1470.

12. Richard Jensen, *The Winning of the Midwest: Social and Political Conflict, 1888–1896* (Chicago: University of Chicago Press, 1971), p. xii.

13. John Webb Pratt, *Religion, Politics, and Diversity: The Church–State Theme in New York History* (Ithaca: Cornell University Press, 1967), p. 201.

14. Quoted in ibid., p. 248.

15. David Burner, *The Politics of Provincialism: The Democratic Party in Transition, 1918–1932* (New York: Knopf, 1968), pp. 234–238.

16. Arthur Mann, *La Guardia Comes to Power, 1933* (Philadelphia: Lippincott, 1965), pp. 138–152.

17. Theodore H. White noted that in 57 of 62 counties the Democratic county chairmen belonged to the Roman Catholic church (*The Making of the President, 1960* [New York: Pocket Books, 1961], p. 287).

18. Cambridge: M.I.T. Press, pp. 306–308.

19. "The Jewish Vote (Again)," *Commentary* 55 (June 1973):81.

20. *New York* 10 (December 6, 1976), p. 9.

21. Patricia U. Bonomi, *A Factious People: Politics and Society in Colonial New York* (New York: Columbia University Press, 1971), p. 7.

22. Jackson Turner Main, "Government by the People: The American Revolution and the Democratization of the Legislatures," *William and Mary Quarterly* 23 (1966):394, 400.

23. Quoted in Alfred F. Young, *The Democratic Republicans of New York: The Origins, 1763–1767* (Chapel Hill: University of North Carolina Press, 1967), p. 5.

24. *The Gansevoorts of Albany* (Syracuse: Syracuse University Press, 1969), p. xiv.

25. *Albany Microscope*, 26 February 1842, quoted in William E. Rowley, "The Irish Aristocracy of Albany, 1798–1878," *New York History* 52 (July 1971):304.

26. *The Decline of the Aristocracy in the Politics of New York, 1801–1840* (New York: Columbia University Press, 1919).

27. Edward Pessen, *Jacksonian America: Society, Personality, and Politics* (Homewood, Ill.: Dorsey Press, 1969), pp. 265–266.

28. Robert A. Caro, *The Power Broker: Robert Moses and the Fall of New York* (New York: Knopf, 1974), p. 9.

29. Wallace S. Sayre and Herbert Kaufman, *Governing New York City: Politics in the Metropolis* (New York: Norton, 1965), p. 690.

30. Ibid., p. xlvii.

31. Anthony Burgess, *New York* (New York: Time-Life Books, 1977), p. 138.

32. *The Abuse of Power: The Permanent Government and the Fall of New York* (New York: Viking Press, 1977).

33. *Addresses on Government and Citizenship* (Cambridge: Harvard University Press, 1916), p. 202.

34. Newfield and Dubrul, *Abuse of Power*, p. 110.

35. *The Government and Administration of New York* (New York: Crowell, 1954), p. 13.

36. *The Megastates of America: People, Politics, and Power in the Ten Great States* (New York: Norton, 1972), p. 197.

37. Richard I. Hofferbert and Ira Sharkansky, eds., *State and Urban Politics: Readings in Comparative Public Policy* (Boston: Little, Brown, 1971), p. 317.

38. Ibid., p. 383.

39. *New York Times*, 12 December 1973.

40. "Governing New York State: The Rockefeller Years," *Proceedings of the Academy of Political Science* 31 (May 1974):123.

41. *New York Times*, 21 January 1976.

Index

Abolition. *See* Antislavery movement

Adams, John, 76, 200

Adams, Samuel Hopkins, 21, 168

Adirondacks, 2, 16–17, 20, 137–138

Adventists, 157

Agriculture, 54, 63–64, 97, 104–110, 134–137. *See also* Farmers; Farm products; Farms

Albany, 2, 4, 25, 27–28, 30, 55, 58–59, 62, 72, 80, 120, 171, 218, 228; and Indian affairs, 54, 67; in 1750, 72; trade of, 21, 57, 107–109, 111–112

Albany Mall. *See* Empire State Plaza

Algonkians, 51, 53

Allen, Ethan, 74

American Federation of Labor, 142–144

Ames, Ezra, 150, 218

Andros, Edmund, 57, 59

Anthony, Susan B., 159

Anti-Federalists, 92–94, 217

Anti-Masonic party, 230

Antislavery movement, 92, 115, 116, 159, 219; political activity of, 206, 230

Architecture, 22–23, 71–72, 150, 152, 164–175

Aristocracy: colonial, 60, 62–68, 71; frontier, 105–107; political role of, 60, 217–221; in Revolutionary era, 76–77, 89–94

Arnold, Benedict, 85

Artisans, 64–65, 71, 76, 90–93, 101, 110, 206, 217

Artists, 71–72, 150–152, 163–165, 171–172

Art. *See* Painting

Arthur, Chester A., 200, 203, 222

Arts, 8, 161. *See also* Architecture; Literature; Music; Painting; Theater

Assembly: colonial, 59–61, 63–67, 69, 79–84; state, 231

Astor, John Jacob, 99, 155

Babcock, Stephen, 135

Baldwin, James, 169–170

Ballet, 174

Banking, 3, 11, 19, 99, 133–134, 140, 207, 228. *See also* Morgan, J. P.

Banking crisis of 1975 (New York City), 96

Baptists, 13, 56, 69, 110, 157, 166

Barnum, Phineas T., 160

Batavia, 106, 113

Bath, 23, 114

Bausch & Louis Co., 3, 46

Beame, Abraham, 193, 196, 216, 226, 235

Beardsley, Levi, 107

Becker, Carl Lotus, 76–77

Bellomont, Richard, 62

Benjamin, Asher, 152

Bennett, James Gordon, 149

Binghamton, 5, 39, 127, 131, 171

Blacks, 10, 29, 33; in colonial period, 26, 46, 70; economic conditions of, 40, 47, 102, 144–145; education and culture of, 169–170, 173, 177; emancipation of, 116, 159, 230; family life among, 40, 145; militancy among, 22, 40, 45–46, 215, 227; and politics, 205, 211, 213–216; in population, 5, 35, 39, 48, 187, 214; as urban dwellers, 39, 45, 194

Blackwell, Elizabeth, 155

Blaine, James G., 208, 231

Library of Congress Cataloging in Publication Data
(For library cataloging purposes only)

Ellis, David Maldwyn.
  New York, state and city.

  Includes bibliographical references and index.
  1, New York (State)—History. 2. New York (City)—History. I. Title.
F119.E447   974.7   78-15759
ISBN 0-8014-1180-7